Anakú Iwachá

Anakú Iwachá

YAKAMA LEGENDS AND STORIES

SECOND EDITION

To Jace

EDITED BY

Virginia R. Beavert • Michelle M. Jacob • Joana W. Jansen

Virginia Beavert
Michelle J

THE CONFEDERATED TRIBES AND BANDS OF THE YAKAMA NATION,
IN ASSOCIATION WITH THE UNIVERSITY OF WASHINGTON PRESS
Seattle

NATIONAL ENDOWMENT FOR THE HUMANITIES

Anakú Iwachá was made possible in part by a grant from the National Endowment for the Humanities: Exploring the human endeavor.

Any views, findings, conclusions, or recommendations expressed in this book do not necessarily represent those of the National Endowment for the Humanities.

Design by Katrina Noble
Composed in Noto Serif, typeface designed by Google
Frontispiece: Ḵw'ashḵw'ashyáy ipáwawaykika pɨnmínk wɨx̱á. Crane pole-boated his leg across.

25 24 23 22 21 5 4 3 2 1

Printed and bound in Korea

UNIVERSITY OF WASHINGTON PRESS
uwapress.uw.edu

LIBRARY OF CONGRESS CATALOGING-IN-PUBLICATION DATA

Names: Beavert, Virginia R., 1921– editor. | Jacob, Michelle M., 1977– editor. | Jansen, Joana W., editor.
Title: Anakú Iwachá : Yakama legends and stories / edited by Virginia R. Beavert, Michelle M. Jacob, Joana W. Jansen.
Description: Second edition. | Seattle : University of Washington Press, [2021] | Includes bibliographical references. | English and Ichishkíin.
Identifiers: LCCN 2020020794 | ISBN 9780295748245 (paperback)
Subjects: LCSH: Yakama Indians—Folklore. | LCGFT: Folk literature.
Classification: LCC E99.Y2 A56 2020 | DDC 979.7004/974127—dc23
LC record available at https://lccn.loc.gov/2020020794

♾ This paper meets the requirements of ANSI/NISO Z39.48-1992 (Permanence of Paper).

Cover design: Katrina Noble
Cover illustration: Ttmayíma papnúshana x̱ alúkt tiichámpa. The maidens were sleeping underground. Yakama Nation Artists.

Contents

Foreword by the Yakama Nation

DELANO (SHI'I) SALUSKIN
Yakama Nation Tribal Council Chairman
Vice-President, Affiliated Tribes of Northwest Indians

It is with great pleasure and hope that I write this foreword introducing the latest work of Tux̱ámshish (Dr. Virginia Beavert), Dr. Michelle Jacob, and Dr. Joana Jansen. This new edition of *Anakú Iwachá* makes this collection of precious stories available for the current and future generations. I remember when the first edition of *Anakú Iwachá* was published in 1974, and it has served as a valuable resource for our Tribal people and educators. Our stories are precious to us because they are the teachings of our Elders who share important lessons through storytelling. It is an honor to be part of the Tribal Council who has supported this project, which helps fulfill the vision of Dr. Virginia Beavert. Dr. Beavert has dedicated her life to educating our students on the importance of Yakama language and culture, and she was the original project director of *Anakú Iwachá*. Dr. Beavert has carried out the important vision inspired by my grandfather, Alex Saluskin, who encouraged the attainment of a college education in a commitment to Tribal sovereignty.

On behalf of the Yakama Nation, I thank Virginia, Michelle, Joana, their students at the University of Oregon, Yakama Nation Fisheries, and the University of Washington Press for the work and time they have dedicated to make this new edition of *Anakú Iwachá* possible. Kw'ałanúu.

TOPPENISH, WASHINGTON
FEBRUARY 2020

Note on the New Edition

Anakú Iwachá is a precious gift to our people. It is a remarkable educational and cultural resource that generations of the Yakama Nation have learned from and enjoyed. We decided it was time for a new edition of *Anakú Iwachá* because the beloved original version is now out of print and very difficult to find, with rare booksellers occasionally charging hundreds of dollars for one book. We wanted to make the collection of stories available for Tribal community members, educators, and anyone interested in learning from our traditional stories—all of which contain important teachings.

Preparing a new edition of a book is a time-consuming and very detailed process. We knew that *Anakú Iwachá* could be updated to build upon the work done in culture and language education since the book was first published in 1974. Much has happened. We discuss that history in two new essays in this edition of the book. To make this edition possible, we collaborated with the University of Oregon and applied for, and were awarded, a grant from the National Endowment for the Humanities. We are grateful for the opportunity to realize our collective dream of *Anakú Iwachá* being in print again and ready for use in classrooms, homes, and Tribal offices.

We have left the original text of *Anakú Iwachá* intact, per the request of the Yakama Nation Tribal Council, who wish readers to see the original text as it was first published. We have, however, updated the Ichishkíin spellings in the original text, using the written system for our language that Dr. Virginia Beavert has created in her work over many decades to help revitalize our Indigenous language. This will make it easier for readers, teachers, and students to use their dictionaries and the book's glossary, which has been updated as well and placed at the end of the new edition. We have added new material, including a map, artwork, essays, and annotations to help readers, teachers, and students engage with the legends as teaching and learning tools.

We thank the Yakama Nation Tribal Council and Yakama Nation Fisheries Program for encouraging us to publish this new edition of *Anakú Iwachá*. We are grateful to our families for also encouraging us in this project. Finally, we dedicate this book to the young people and future generations, who have always been the source of inspiration for *Anakú Iwachá*.

VIRGINIA R. BEAVERT
MICHELLE M. JACOB
JOANA W. JANSEN

Acknowledgments

This project was supported by a National Endowment for the Humanities (NEH) Scholarly Editions and Translations Grant: "Anakú Iwachá (The Way It Was): A New Edition of Yakama Legends and Stories." We are grateful to NEH Program Analyst Lydia Medici. Any views, findings, conclusions, or recommendations expressed in this book do not necessarily represent those of the National Endowment for the Humanities. The Endangered Language Documentation Programme and the Jacobs Research Fund provided funding for the recording, transcription, and translation of two of the new legends included in this volume.

We are grateful to all of the following people who have made substantial contributions to this new edition: Regan Anderson, Gregory Sutterlict, Shayleen EagleSpeaker, Sia Aronica, Hobie Blackhorn, Ken Doxsee, Robert Elliott, Stephany RunningHawk Johnson, Allyson Alvarado, Department of Education Studies students at the University of Oregon, Ichishkíin students at the University of Oregon, Roger Jacob Jr., Delano Saluskin, Arlen Washines, Elese Washines, Elizabeth Nason, Leslie Martinez, Teodoro Reyes-Ramirez, Janne Underriner, and the Northwest Indian Language Institute at the University of Oregon.

History of the Project

In the late 1960s, Indian* parents of several school districts on and around the Yakama** Reservation came together to create a Johnson O'Malley Advisory Committee for each school district that served Yakama children. These committees sought available funding for Indian education and, in 1973, were incorporated as a Johnson O'Malley Consortium of Region IV in the State of Washington. Such organizing was part of the self-determination movement in Indian education at the time, following a wave of Red Power protest movements all across Indian Country. This book, *Anakú Iwachá*, is unique in that it represents the first large-scale, multi-district organizing effort involving state and federal funds for education. It was the first time that Yakama parents took control of Indian education funding to create and manage a project that would forever become a powerful teaching resource for the future generations. *Anakú Iwachá* was the first example of this Indian parent-led work to intervene in K–12 curricula and is a critically important resource. However, coming together to benefit future generations through the power of storytelling and recognizing Elders as revered teachers was not new; indeed, that is how our people have always survived and organized ourselves.

While the parent committee had the vision and political savvy to organize and access the funding needed for the project, they needed a fluent

* The original edition of *Anakú Iwachá* uses *Indian*, as is still common practice among many American Indian and Yakama peoples. Also of use today are identities such as *Tribal* and *Indigenous*, although these terms were less common in the late 1960s and early 1970s when the book was first published.

** The Yakama Nation Tribal Council voted in 1993 to use the spelling *Yakama* rather than *Yakima*. We updated the spelling to *Yakama* in the legends in the new edition, and *Yakima* is used for names of places, such as the Yakima River and Yakima Valley.

speaker in multiple Ichishkíin/Sahaptin dialects, an educated person who could speak, read, and write the languages and English fluently. They needed someone who was also grounded in Tribal cultural ways and could approach and work with Elders and youth, who would be the important contributors to the project. Tux̱ámshish Virginia Beavert became Project Director because she was recommended by the Yakama Nation Tribal Council. She was one of the very few people who knew all the dialects that the storytellers would use. Deward Walker became involved in the project because the Consortium was familiar with his work in and around the local area, including working with place-names. Dr. Walker had already completed a similar project for the Nez Perce with Dr. David Warren of the Institute of American Indian Arts in Santa Fe, New Mexico.

For the original edition, Virginia gathered the legends from many different storytellers, twenty-three of whom have a brief biography in the book. Additionally, seven Tribal illustrators, mostly young people, contributed illustrations for the book. Virginia worked out of a small office in Toppenish, Washington, on a very modest project budget. She traveled all across the Columbia River Plateau to gather the legends for the book. The process was intense, and only one year was allotted to the project, so Virginia drove her own car across a vast area to visit Elders. She remembers driving her Dodge through snowstorms to get up north and feeling the responsibility to meet the deadline for the project.

At the time, legends were rarely recorded for purposes of publication. The Elders were comfortable sharing with Virginia because in many cases she was their family member. Especially when they learned X̱ax̱ísh was her great-grandmother, they were happy to share. The Elders selected the stories that they wanted to share; they wanted the stories to be available for the children. Not every Elder Virginia approached was willing to share. An Elder in White Swan said she was cautious to reveal her legends, noting that "White people just take it over, I think I'll keep it in my family."

When Virginia recorded the Elders' stories, usually in different dialects, the Elders shared some brief biographical information, which was also translated into English and included in the original book. Translating the stories into English, in addition to the extensive travel required to gather the stories, made up the bulk of the work, which was detail oriented and intense, as anyone who has worked with recordings, transcription,

History of Ichishkíin Language Education and *Anakú Iwachá*

Around the same time that the Johnson O'Malley Advisory Committees were forming, an interest in incorporating Ichishkíin language teaching in classrooms was building. In the late 1960s, teachers started meeting together to study language, literacy, and language teaching. At that time, the language was spoken and heard in households and wherever people gathered.

The Yakama practical alphabet—the spelling system used in this book, the dictionary, and many classrooms—was established and began to be used at this time. Alexander (Alex) Saluskin and Dr. Bruce Rigsby, working with other Elders, had developed a practical spelling system that represented all the sounds of the language and that could be typed on a standard typewriter. Alex had retired from Tribal Government work and was a curator at Fort Simcoe. Bruce met him there while researching varieties and dialects of Ichishkíin. Together, they traveled to meet with people across the region. From their work, the first modern and available dictionary of Yakama Ichishkíin was developed (Beavert and Rigsby 1975).

At the end of each work day, Alex and Bruce also taught the practical spelling system to a small group of teachers from White Swan, Toppenish, Celilo, and Lyle. Teachers saw that the children were using mostly English language at school and wanted to be sure Yakama was not left out. Teachers also thought that by learning to read and write their own language, the children would strengthen their skills in English or any other language. The Bilingual Education Act of 1968 encouraged the use of a child's home language in the schools as a way to transition students to speaking English and to support their home language and culture. Although the legislation was developed with immigrant communities in mind, and with the goal of developing speakers of English, bilingual education was also a civil rights issue and a way to gain financial and district support for incorporating Indigenous languages. When *Anakú Iwachá* was first published and copies were provided to all the local schools, interest in the language grew. At Lincoln School in Toppenish, Ichishkíin, Spanish, and English were all taught. The Yakama Nation Tribal School, established in 1980, emphasizes the importance of language and culture. The first teachers there had been a part of Alex and Bruce's classes.

One of the first colleges to include Ichishkíin language education was Central Washington University, where Dr. Beavert incorporated the alphabet in her ethnic studies classes as she taught local culture, geography, and history. Later, after Heritage College (now Heritage University) was established, Dr. Beavert began teaching history and culture there and advocating for Ichishkíin language to be taught given the school's location and student body. An early administrator obtained grant funding, and the language class began. At that time, Dr. Beavert emphasized reading and writing, as most students had Elders and family members to converse with. This focus has continued in her classes, although now she equally emphasizes listening and speaking.

Understanding and speaking a language are critical to using a language. Reading and writing can support this learning. Those who wish to write Ichishkíin words—then and now—may use the Yakama practical alphabet or may use their own spellings based on the English alphabet and sound system as a way to remember those words. This works well in many instances, but when creating books and lessons to be used by more than one teacher, and especially to represent the sounds that are not used in English, an individual writing system does not always work. The practical alphabet has a one-to-one correspondence between a sound and a symbol, which means that a written word contains the information needed to pronounce it correctly. For example, the Ichishkíin diphthong *ay*, as in *áy'ay* (magpie), is always pronounced the same way. It rhymes with the English word *try*. It is the only combination of letters that is pronounced that way. Sounds that are not shared between Ichishkíin and English, such as *x̱*, as in *x̱átx̱at* (duck), and *ł*, as in *łkw'i* (day), have their own symbols. Classes today often include learning about the spelling system and sounds of the Ichishkíin language, and this knowledge helps students to accurately pronounce the words and phrases in printed books.

Ichishkíin is taught today in community classes, and the language is more widely used across Tribal programs, including in program names, reports, and signage. A Yakama Nation Head Start Program is helping to teach the youngest students the importance of language and culture. Ichishkíin is also being taught to K–12 students in and around the Yakama Reservation and at our sister reservations as well as in the Yakama Nation Language Boot Camp summer program. The summer program uses curricula developed by multiple instructors and students, including some of Tux̱ámshish's students from the University of Oregon.

University programs promote Ichishkíin language. The Northwest Indian Language Institute (NILI) at the University of Oregon offers intensive language education and professional development training in a two-week summer institute each year and has taught Ichishkíin language and linguistics at the summer institute for over twenty years. The Sapsik'ʷałá Teacher Education Program provides Ichishkíin instruction through a partnership with NILI through which preservice teachers attend the summer institute. Heritage University has a Language Center that features Ichishkíin, and the University of Oregon—in addition to the remarkable resources of NILI and the Sapsik'ʷałá Program—offers two full years of Ichishkíin language, which university students can take to fulfill their language requirement for graduation. Dr. Virginia Beavert worked with her students to develop the language curriculum offered at both Heritage University and the University of Oregon. This curriculum inspires much of the work being done in K–12 classrooms.

In reflecting on this history of language education, all of which is rooted in Virginia's early work on *Anakú Iwachá*, Virginia shared that it was always Alex Saluskin's strong belief that language classes and learning materials should be available to anyone who wants to learn and help preserve the language and that those who have an interest in the language will be supporters and advocates and strengthen the work of revitalization and teaching. She offers these words of encouragement to teachers and learners: "There have always been those who have supported language teaching, who have come to Elders to ask how it can be done. It takes a long time to learn a language."

We feel hopeful that the Ichishkíin language and all Ichishkíin-speaking peoples have a strong and healthy future ahead.

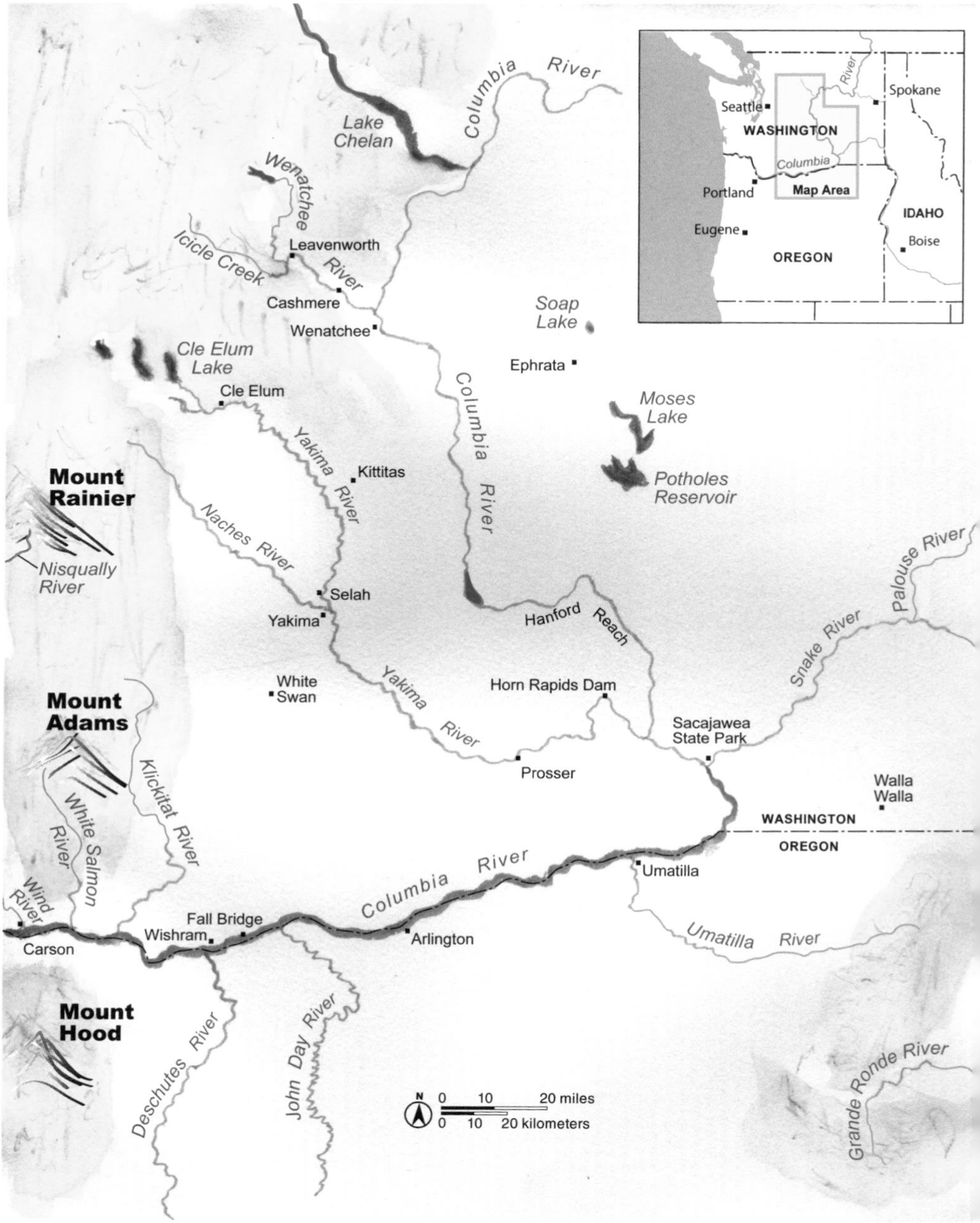

The land of Yakama legends. Map by Robert Elliott.

Anakú Iwachá

The Way It Was

(ANAKÚ IWACHÁ)
(YAKAMA LEGENDS)

THE CONSORTIUM OF JOHNSON O'MALLEY COMMITTEES OF REGION IV
STATE OF WASHINGTON

Virginia Beavert
PROJECT DIRECTOR
YAKAMA TRIBE

Deward E. Walker Jr.
TECHNICAL ADVISOR
UNIVERSITY OF COLORADO

PREFACE

In the beginning, our Creator spoke the word and this earth was created. He spoke the word again and all living things were put on earth. And then He said the word and we, the (Indian) people, were created and planted here on this earth. As though we were recreated again.

We are like the plants on this earth. Our food was put here as plants to feed us: just like when we plant a garden. That is the way our earth was in the beginning.

There was salmon, deer, elk, and all kinds of birds. It is as if our bodies are the very end of this earth, still growing while our ancestors are all buried in the ground.

He named everything He created. He put water on this earth. He made it to flow into the rivers and lakes to water this great garden, and to quench the thirst of the people, the animals, plants, birds and fish.

He took the feet of the people and made them walk on this earth. He created the horse: which is like a human being. He put the horse and the people together to help one another.

All of the land where we live and where our ancestors lived was created for the (Indian) people.

Now I see it diminishing gradually little by little until some of us have no place to live. The land changes as our children are changing, and it makes me sad.

Popkiawahnee Hienstulle, Annie Jim

Introduction

THIS book has been completed under the sponsorship and direction of the Consortium of Johnson O'Malley Committees of Region IV. This book represents the culmination of a one-year project, funded by the Bureau of Indian Affairs and the Washington State Supervisor of Indian Education. This project became a reality because of the cooperation and the endorsement from the Yakama Tribal Council and the government agencies. We wish to extend our special appreciation to Dr. Dave Warren, Director, Research and Cultural Studies Development Section, Bureau of Indian Affairs, and Emmett Oliver, Supervisor of Indian Education, Washington State, for the financial support and valuable advice they provided this organization. We also want to express our gratitude to the traditional and the contemporary participants for recording the legends for this book. The artists are also due thanks for illustrating the legends in their individual artistic expression.

The Consortium is a non-profit incorporated body under the State of Washington, which has as its principal purpose the improvement of education for Indian youth. The Consortium members now represent six school districts. Organizing acceptance of the Consortium concept was not easy. Initially, opposition was expressed by state officials, local schools, local citizens (both Indian and non-Indian), and countless others. Indian parental determination overcame this opposition; however, a full year of struggle was necessary before the Consortium became recognized as an organization capable of administering and developing educational programs specifically for local Indian children.

The present officers of the Consortium are: Chairman, Elmer Schuster; Vice-Chairman, Lila Porter; and Secretary/Treasurer, Leona Smartlowit. District representatives are: Joe Sampson (Mt. Adams School District); Larry Porter (Wapato District); Joe Jay Pinkham (Toppenish District); Evans Dick

(Granger District); Francis George (Goldendale District); and Ladd Kahclamet (Klickitat District).

The major responsibilities of the Consortium now include this project; the coordination of Johnson O'Malley funds allocated to the schools of Region IV by the Washington State Supervisor of Indian Education; and the supervision of the Native American Component of the Migrant and Indian Education Center, located in Toppenish, Washington. During the summer of 1973, the Consortium also completed a project which surveyed the educational resources of the Yakama Indian Reservation.

Currently, the Consortium is seeking additional financial support for more books dealing with the Yakama written language and culture and history to be used by the schools on the Reservation.

The Consortium intends to continue supporting and helping to implement projects to improve the school systems of the Reservation and other Indian communities of the Northwest. It is hoped that the efforts of the Consortium can be pursued cooperatively with other Indian parents throughout the country who are concerned with improving the education of their youth at the "grass roots" level.

The present Yakama Tribe consists of fourteen different bands that were brought together under the Treaty of 1855 and which are now located on or near the Yakama Reservation in central Washington State. These bands of Indians are united by several different dialects of a single language called Sahaptin. This language and culture are closely related to tribes on the neighboring Nez Perce, Umatilla, and Warm Springs Reservations. Some of the people came from the Wenatchee, Entiat, Chelan, and Columbia tribes who speak the dialect of the Mid-Columbia Salish language. They were located on the Columbia River to the north of the present Yakama Reservation and are now living on the Yakama, Umatilla, and the Colville Reservations.

Traditionally, the people depended on the salmon runs, which annually ascended the Columbia River and its tributaries. These formed their principal food supply and together with game, roots, and other vegetables and fruits provided a very bountiful supply of food. They lived in mat-covered Longhouses, and they preserved their food by drying and storing it in caches.

The Yakama people lived in small bands with permanent settlements along the various tributaries in this region. In the summer months, they left these settlements and ascended into the high country to collect the foods that grew wild there. They gathered all of the products of the forest, which are used in many ingenious ways. Many of their ancestors possessed horses and traveled even as far as the plains country to hunt buffalo. On these trips they often were accompanied by members of neighboring, friendly tribes. Other tribes made extended trips to the Pacific Ocean where they traded for valuable shells and other useful and valuable objects made by the tribes who lived close to the ocean. They also went to Klamath Lake to gather water chestnuts which they ground and made into flour.

The following legends which make up the bulk of this book have been brought together and published through the combined efforts of many people. Our Tribal Elders have consented to let us record this part of their knowledge of traditional Yakama culture. In order that these legends are as genuine as possible, they were collected in several dialects and then translated into English for presentation in this book. Considerable time and energy have been expended in translating these legends in order to convey the proper meaning. Recounting these legends is a skill the Elders acquired from their Elders when they were small children. It is hoped that by recording these legends the youth (many of whom do not speak the Yakama language) will become more interested in their culture and language.

These legends contain much traditional wisdom, especially lessons about how to be a proper Yakama. They instruct youth in the responsibilities of parents, other relatives, and Tribal membership. They reveal the crucial role of the grandparents in passing on the traditional knowledge. This point is covered in the following account of traditional child raising contributed for this book by a Tribal leader.

he will grow up the same way. The child is unable to absorb any kind of training because he does not have a firm foundation. The parents must maintain this balance by being good examples, by practicing self-discipline and belief in the Higher Powers. Avoid the bad influences on this earth just as the Elders did a long time ago. Avoid overindulgence; it will only bring you sorrow, it will enslave your soul, and it will drag you to your grave. Listen to your Elders, don't brag. Maintain your dignity.

Traditionally the legends are told by grandparents to children in the cold months of the year. The setting was in a warm winter house with lots of food and many young children surrounding the Elder who was recounting the legends. It was essential that each child listen attentively and learn the various lessons being conveyed. The legend-teller would gain their complete attention by saying, "Áwacha nay!" (This is the way it was). The children would respond loudly, "Ii" which means "Yes." There were times when there was more than one storyteller involved which made it a longer and more interesting evening. Many questions were answered in the minds of the children; for instance, why did the characters in the legend do things five times? It was explained that this was a part of our lives, the parts of our bodies, the parts of the religion, and many other things we take for granted in our everyday living. The child learned that sex was a part of his life too. This part of his training was not secret, because secrecy creates bad results. They learned about sex early in life, and it was emphasized that the Creator was involved as the important part of it, and without Him the stories probably would be classified as "dirty."

We hope the reader will bear in mind that these legends are drawn from the myth age when animals were people—a time before the coming of the human beings. It is believed that in various ways the animals helped prepare the earth to receive the human beings. The most prominent character for us in this time was Spilyáy, the legendary Coyote, who by his various antics showed the human beings and especially their children how to live and behave properly. Although humorous, Spilyáy's antics have many important lessons and even offer explanations for why the world is as it is today. Other characters in this book are equally important, but they are less often mentioned. Not all of the characters in the myth age were animals. A few were human beings with extraordinary abilities beyond the limits of present human beings.

The legends presented here contain only a portion of the many characters and motifs that appeared in our traditional cycle of legends. Together they make a bigger picture, an outline of the world as our ancestors knew it, and how they succeeded and failed in dealing with it.

We hope that this book will bring to the attention of the Indian and non-Indian friends alike a better understanding of the nature of our culture and history. It is only by communicating that we can hope to understand each other. This small glimpse of a time long ago will allow readers to appreciate the historical and cultural foundations of present-day traditional Tribal life. It is not a complete picture but one that we hope will stimulate questions that can be answered by our Tribal members and by future books that we are planning to complete in the near future.

Now, Dear Reader, let your imagination delve into the wonders of Indian mythology. Imagine yourself in the forest, around a campfire; it is pitch dark all around. The stars are shining brightly overhead, and a soft warm breeze is blowing around you—just enough to keep down the mosquitoes.

The fire is merrily jumping up and down, and an old Indian couple are seated near this fire, their faces weathered and lined with ancient signs of life, their pure white hair hanging in skinny braids down around their chest. They are ready to begin a legend . . . You are waiting breathless with anticipation . . . "Áwacha nay!"

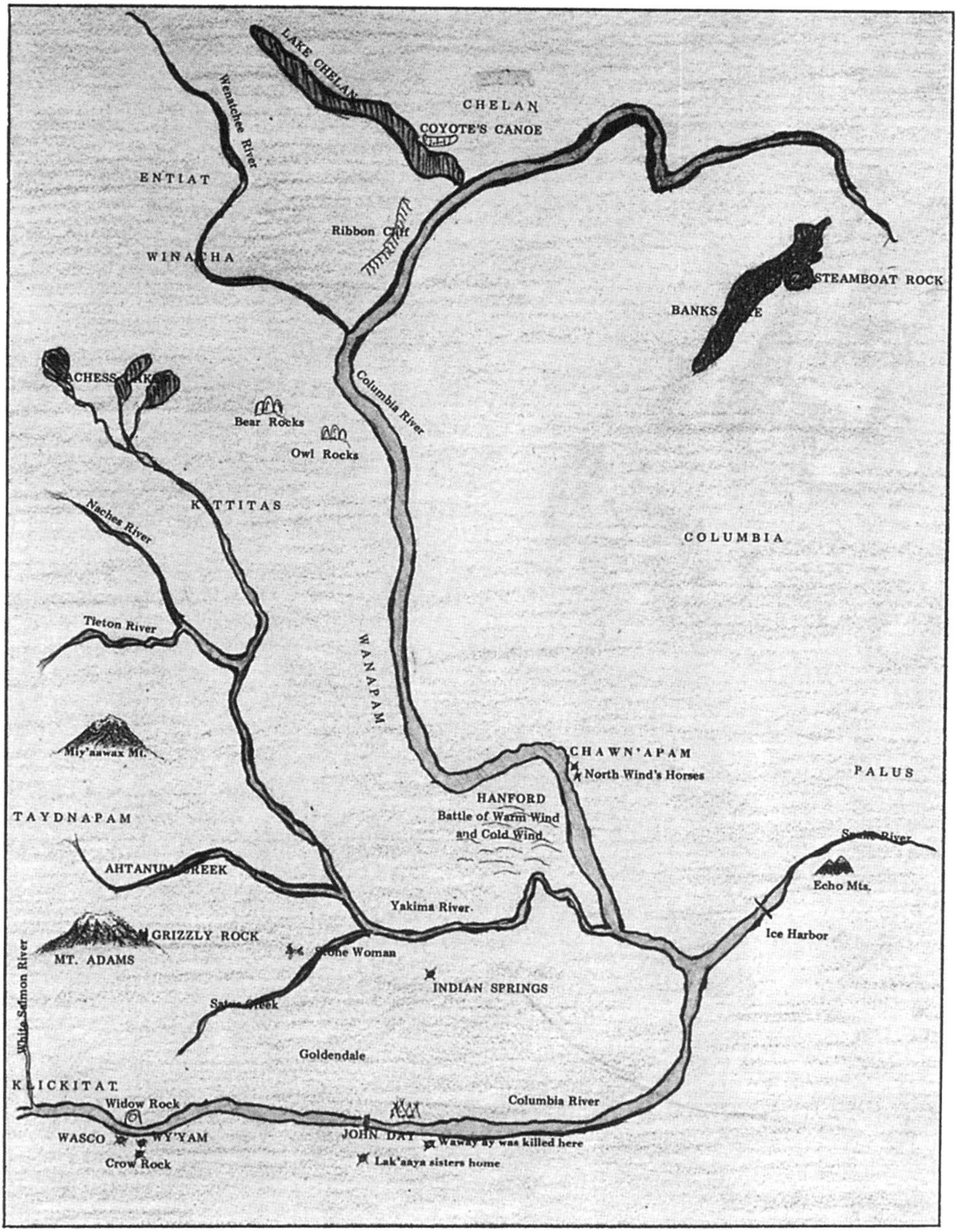

LAKE CHELAN
CHELAN
COYOTE'S CANOE
Wenatchee River
ENTIAT
STEAMBOAT ROCK
BANKS
Columbia River
Bear Rocks
Owl Rocks
Naches River
COLUMBIA
Tieton River
WANAPAM
Miy'aawax Mt.
CHAWN'APAM
North Wind's Horses
PALUS
HANFORD
Battle of Warm Wind
and Cold Wind
TAYDNAPAM
Echo Mts.
Yakima River
Ice Harbor
GRIZZLY ROCK
MT. ADAMS
INDIAN SPRINGS
White Salmon River
Goldendale
Columbia River
Widow Rock
WASCO
WY'YAM
JOHN DAY
Crow Rock
Lak'aaya sisters home

CHAPTER I

Legends and Stories of Explanation

A large part of the Indian child's education was learning about the animals, plants, and natural phenomena around him. This group of legends explains how things came to be in the way they are today. They tell us why there are no buffalo in the Northwest country, how the heron, blackbird, and coyote got their markings, and why many other things are as they are. Although most of these explanations differ from modern scientific ones, they served the same purpose for the traditional youth. They made the world understandable to him and helped him learn what to expect from the things around him.

Amushyáy and Wɨx̱inshyáy

(Monetaria Sea Shell and Abalone Shell)

This story deals with the many pitfalls of life, such as: it is unwise to be vain as Eagle discovers, unwise to be cruel because someone might take drastic action to stop you as Heron discovers, how foolish it is to ignore the pleas of your brothers as Coyote discovers, and how important it is not to be selfish as Wɨx̱inshyáy finds out.

ONE time at Wíshx̱am, Spilyáy (Coyote) had a son living there. He was Eagle, a young man of distinction, of royal blood, and of marriageable age. All of the young virgins were eagerly waiting to become his wife. They would come from all over to court this famous young man, but he would not accept anyone, he would tell them to leave him alone. He did not want to be bothered. He would make them go away.

Way down by the ocean on an island lived an old woman and her granddaughters, two beautiful maidens. She decided to send them to this young man. They heard about how hard he was to please, and he was turning everybody away. One was Amushyáy (Monetaria Sea Shell) and the other one was Wɨx̱inshyáy (Abalone Shell). They argued about when they should go, in the day or evening. One insisted on evening, but the other wanted to go in the daytime so she would show up better and Eagle would recognize her. Wɨx̱inshyáy was more aggressive and she picked her own time. She wanted to be first. The other sister waited until her sister went ahead. She went in afterward.

When Wɨx̱inshyáy went in to see Eagle in the evening, it annoyed him very much because he was trying to get some sleep and this made him cranky. He told Wɨx̱inshyáy to leave. "Why are you disturbing my sleep?

Can't you wait until it is daylight before you come around annoying me?" She would not go, he hit her on the face and her nose began to bleed. She ran outside crying, holding her hands over her face. Her sister saw her and was alarmed, "What happened to you, sister?" "Oh, Eagle hit me in the face," Wɨx̱inshyáy cried.

Then Amushyáy rushed inside to find out what was wrong, and he hit her too. "You people keep me awake all night and I can't get any sleep; can't you find another time to court me?" Amushyáy walked outside sobbing and holding her bleeding face. Young Eagle lay in bed afterward, and he began to think, "I believe I did something wrong; their skins felt so soft and smooth, unlike some of the low-class ones with scaly skins. I did not recognize them in the dark. I don't think they are from around here!" He went outside and found small shells lying around, here and there, where the blood dripped down on the ground. He looked a little closer and found small bits of mother of pearl from the Abalone lying where Wɨx̱inshyáy's blood dripped on the ground. "Oh! They are the girls I've been waiting for all this time. I must follow them immediately!"

He chased them but could not catch up. Soon he came to the edge of the ocean where Old Man Heron, grey and long legged, sat by the ocean. Heron was the ferry man. He helped people to get across the ocean onto the islands. All he had to do was stretch his long legs across the water and people walked across it like a bridge. Heron coughed, "Hah, hah, hah," towards Eagle. He spat all over his beautiful robes. He was very disrespectful and rude to Eagle because of the way he had treated the ocean girls.

In the meantime, back at the village where Eagle lived, everybody was alarmed because they could not find him. "Oh, the chief's son is gone!" All the creatures were scrambling around looking for Eagle.

Nearby were five small mallard ducks swimming around in a pond. The head of the search party came and asked them if they would help them find Young Eagle. "We must find him immediately," they said. The ducks said they would help, and they prepared for a long journey. They took off into the air flying in formation with their eyes looking around where they thought Eagle might be found. They searched for five days. Before they left they told the villagers that when they returned in five days, if they fly over the village and circle around in the sky, then they will have found him. But if they come straight to the water and land, they have not found him. This was the signal set up by the ducks.

They flew around for several days, and on the fifth day they found Heron still coughing and spitting on Eagle, laughing, “Ha, ha, ha, ho, ho, he, he,” and spitting on his clothes, ruining them. The ducks observed this, and they flew back to the village to spread the news that they had found Eagle.

When they reached the village they flew over the village, “Whew!” All the villagers heard this and they came to hear the news about Eagle. The ducks told them their young chief was pitiful, and they told them all about how Heron was spitting all over Eagle with his awful cough and making the chief’s son very ill. “His skin is turning dry and scaly from hunger and disease.”

All of the creatures who are swift—Wolf, Grizzly, Hawk, Snake, Salmon—said they would go immediately. Chinook Salmon said, “I guess I’ll go in the river as I can travel fast in the water!” Spilyáy said, “I’m going too, I’m going with Chinook Salmon and all his brothers.” They tried to persuade Spilyáy not to go, but he insisted. They told him he might fall off and drown, but Spilyáy said, “No, I’m going!” So Spilyáy climbed up on Chinook’s back. Chinook ducked down and up and he was at the rapids! There sat Spilyáy telling stories. Again Chinook dipped under the water and they were at another rapids! Spilyáy still sat on top of Chinook telling stories. This happened five times. The fifth time Spilyáy was no longer sitting on top of Chinook. He fell off and drowned, just as he was warned by his friends.

Then they came to the place where Young Eagle was sitting by Heron. They called a council and decided he could still be saved, and they cleaned him up and changed his clothes.

Old Heron, the ferry man, sat close by, amused at all the activity. Young Hawk said he would teach Heron a lesson. “It is not right for this old man to destroy people at his own will by coughing and spitting on them. He must be stopped from destroying people.” Young Hawk painted himself all up with warpaint, around his eyes and his face. Then he flew way up in the air and he came down like a bullet hitting Heron between the eyes and killing him.

In the meantime the Salmon brothers formed a bridge across the ocean onto the island where the two virgins were hiding. Wix̱inshyáy argued that she was the chosen one for Young Eagle and she was to walk across first. But her sister thought it better if they both crossed over together.

Old Man Turtle saving Shell Girl

Wɨx̱inshyáy was angry because she did not have her own way and she was pouting. Chinook Salmon was observing all of this and he did not approve of Wɨx̱inshyáy for the young chief's wife. She still wanted to be first, and she walked on ahead of her sister. When Wɨx̱inshyáy came up to Chinook Salmon, he dipped down into the water and Wɨx̱inshyáy fell into the ocean. Then Amushyáy was allowed to come over and she became Eagle's wife.

Afterwards the creatures had a large council. "Wɨx̱inshyáy fell in the ocean. Who is going to save her?" It was decreed that the one who saves her life will take her as his wife. All the young ones tried to dive down, but they could not reach her; she was too far down in the bottom of the ocean. There was another Spilyáy there and he tried to dive down and save this young Shell woman. He dove down with all his might, but they could still see his tail sticking up quivering in the air! When he came up again, he lied, "I nearly had her; it was just a few more inches and I could have reached her!" All the people saw his tail sticking out on top of the water and they did not believe him. Nobody could save her.

Old Man Turtle lived not far from there. They called on him to come and save this young girl. The chief sent word to him, "If you save this young girl, you can have her for your wife." The old man said, "Oh, no, I am an old man. I could not take that young girl for a wife!" Then he very reluctantly consented. He told them, "I want a reward if I bring her up, but I do not want a wife." So the chief told him he would reward him with a beautiful robe. The old man agreed, and he was taken to where Wɨx̱inshyáy fell in the water.

Old Man Turtle walked on the floor of the ocean searching for her, looking right and left, as he crawled slowly along. In a little while he brought Wɨx̱inshyáy up in his arms safe but scared. They again tried to persuade him to take her for his wife. "No," he insisted, "I want my pay." So they gave him the reward he was promised. If you look carefully, you will see the old turtle wearing a beautiful robe on his back. That was the reward he received for saving the life of Wɨx̱inshyáy. But she had to promise not to be selfish anymore, that other people are important too.

Since that time it was decreed that the woman is to walk behind the man. She is not to be the aggressor. This is the traditional way of our tribe.

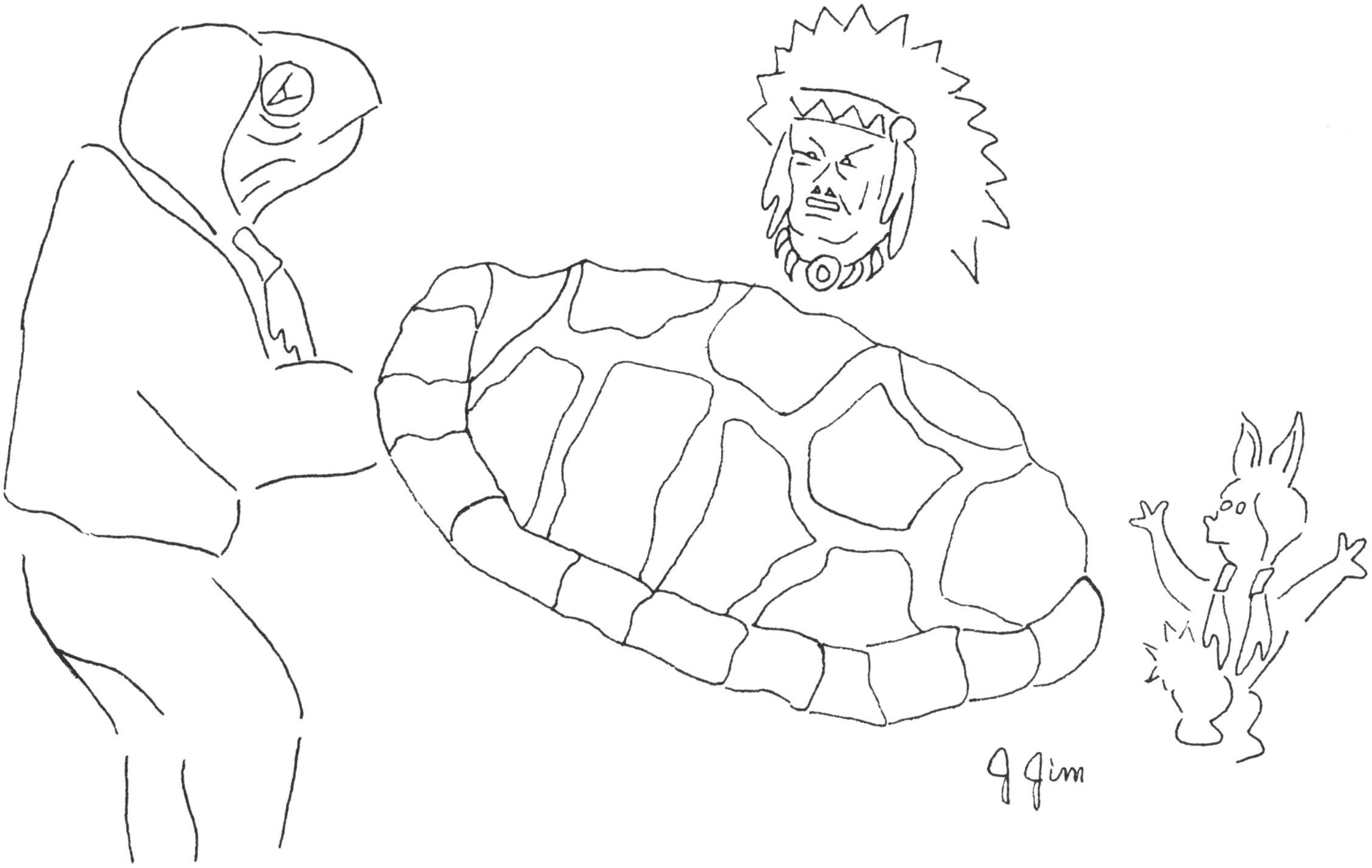

Old Man Turtle receiving his reward

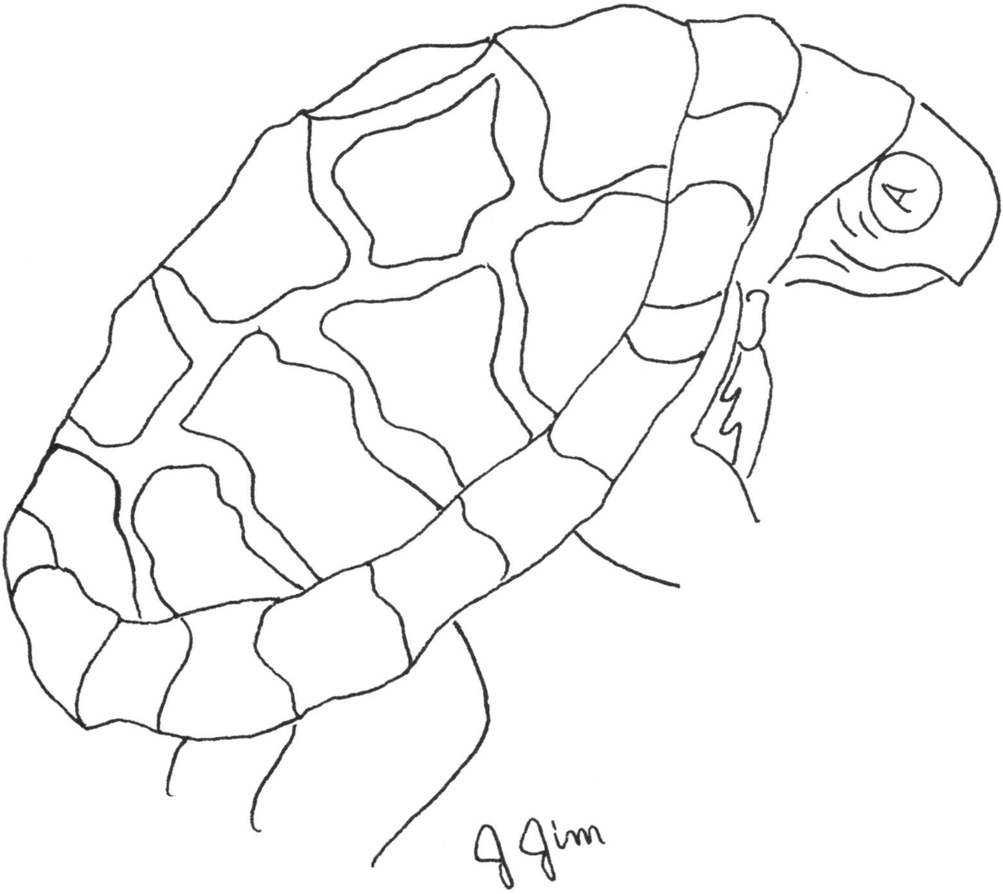

Turtle walking away, wearing his reward

Legend about Winaawayáy

(South Wind)

This is the story of how the North Wind almost took the Chawnapamípa land, and how he was finally stopped by the South Wind, grandson of Tick and Louse. It explains how certain landmarks came to be. It also shows why one should always be physically and mentally prepared.

ONCE there lived a man and his wife. The man was Tick and his wife was Louse. They had five children and they lived in Chawnapamípa, the land of the Chawnápams near the Columbia River. (Today this is Hanford, in the Tri-Cities area.)

The climate at Chawnápam was wonderful. The weather was ideal, not too cold and not too hot. This family living there never experienced any problems and they never suffered any hardships. They were very happy.

One day Atyayáaya (North Wind) and his brothers came along. They were riding beautiful horses. They came up over the White Bluffs at Chawnapamípa (there are white cliffs northeast of Hanford) and looked down on the beautiful valley—everything was there, food, good weather, everything they were looking for. There was plenty of fish, all different kinds of meat to eat, and all kinds of roots to eat all year round, and Atyayáaya wanted that place for himself.

Atyayáaya told his brothers, "Let us go down there and kill all those people and take their land. We will freeze them out. This is the kind of land we want to own, so we must kill them off." They all agreed. They had one sister named Tayatkíisya (the cold wind that makes icicles), who took her wrath out on everyone because she was crippled.

They brought their belongings on two horses; one was white and the other one, it is said, was an Appaloosa. They left these horses standing overlooking the Columbia River at the top of the White Bluffs in Chawnapamípa land. The horses were still standing there until a few years ago (20–30 years). One horse's head fell off, and finally they both toppled into the Columbia River and are now at the bottom of the river. They were perfectly formed with flying manes and tails out of rock salt, which is nearly like ice. It is thought they were also frozen solid.

The oldest brother of the Cold Wind family, Atyayáaya, was the first to descend into the valley, blowing cold and freezing everything. He froze the river so that the Tick family could not catch any fish, and he also froze the plants so that they could not get roots for food. (At one time in the Chawnapamípa land there were ticks in abundance. Also, there were lots of lice.)

Finally, the eldest son of Tick, who happened to be Warm Wind, decided to do something about this intruder who was freezing everything. He asked Atyayáaya, "Why are you doing this to our happy home?" Cold Wind told him, "I want this valley and if you want to prevent me from taking it, then you have to fight me." Cold Wind taunted him, and they argued—blowing back and forth, hot and cold.

Each time Cold Wind would blow he would freeze everything, and Warm Wind would come back and thaw everything again. Finally, Cold Wind lost his temper and challenged Warm Wind to a wrestling match to the death.

This was a big event to all the creatures, and they came from all over the land, east and west, north and south, to bet on the wrestling match. Many had great confidence in the Warm Wind, mainly because he was well liked.

When they were ready to wrestle, Warm Wind blew warm and thawed the ground. Immediately, Cold Wind blew his cold breath over it and before Warm Wind could do anything, Cold Wind grabbed him and threw him to the ground and killed him. He killed the oldest son of Tick. He stepped all over him and crushed him to pieces and stomped him into the ground.

The next eldest son thought, "How long is this going to go on? They must not be allowed to do this to us." Then he challenged Atyayáaya. He was a little younger and stronger than his older brother, and he had lots of confidence in his ability to wrestle, and all his friends did too. When he challenged the Cold Wind he was told to blow first, but he hesitated. Cold Wind kept on telling him five times until he was forced to blow first. He blew real hard and tore up all the icy ground and melted the ice and snow. Then Atyayáaya blew and froze everything again, covering everything with thick ice. He grabbed Warm Wind and threw him to the ground because the ground was too slippery for Warm Wind to brace his feet. He was overcome and thrown to the ground, killed and stomped to pieces into the ground.

It was after the second brother was killed that the youngest son of Tick decided he should go west of the mountains to the Northwest Coast. He went there to tell the creatures about their trouble with the North Wind people. He thought he might get some help from somebody there. When he arrived, all the creatures from the coast gathered together and held a council to listen to his story.

While he was there, he found a beautiful maiden and married her. He knew that they were powerful people from the ocean. The young maiden had a grandmother named Pityachíishya (Ocean Woman) and they lived in the bottom of the ocean. They knew many strange things. Before long he found his wife was to have a child. He had to return to his home, and he left his family (child-to-be) and wife, telling her he would return after he defeated the Cold Wind brothers.

When he returned to his home, he found the rest of his brothers had also been killed and stomped into the ground. He learned that the strategy the Cold Wind brother was using was to make Warm Wind brothers blow first, then he would freeze the ground and throw them and defeat them. Spilyáy wanted to change these rules but Cold Wind refused. He said, "This rule was set up from the start, and when the Warm Wind brothers throw me, they can change the rules to whatever they want." Spilyáy was losing everything betting on Warm Wind. When his wise sisters would caution him, he would tell them, "I want to double my bet and get everything back." (This is what happens when people gamble and lose. They think if they double their bet they will get it all back. It has been that way ever since.)

It was time for the youngest son of Tick to challenge the Cold Wind. Before he went out to meet Atyayáaya, he sent messengers to his wife and her grandparents, giving them some instructions. He told them, "I do not expect to win. If we have a son, this boy must prepare to defend his land."

He told them, "All these things must be observed in preparation for this battle with the Cold Winds."

He told his mother, the Louse, "Here are two feathers; one is a black-tip eagle feather which will represent a boy, and the other feather is a soft down feather called púkła (that grows next to the body of the eagle) which will represent a girl." He told his father, "If this black-tipped feather falls to the ground my child will be a boy. But if this downy feather falls to the ground it will be a girl."

His parents were nearly frozen stiff by this time, and he tried to make them as comfortable as possible before he left them. He filled in the cracks in their house and fixed their doorway so that the cold air would not blow inside the house. It was thought the house was made of stone or rocks where the old man Tick and his wife lived.

They still had their wealth put away inside this house because the Cold Wind people were not able to get inside. They had worked hard for years to gather all sorts of food. Tick would suck blood out of other creatures and store it, as would his wife, Louse. While she was feasting on something, she would store some for the future. This was what they had left in the house, and it was their only means for survival. Young Warm Wind saw this and he was confident they would last long after he was gone until his son would come to avenge him if he should be defeated.

Warm Wind prepared himself for battle very carefully and with much ceremony. At first he tried to persuade Atyayáaya to blow first, but this request was met with a big flat, "No." He told Atyayáaya, "I'm feeling weak," which gave the Cold Wind some confidence. Warm Wind blew softly, barely melting the snow. This gave Atyayáaya more self-confidence. He said to himself, "This is going to be easy. This boy is very weak." Finally, the battle became a little stronger and stronger. They blew hot and cold, back and forth (like it does in the spring when our fruit orchards have a hard time and some of our fruit trees freeze) until things became more fierce and Cold Wind finally overcame Warm Wind and threw him down. This time he did not stomp Warm Wind into the ground as he did his brothers, because he really believed young Warm Wind was too weak to fight. Instead he threw him into the canyons in high places where he still blows today warm and cold down the canyons, and he is called Wítx̱uupt by the people. So the fifth son of Tick was defeated. The Cold Wind people were very happy. They were sure they would soon own the beautiful valley after the old couple died from starvation and cold.

When Atyayáaya defeated the youngest (Warm Wind) son of Tick and Louse, he moved down into Chawnápam land to await the death of the old people. (People lived there all along the Columbia River clear down through Snake River into Idaho. They lived where there was abundant food and salmon and game.)

One day the black-tipped feather fell down. Louse grabbed the feather and coddled it saying, "Oh my beloved grandson, we are so pitiful. Tayatkíisya (Cold Wind sister, icicle maker) is treating us badly. She makes us wipe her bottom with our heads, and if we don't do it she threatens to tell her brothers to kill us. Our heads are all stiff and sore from wiping her. That's how we are—pitiful!" She continued, "We are so glad you are a boy. You must hurry and come help us." Then they both stroked the feather just like it was a person.

In the meantime they had been making small bundles of rye grass, thorn bushes, thistle, and wild rose bushes, anything that would scratch, just as they had been told by their youngest son. Even though they were weak and sick they still gathered a few at a time and tied them into five bundles.

The Cold Wind brothers were becoming more anxious and they kept sending their sister to the old couple's home to find out if they were still alive. She would swoop down on the house, fling open the door, and stick her bottom in the doorway expecting them to wipe it with their heads. This would show whether they were still alive or not. Then she would run home to tell her brothers that they were still alive. When the old folks found out they had a grandson, they did not mind wiping her bottom anymore.

The reason Tayatkíisya enjoyed humiliating them was because she was crippled and was shunned by other creatures. She enjoyed doing mean things to people because it made her feel important. (This is the way it is today, when people who feel bad about themselves enjoy humiliating other people just to make themselves feel important.) You can still feel Tayatkíisya in the wintertime when she comes blowing around your house making icicles over your doorway and around the roof of your house. People used to say, "Never leave a receptacle outside with food or water in it or Tayatkíisya will sit on it and crush it." That's what happens when you leave a bucket of water outdoors during freezing weather; it bursts open when it freezes and sometimes it will flatten out.

South Wind with his sea creature grandparents

In the meantime when baby Winaawayáy (South Wind) was born over on the Northwest Coast, he was immediately dipped in ice cold water to make him strong. His mother died at childbirth, so he lived with his maternal grandparents who were sea creatures. They lived in the bottom of the ocean.

When Winaawayáy began to mature enough to understand things, his grandfather called him to his side and told him, "The bird messengers have told me that your uncles have all been killed by Atyayáaya (North Wind), and your father was also killed. They say that your grandparents are pitiful, and they are not expected to live much longer. It is time to challenge Atyayáaya. You must prepare carefully because the Cold Wind brothers are very crafty."

Winaawayáy began to train. He began by blowing straight up out of the bottom of the ocean into what is known as a sea gale today. Then he blew inland, which is now called a tornado, blowing over trees and tearing them up by the roots. Each day he grew stronger, making huge tidal waves and pushing hillsides over and taking tops off mountains. His grandfather was watching all this time, instructing him carefully. He trained like this for many years until he was so powerful it was frightful! Soon his grandfather told him, "You are ready." He told him, "There are several things that you must observe on this mission. Your grandmother will go with you."

His grandmother told him, "Grandson, it is time to make our medicine. We must gather the most ferocious monsters of the sea—killer whale, shark, electric eel, the walrus—kill them, and melt their fat down into grease." Winaawayáy did as he was told, because by now he was so powerful that he could kill anything. They put the grease into five containers and stored them. Then she said to her grandson, "We are ready."

Grandfather called Winaawayáy before him and told him that he must exercise all the way over east of the mountains while his grandmother followed carrying the grease. His grandfather instructed him five times, and then he was ready. He went ahead of his grandmother tearing up trees, blowing over mountaintops, tearing chunks out of rock boulders, and smashing the Cascades, which were long smooth mountains at that time. He came along and tore off the top of Mt. Rainier, tore a chunk here and there from Mt. Adams, gouged out the earth along the way, made deep lakes in the mountains, and carved deep canyons everywhere.

When he reached what is now called Bickleton Ridge, he looked down towards White Bluffs (Hanford) and saw the land all frozen. He saw how pitiful his paternal grandparents were, the father and mother of his beloved father. He thought about his uncles and father, and how pitiful his grandparents were, and he lay down on the ground and wept. There is an artesian spring there today called Pánatk̠'pt (Indian Spring), which represents the tears that he wept. This spring never ceases to flow.

He saw his grandparents, stiff and still, but he did not know if they were alive. Then he went down there and blew softly around the home of Tick and his wife, Louse. The icicles began to fall all around making musical sounds like the wind chimes. The old lady heard this sound and she knew immediately that her grandson had arrived. She nudged the old man Tick and said, "Our grandson has arrived." Then she said, "Áana, chxw ála (Oh my beloved grandson) we are so glad you have arrived at last. We are just pitiful. Tayatkíisya is treating us badly. We have to wipe her bottom every time she comes, or she will tell her brothers to kill us." Their heads were all stiff and sore from wiping Tayatkíisya. Then she told him of their hardships and how Winaawayáy's father was killed by the Cold Wind.

Winaawayáy blew softly around the house on the outside, melting the snow and ice. Then he went inside the house, "Shux!" melting the snow, and the icicles fell down, "Shay . . . !" making musical sounds. Then he blew warm air all around the house making it warm and comfortable for his grandparents. He asked them if they had prepared the five bundles of rye grass and thorns, as they were instructed. They showed him where they had hidden them.

They heard Tayatkíisya coming and he hid. She came to the door, flung it open, and peered inside to see if the old people were still alive. She pushed her bottom in the doorway to have it wiped. Winaawayáy signaled his grandmother to wipe her with one of the bundles. She wiped her with a bundle of thistles, and Tayatkíisya cried, "Ana, na, na, na. They hurt me!" She then ran home to tell her brothers.

When she told them what happened, they only laughed at her. They thought their sister was getting tired of running errands and was making up stories. She tried to tell them about the warmth around the home of Tick and Louse, but they ignored her. They knew that all of Tick's sons were dead, so what was causing this to happen?

Grandfather coaching South Wind

The next day Tayatkíisya was sent on her errand, but this time she did not want to go. She found it warmer than the day before, so she cautiously peered inside the door and found they were still there. She shoved her bottom inside the door to be wiped, and the old lady Louse took a bundle of thorns and wiped her with it. She hollered, "Ana, na, na, na! That hurt more than ever," and she ran home to tell her brothers.

The next day this happened again. Finally, one of the brothers went down to check on her story. But Winaawayáy had powers inherited from his ocean creature people, and he wished everything to be as they were before. The Cold Wind brother saw only frozen ground and the old people all covered with ice and frost. He returned to his home and reported that everything was the same; there was no warm wind or anything like their sister had been telling them.

The next day they sent her again. She was very, very reluctant to go. She was afraid of her brothers, but she decided this would be the last time. She swooped down on the home of Tick and Louse, finding it warmer than ever. She flung open the door and peered inside. They were the same as before, but it was warmer inside. She turned around and pushed her bottom inside the doorway, and this time the old lady wiped her with a thornier bundle, scratching her all the way down to her thighs. Tayatkíisya cried out, "Ohla, lala , lala, lala! That hurt more than ever. I am not returning anymore!" She ran home again to tell her brothers. When they saw the scratches they believed her. So they came down to investigate it. Again, they found everything as it was before, but then they suspected that something was wrong.

The next time they put a thick, hard covering of ice over Tayatkíisya's bottom (that's when panties and pants were first made). They told her that the covering would protect her from the sharp thing that was hurting her. So she went again. By this time she was so sore she could hardly walk. She went down there and peered inside the door. It was warm and cozy inside. She turned around slowly and put her bottom through the doorway to be wiped. This time Winaawayáy grabbed the last and thorniest bundle. He wiped her with all his strength tearing her all up and knocking the thick ice off. Tayatkíisya cried out, "Ana, na, na, na, na! That hurts more than ever," and she ran away, stumbling and falling. Winaawayáy chased her, wiping her with all his strength, until Tayatkíisya fell down writhing with pain. She died from the pain without revealing the identity of Winaawayáy.

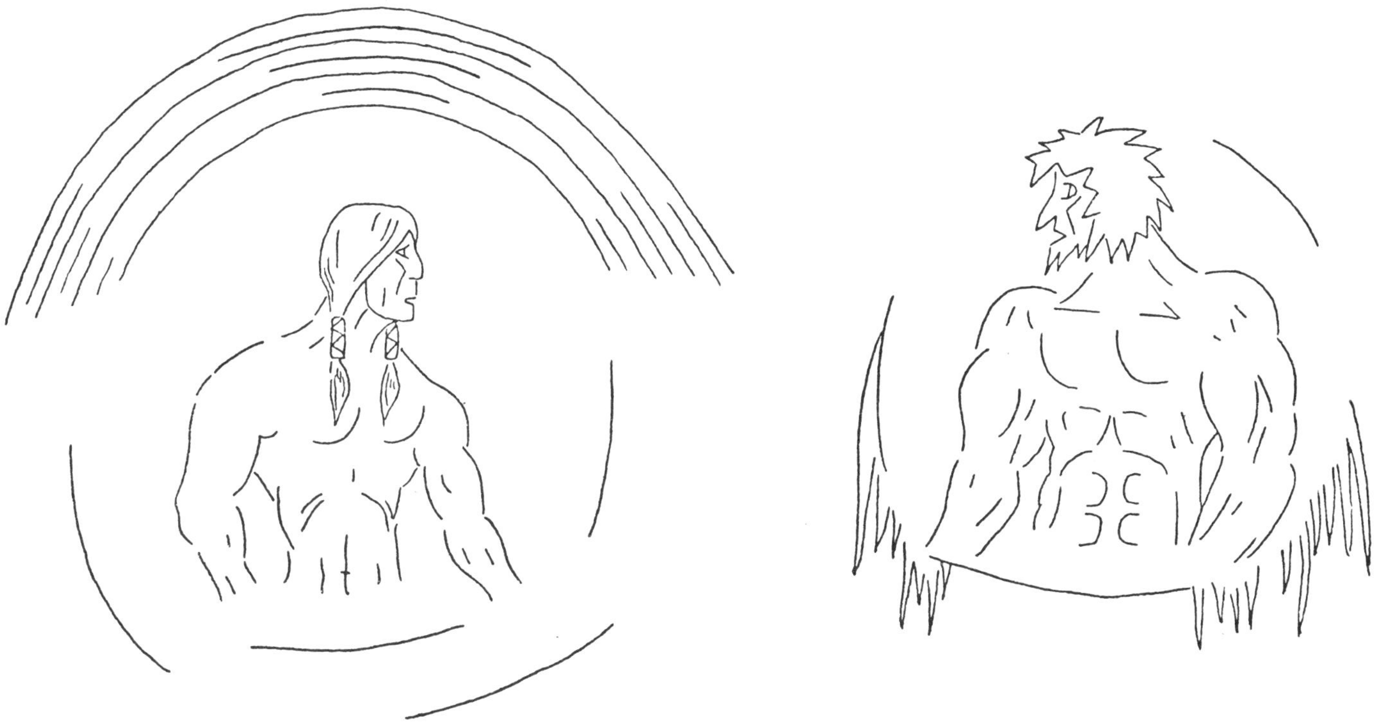

South Wind challenging North Wind

When the Cold Wind brothers discovered their sister was killed, they were very angry. An informant told Atyayáaya that Winaawayáy killed Tayatkíisya. The oldest Cold Wind brother challenged Winaawayáy saying, "All right, you think you are so powerful just because you killed my little sister, then you must defeat me!" Winaawayáy told him, "I am only a little boy; how do you expect me to defeat a powerful man like you?" But Atyayáaya was determined to avenge his sister. He called him five times until Winaawayáy was forced to accept. Atyayáaya was suspicious of the Warm Wind. He looked him over, but he couldn't figure out what he was, this strange-looking creature. He decided to use caution in dealing with him.

Winaawayáy prepared for the battle by painting the skies fiery red with his grandfather's (Tick's) paint. Because he was part tick he was able to use this paint. You will find red earth that looks like Indian paint in the land of the Chawnápam. When Atyayáaya saw this, he was afraid, but Winaawayáy assured him that he was a stranger only passing through, that he only stopped to visit. Atyayáaya tried to find out the identity of this stranger. None of the creatures would tell him. Winaawayáy had to delay until his maternal grandmother, the Sea Creature, arrived with the medicine, the five containers of sea creature grease. Finally, Sea Creature arrived with the five containers of medicine and everybody began to wager. The two old women got together on what they were to do.

Atyayáaya was still suspicious of Winaawayáy, so he decided to change his tactics. "I will give you a chance. I have this rule giving you the first chance to blow, but I will blow first this time."

Spilyáy (Coyote), sensing a scheme, immediately objected. "You are changing your own rules. You said before that this rule would not change until you were defeated!" Crafty Spilyáy did not want to spoil his chances of doubling his winnings because his five sisters had already counseled him. "Besides," Coyote said, "I have been a witness to your rules all this time while you were fighting the Warm Wind brothers. You cannot change it now!" Winaawayáy taunted him too, "It was your sister that was killed. Why do you want to give me this chance? Besides, I am only a small boy. You should not have any trouble throwing me and killing me!" He pretended to lose his patience and said, "I don't know what you have to fear. I am only a poor, weak person. What could I put on the ground that would be more superior than yours? We are only wasting time. Let us go ahead with it so you can kill me sooner."

Atyayáaya would look at Winaawayáy and think, "He is a strange-looking creature indeed. He is so ragged, puny, and his body looks so grey." With his supernatural powers, Winaawayáy was able to hypnotize North Wind into seeing him like that. Atyayáaya changed his mind, "Why should I fear this creature?"

Atyayáaya was elegant in his raiment with his hair all stiffened over his forehead and his face all painted up. He looked over the red sky that Winaawayáy had painted, and he likewise painted the skies with northern lights, trying to outdo Winaawayáy's red sky.

Observing all this, Atyayáaya decided he had nothing to fear, so he consented to the original rule. He thought, "This is going to be easy. What can this puny looking creature do to me? I will make short work of him," and he blew with all his might, "Whooooo!" freezing everything on the ground.

Then the young Winaawayáy grew taller and taller, bigger and bigger, until he towered over Atyayáaya. The sky turned fiery red. Winaawayáy made a huge arch with towers of rainbows at each mountain peak. That's how he dressed himself. Then he told Atyayáaya, "I don't want to soil your ground. I will go up a short way before I lay my ground."

The Cold Wind brothers thought he was trying to run away, and they laughed at him, saying, "Oh, you just want to run away! We will follow you no matter how far you go." Then Winaawayáy released a powerful gust of wind, gouging out a huge hole in the ground, there at Lilíik which is now a valley at Chawnápam. At the same time the grandmother lifted up one container of the sea creature grease and poured it over the ice that Atyayáaya had put down. Cold Wind tried desperately to freeze the grease, but it would not freeze, and Winaawayáy stepped on it, stood fast and threw Atyayáaya down. Warm Wind said, "I will not kill you and stomp you to the ground like you did my uncles and my father." Instead, he cut him into five little pieces and threw him into the canyons and gullies.

Spilyáy, the referee and judge, decreed Atyayáaya will blow only a few days at a certain time. He will no longer kill things. Spilyáy was generous because he had won back his losses. He said, "There is a different kind of human to be created soon. They are coming closer. The People will be

Wrestling match between South Wind and North Wind

living all over this land. When you blow in season, they will say, 'Oh, 'átyasha' (Oh, it is blowing cold wind)."

It was the same with the next eldest brother of the Cold Winds. Winaawayáy defeated him and threw him into the canyons and gullies, and the same declaration was made by Spilyáy. Then the third and the fourth were thrown. The youngest Cold Wind brother was alarmed and he did not wish to die, so he asked for mercy. He said, "Take pity on me. I want to live!" Coyote wanted to win some more, so he taunted the young Atyayáaya. "It can't be true! You, Atyayáaya are supposed to be fierce and strong. You have killed many people. You froze everything, all the food and Waykáanash (Salmon). You left nothing, why are you pleading for mercy? This is disgraceful!"

Atyayáaya ignored Spilyáy and still persisted. "Take pity on me, I will never bother you again. I will never challenge you to a fight. My powers also have some benefit. I can blow for a short while, and I will make things grow. My medicine will water the food, provide paths for the Waykáanash, and survival for animals." Spilyáy was becoming desperate, and he told Atyayáaya, "Go home and get ready to fight. I want to win some more." But Atyayáaya refused.

Finally, Atyayáaya knelt down humbly in front of Winaawayáy and asked him five more times. At last Winaawayáy decided to let him go free. Although the revengeful grandparents urged him to kill Atyayáaya, Winaawayáy was merciful. (It is not right to take revenge.)

Spilyáy further decreed, "If Atyayáaya blows more than three days (if he should blow five times), then the People who are coming will take hot ashes and fling it against the wind saying, 'Páax̱amuni!' (five times more), and the wind will die down." This is practiced today by some people. So that is how it is today.

Now the white people have discovered our secret. At the land of the Chawnapamípa, where Louse and Tick lived, there were all kinds of food stored there. Now the white people have discovered some of these things and are making a living from it. They discovered uranium, which is made into medicine and ammunition. This is the animal grease that the grandmother poured on the ground and the ice that Atyayáaya laid down is still there. You can see a layer of white substance, a layer of crystal substance, a layer of red earth, and a layer of powdery substance. The powdery substance is made up of the Sea Creature medicine used to defeat Cold Wind.

Grandmother Sea Creature pouring medicine, and South Wind throwing North Wind down

When young Winaawayáy left Chawnapamípa land, he said he would return whenever there is trouble for the People. Today we experience many bad things. Our water is becoming so polluted that our Waykáanash and small fish are dying. The mountains do not provide enough moisture to give us water for our plants and animals, and our huckleberry bushes are drying up. Every day we hear about the tornadoes blowing and tearing down homes leaving people homeless. The sea gales toss ships around on the ocean. Perhaps Winaawayáy knows about how we are abusing our environment, and he is going to return to do something about it.

After everything was finished at Chawnapamípa land, old lady Pityachíishya was returning to her home at the bottom of the ocean, when she lay down to rest at Toppenish Ridge (she is still there). There is a trail they call Zig Zag Trail going up there. The Indians call it Eel Trail because it reminds us of an eel swimming the water—all twisty—back and forth. If you want to make a wish, give the old lady a gift and make a wish. She will grant it for you. It is now called the Wishing Rock.

Race between Eel and Rattlesnake

Rattlesnake wanted to exchange bodies with Eel, but Eel would have nothing to do with it. Finally, under pressure, Eel agreed to have a race and the winner would get his way. This legend shows how gambling could cause great misfortune. We learn why there are a lot of eels and rattlesnakes around the falls of the Columbia River at Wíshx̱am.

A LONG time ago Wáx̱push (Rattlesnake) lived way up in the hills. He had a very comfortable home, no worries, and plenty of food, but he was very lonely. All of the other creatures were afraid of him because he was not easy to live with, and they stayed away from him.

In another part of the country, Asúm (Eel) was having a hard time. He could not find a suitable place to spend the winter. He looked everywhere—in the river, lakes, the sloughs, the creeks, everywhere. He traveled up the river (Yakima) to Satus Creek, back down again and up Toppenish Creek, on up the hills farther and farther until he came to Mill Creek where he found Wáx̱push. Wáx̱push was glad to see him and he was also surprised to see him so far up in the hills. He asked, "What are you doing way up here in the hills?" Eel answered, "I am looking for a place to live for the winter. I went up the other way but I could not find a suitable place. I came up here in hopes of finding the kind of home which will be comfortable through the winter." The Snake found an opportunity for some company and he immediately responded to the chance. "Oh, this house of mine is all finished and there is plenty of room for both of us. Let us live here together for the winter. It's getting too cold now to be building a house anyway!" Eel was not too enthusiastic, but he agreed that it was rather late to be building a house. He agreed to live with Rattlesnake for the winter.

When spring was approaching, Rattlesnake told the eel, "You have had the name Asúm for a long time now, and my name Wáx̱push is old. Let us exchange names. From now on you can be Wáx̱push, and I will be named Asúm." Eel was definitely opposed to this and he answered, "No! That would not be right. The Creator named me Asúm and he created you and gave you the name of Wáx̱push. It is not proper for me to change my name." However, Wáx̱push insisted, and he asked Eel five times to exchange names with him. But Eel still said, "No!"

Finally it was warm enough to come out of the den, and Eel did not want to stay in that cave any longer, so Rattlesnake challenged Eel to a race. He told him that if he beat him in this race then they would exchange names legally, and they would also exchange bodies. At last, in exasperation, Eel accepted the challenge and agreed to race against Wáx̱push. They plotted out a route towards the Columbia River to end at a place called Spearfish (now called Horsethief Lake) at Wíshx̱am. The rules set up for the race were that the one who won would abide by the other's wishes; if Snake won, Eel had to exchange his name, body, and everything with him; but if Eel won, they would not exchange anything.

There was much preparation as they went over the route again and again to make sure each one understood. Finally they were ready to start. Rattlesnake, however, did not wait for the starting signal. He started right out ahead of Eel, bolting around the mountain. Asúm was caught by surprise. He jumped up and started over the mountain in hopes of catching up, but he was a little too late.

They battled over the mountains, down the hill, and around the bend but Eel could not catch up with Snake. Snake knew that Eel could not travel fast on the ground and he kept the route away from water as much as possible.

This kept up until they reached the bank overlooking the Columbia River at the point where Wíshx̱am is located, where Horsethief Lake is now. When Eel saw the water it gave him more confidence and he plunged ahead with every bit of strength he had left. He plunged, "Pow!" into the water, surging an inch ahead of Snake. "Ay! From now on you will remain Wáx̱push for the rest of your life and I will remain Eel."

From that time there have been lots of eels at the falls of the Columbia River near Wíshx̱am, and people come from all around to catch eels to

Race between Eel and Rattlesnake

put away for the winter. Also, there are a lot of rattlesnakes around there. There is a large snake pit covered over with a huge stone. Whenever the children would slide down the slanted stone (which is like a slide at the playgrounds) they could hear the rattlesnakes making rattling sounds which sound like a swarm of bumblebees, "Shayyy!"

Spilyáy and the Monster

In this tale Spilyáy kills the monsters that were swallowing all the people, gives many animals the colors they now wear, and exiles the monsters so that people could live in peace. It shows how cowardice can defeat human beings. Special attention should be paid to the middle of the tale, where examples of this are pointed out.

In the land of Winátsha (Water Pouring Out), and the canyon going up towards Omak, where there is a high rocky mountain, there lived a man-eating monster in the water. He was the leader of other monsters living in this area. All kinds of creatures used to travel through there, and this monster would surprise them and capture them. The monster resembled a dog and when he inhaled anything he would howl, "Whuu" five times; then he would swallow them.

One day Spilyáy was sauntering along the trail on top of the mountain. He was famished because he hadn't had anything to eat for many days. He strained himself five times, letting out five piles and these mounds turned into his sisters. He asked them where he could find some food. His sisters knew everything and when he was in trouble he usually accepted their wise counseling. This time they were reluctant to give him any information. "Oh, we don't want to tell you because when we tell you what to do, you always say, 'Just as I thought.' That's why we don't want to tell you." He was real angry with them and he said, "Oh tamkw'íkw'i (hail) come down and smash these selfish things to pieces. They don't want to help me! And I waste my energy carrying them around!" Finally, they consented to tell him. They told him, "You are near the home of a man and wife. They are informers for a water monster living at the bottom of the river. He has some resemblance to a huge dog. When you get there they will tell the monster and he will come and get you. He will inhale you inside his mouth." Spilyáy decided to go ahead, anyway, and find out.

He prepared himself carefully. He put on his best clothes and proceeded on up the trail towards this place his sisters told him about. He began to sing, "Ah, haha, ya haaaaa, ha hu ha huu, ah hu ha ihuh huu," sauntering along as if he did not know there was a monster living there.

Yiityíitya (Sandpiper) and his wife heard this song, and they were alarmed. They thought it was some sort of ferocious being. Pretty soon the song seemed to hypnotize them and they began to sway with the rhythm of it, and the music seemed to echo and reverberate up and down the canyon. It hypnotized the Yiityíitya and put them in a deep trance. Coyote walked up to them and grabbed one of them by the head and throat and he cut off its tongue. But before he could cut the second one's tongue, it managed to let out a yelp, "Yiit!" He told them if they didn't tell the monster about him, he would reward them with a beautiful robe and decorations.

The monster heard the very weak "Yiit!" and he decided to investigate. Usually they made loud sounds, but this was very faint and weak, and usually they swam out in the river to warn him, too, and they were not out there.

The monster came up to the surface of the river and peered around. Again he heard a faint "Yiit!" as Yiityíitya was vainly struggling to warn the monster. Then the monster climbed out of the water to find out what was happening. He climbed up the steep cliff to the top of the hill.

Spilyáy was waiting at the top of the hill for this monster, who truly resembled a huge dog. Spilyáy had rigged up a trap for this monster. When it climbed up and reached the top of the mountain, Spilyáy cut the vines. The monster fell down the cliff to his death, splattering blood all over the cliffside. Today when you are driving along Highway 97 between Entiat and Chelan, you will see the cliffs all covered with red streaks and splashes of blood on the stone cliffs. This place is Ribbon Cliff.

While the monster was catapulting down the canyon, Spilyáy was nonchalantly singing his song, "Ah ha, yahaaaah ha haaa, ihaaaaa, ah ha ha hu ha hu ihuh huu, ah huu!"

Then Spilyáy climbed down the cliffside, and he discovered all the creatures that the monster was holding captive in his stomach. He turned everything loose. He found Wáx̱push (Rattlesnake) inside. When he became angry—"Shay!"—Spilyáy told him, "Ah, indeed you must be ferocious. Then why have you turned into waste inside this monster?" He turned everything loose. That's why we have all these birds and animals back again because Spilyáy turned them loose after the monster had swallowed them.

He told Yiityíitya and his wife, "Although you are spies, I will reward you nevertheless." He painted their hands (bird legs), painted even their fingernails red, then he made paint from the blood of the monster and painted their feathers. On their faces he painted their eyelashes black from parts of the monster's body (like the girls do these days when they paint their eyelashes) and he drew heavy lines around their eyes. He fixed them all up, and they were so proud. They ran down to the river's edge and looked at their reflection in the water. They were proud of their decorations. The female had some yellow paint mixed in with the paint on her feet. Then he massaged their tongues with his hands, making them long again.

When you look at Yiityíitya running along the riverbanks today, you will notice how they are decorated. Coyote predicted, "You will always be together living near the water."

Then he walked on down the trail again, along the river. When the other monsters heard what he did to this dog monster, they held a council and warned each other to avoid this Spilyáy because he wanted to kill them. He kept on walking and singing his song sitting on top of the hilltops, hoping somebody would answer him. But all the monsters had warned each other not to fool with this creature, so there was no answer to Spilyáy's song. (This is the way he sings today, sitting on top of the hill. He will also let his sisters sing too. That is why you think you hear a whole pack of coyotes singing at night, when actually there is only one.)

Little Sagebrush Mɨsɨ́s (Grey Ground Squirrel) would run down there and cautiously peek at him, "Yes, that's Spilyáy," then he would run quickly back and tell the monsters from Banks Lake, "Yes, it's Spilyáy!" They all hid themselves, and poor Spilyáy would not get any response from the monsters.

That's the way it should be; when you know there is something around that might harm you, stay very still and hide. Don't try to be brave and confront something that might harm you. If you know there is a person who could do you harm, avoid him and don't try to have anything to do with him.

As Spilyáy was walking along the river, he came up on a monster that was not warned. He approached him at Sundale, north of the Columbia River. The monster was huge and powerful like those we call prehistoric monsters. This monster used all his strength and tried to swallow Spilyáy. But Spilyáy fought against the monster as it tried to inhale him.

He prepared to outwit this monster. He went out and gathered vines that grew along the Columbia River. (These vines are there today and are used for many things.) He braided them into ropes. Then he prepared some pitch wood and made shavings out of this and hid it. He tied himself to a big rock with the vines and called out to the monster, "Oh, ho, ho, ho, ho, ho! Oh, hohohhoy! How come you are asleep?" But the monster ignored him. "Oh, I'm so afraid of you. Are you so afraid of me that you don't answer me?" Finally, the monster became angry, and he came up out of the water and he inhaled with all his strength. Coyote slyly told the monster, "Oh, nephew, what is the matter with you, don't you recognize me? This is I, the old man!" The monster sucked and sucked, tore one vine off the rock, then another, and Spilyáy said, "My, my! He just does not recognize me!"

He tried to convince the monster of his identity. Finally the monster broke all five ropes and swallowed him. Then Spilyáy walked inside, and the first one to greet him with a "Shayy" (rattling sound) was another rattlesnake. Spilyáy said to him, "Shayy! indeed. Look at you making all this racket, and you are nothing but waste." He told the rest of the captives, "Why are you growling at me? How come you didn't use all that meanness on the monster when he swallowed you?"

Some of the animals inside were very cold; they were huddled together shivering. Spilyáy decided to build a fire. He had some flint and he built a fire with the pitch shavings he had hidden inside his robe. He made sure to build this fire right beneath the heart. The small creatures recognized him and they called him "uncle." They were scurrying around helping him gather bits of wood. Some even tore their clothes to help build this fire. They told him, "We are hungry and cold." He told them, "What's the matter with you? Don't you see all this fat dripping around from the inside of the monster?" Then he said he would cook for them. Pretty soon the fat began to drip from the heart of the monster, as the heart began to bake.

Coyote sat nearby licking the drippings. "This is what I thought. I knew that this monster was nice and fat and would fill my stomach." He cut up the vines still hanging on his body and added them to the fire. Then he invited the creatures to come and help themselves to the bits and pieces of fat that began to fall off the monster's heart. "Don't be so stupid. Don't you see all this food around?" Then he invited them to sit down and eat.

All the creatures began to feast and they began to feel alive again, because they were nearly starving to death. There was Whippoorwill tearing at the heart and Blue Jay drinking fat.

Suddenly they heard a funny sound like groaning. "Hah, Hah, Hah." Spilyáy said, "Hurry, gather some more firewood; let's build up our fire." And they all ran around picking up debris and breaking off pieces of their clothing to make more fuel for the fire. The flames shot up against the heart. Then they began to heave around inside and they felt they were tipping over, and they heard a sound, "Haah!" which sounded final. Spilyáy told them, "Quickly head for an opening" (anus) and they all swam right into the water. Some swam to shore, and some flew away. Some of the creatures were affected by the smoke inside the monster. Old Heron's wings were scorched at the tips; that's why you see the heron with black wing tips. Other birds were streaked with black and gray. Some became all black, like Blackbird. Even Spilyáy was scorched here and there on his body. Some parts were yellowed with smoke and there were dark patches on his body like burns. That's why he looks scorched. Some of the creatures nearly died. He would shove them out saying, "Oh, you're just faking around; you don't want to die. Look at me; I am an old man and I'm not dying."

Since that time, when Spilyáy killed his second monster, he made a decree. "There will no longer be monsters to kill people." He told the monsters, "You will not kill people anymore. Others should have a chance to live too." The monsters that didn't want to observe his decree immediately left the area, moving to deeper waters, so they would not have to encounter Spilyáy anymore. Some, like the shark or killer whale, still kill people. But in this area there are no killer monsters in any of our rivers or lakes.

Legend about Pyax̱í

(Bitter Root)

Spilyáy gives bitterroot a good taste and thus helps the human beings with food sources before their arrival.

A LONG time ago, in the animal world, Spilyáy happened to be temporarily living in the mountains around Ḵw'ayḵw'áylɨm (K'úsi Creek area), where the pyax̱í (bitterroots) grow in abundance. We Indian people go there to dig our supply for the winter every year in the springtime. The bitterroot is a basic food for us. It is an important part of our diet containing the necessary food value to provide healthy bodies but no excess fats. It is a vegetable. The leaves are green and they lie flat on top of the soil in a circular shape the size of a dollar. The blossoms are pink clusters which look like small rose buds. In full bloom they are like hydrangea blossoms.

Spilyáy wanted to eat some good pyax̱í. There was a lot of it around, but the plants appeared smaller than he wanted. He decided to taste one, then he tasted another, until he became really concerned because they were tasteless and flat. He was very disappointed. He wanted a vegetable with a little more taste.

Spilyáy called forth his wise sisters for counsel. They told him, "In the north, there is a land where the pyax̱í plants grow into very large plants." They told him where to go. He told his sisters, "I knew this all along," and they were disgusted with him because they thought they were helping him. Spilyáy said, "I will go to this northern country and see for myself if they really have such large pyax̱í!" Spilyáy journeyed to this land of big pyax̱í, a place now known as Coulee Dam.

Spilyáy was desperate. The more he thought about pyax̱í, the more he craved it. (People actually crave pyax̱í, it is such an important part of their diet.) When he finally arrived at this place in the north, he found huge pyax̱í plants scattered all over the flat lands. The blossoms looked three times larger than those at Ḵw'ayḵw'áylɨm.

Spilyáy was very impressed with the pyax̱í he saw growing in the north. They were large, long, and tender. But when he tasted it, he could hardly keep from spitting it out again. It was ever so bitter! Then he thought about the small and short pyax̱í at Ḵw'ayḵw'áylɨm. How shaggy and dry they appeared. Not as large and tender, growing as deep into the ground as these in Coulee. He, again, asked his sisters for counsel. This time they were reluctant to counsel him because he always told them he already knew everything. Spilyáy called up to the sky, "Come down hail and beat these ungrateful sisters to pieces!" The sisters pleaded with Spilyáy not to allow the hail to come down and beat them into the ground. Then they told him, "Take these plants, bundle them into five bundles and carry them back to Kw'aykw'áylɨm and plant them with the other plants." Spilyáy said, "I knew this all along, sisters. That is what I will do."

Spilyáy looked for the biggest plants he could find. Although they were bitter, he still picked them and made five bundles as he was instructed by his sisters. He tied them into five bundles and he brought them back to this land. When he arrived he stood up on a high hill and picked out the place where he would plant these huge pyax̱í plants. He took the five bundles and began to plant them, mixing them up with the small plants all around the hills where they grow today. (There are several places where the pyax̱í is dug today. Some are bitter and some do not have as much bitter taste. I am sorry to say that pollution is gradually destroying this necessary food for Indians. There are sheep and cattle eating it up before the Indians can dig it.)

When Spilyáy finished his work, he threw five bundles in all directions, so that they were mixed with the other plants, saying, "This is where we will plant our bitterroots, pyax̱í!" He worked for five days before he was finished. Then he said, "Soon there will be People living here. This is their food. They will dig it for food. Some will prefer the bitter ones, the other will want the more bland ones. They will seek out their own taste, but this is their food!" The pyax̱í grew up after that as large, tender, and long-rooted pyax̱í plants. Some were bitter, some mild. This is how Spilyáy predicted we would have food called pyax̱í, and this is how he brought the flavored bitterroots to our country.

Spilyáy Breaks the Dam

At one time no salmon could swim up the Columbia River because the Swallow Sisters had built a dam. This legend tells how Spilyáy outwitted those sisters and liberated the salmon for everyone to use. If the younger sister had followed her better judgment, Spilyáy would not have succeeded.

SPILYÁY was traveling down the Columbia River near Spearfish (Wíshx̱am) and he was told by some creatures that there was great concern because the salmon were blocked off from traveling up the Columbia River. It was rumored that there were five Swallow Sisters damming them up and trapping them to keep them from escaping and going up the river. The sisters had this trap built right there between Wíshx̱am and Celilo Falls. (Wíshx̱am is across the river from Celilo.)

Spilyáy pondered and schemed on how he would release the fish and get them to the upper part of the Columbia River, because the people were starving. Finally, he thought of a way. He would play on the sympathy of the five sisters.

He caused a lot of rain and it flooded the river and then he rigged up what looked like a battered old house, with torn up tules crushed up like they were smashed, and tent poles all bent up and broken. Then he made it float down the river, as if this home was torn down by the wind. He made himself into a little tiny baby, wished himself into a baby board, and floated down with the tules and tent poles, crying, "Waaa, waa, waa!"

The five sisters saw the baby and they said, "Oh, somebody's home must have been washed out and this baby is the only survivor! Poor thing." They picked him up out of the river, "He's a cute little baby." But the youngest sister was suspicious of this baby. She said, "I don't want to hold that baby; there's something peculiar about it!" But the others were still sympathetic and they scolded their younger sister for being so cruel.

They took him into their home and they gave him an eel tail to suck like a nipple. Then they tied a piece of dry salmon on his cradle, hanging it down in front of him. He would reach up and grab it, pull on it, and put it in his mouth. The sisters exclaimed, "Oh, he is a smart baby! He can feed himself just like a grown-up!" But the youngest sister was still suspicious.

They were active women, always going around digging roots and preserving food for their home. That's why they were hoarding all the fish for themselves, because they believed in eating well. One day they had to leave the baby at home and go to Warm Springs to dig nunás (mariposa lily). They left him with dried salmon tied on his cradle and hoped he would be all right until they came back.

As soon as they left he turned himself back into Spilyáy again. He already had five shields put away near the dam, and he had five sharp tools to work with on the dam. He took one sharp stone and began to chip away at the dam with it. When the sisters came home, he changed himself into a baby again and jumped into the cradle, where he was innocently sucking on his dried salmon and cooing away. The sister exclaimed over what an intelligent baby he was, how he took care of himself, smiling and cooing. They thought he was so cute.

On the second day it was the same, and then the third day and fourth. Then on the fifth day he was nearly finished with his work and he began to work too eagerly. One of the sisters was digging up at Warm Springs and she broke her digging iron, exclaiming, "Something is wrong at the house! It's the baby. He must be something else, not a baby!" They ran over the hill into the Columbia River and caught Spilyáy chipping away at their dam. They took their diggers and began to strike him on his back over and over, but he threw a shield on top of his back and kept chipping away. When one sharp instrument became dull he would throw it away and grab another until he was on his fourth chipper and his fourth shield. When his fifth chipper put a hole in the dam and his fifth shield was on his back, he ran away as the salmon came bursting out of the trap, swimming up the Columbia River.

The five sisters sat down on the beach and cried when they saw all the salmon swimming away. From that day Coyote decreed the Swallow

Sisters would no longer have the power to trap the fish and keep it from the other people.

Spilyáy continued up the river and soon he became so hungry he could not stand it. Spilyáy went up the river scavenging for food. Soon he became so hungry his insides felt hollow. He was thinking to himself, "I wonder if the salmon will feed me?" Then he called out loudly, "Oh my liberated salmon, jump out here and feed me!"

The Chinook Salmon jumped out of the river and landed on his feet, flapping its tail against the rocky ledge. Spilyáy grabbed it, but the salmon slipped through his fingers and slid back into the river because it was too slimy to hold. This happened five times until Spilyáy gave up. Then he sighted an object that looked like a piece of fat from an animal floating in the river. He thought, "Hmm. This piece of fat must have floated off an animal." He would dive into the water, feel around in the water for the piece of fat, but he couldn't find anything. He'd come up out of the water with nothing in his hand. When he dove under the water, his tail would stick straight up out of the water, wiggling. He kept diving in the water until he was all tired out. Do you know what that thing was in the water? It was the reflection of the moon overhead. He was so hungry that all he could think of was food, and when he saw this reflection it immediately related to food and he thought of the first thing that came into his mind, grease. This is what Spilyáy liked best to eat.

Spilyáy dove around like this for quite some time until he was so tired and hungry he was nearly starving to death. Then he decided to ask his wise sisters who were his counselors. He asked them, "What is the matter? I can't find any food. It's the same with those creatures that I have helped to create, they don't respond to my bidding." His sisters told him, "Oh, if we tell you, you'll only say, 'I knew that all along,' that's what you will tell us. We thought you were the wise one, you are Spilyáy, and here you are diving around blindly grabbing at what you think is a piece of fat. It is only the reflection of the Moon on the water. You are also asking the salmon to come out of the water. Don't you know that if you catch a salmon on top of hard stone, you will not be able to hold him. If you want to catch the salmon, you must go to a sandy beach, then ask him to jump out. He will jump out onto the sandy beach and you can catch him." Spilyáy was flabbergasted that he was fooled by the Moon. He was so hungry, his stomach was growling like a wolf. Then he walked down the river looking for a sandy beach. Then he called the salmon, "Come out my creation! Now is the time for you to throw yourself out of the water." Immediately the salmon came flapping out of the water. It was a great big Chinook Salmon that threw himself out on the sandy beach, and rolled around covered with sand, until Spilyáy clubbed it to death. He walked up to a hillside and he found some flint and made himself a flint knife. Then he cut up the salmon. Afterward he built a fire and then he roasted the salmon on a stick by the fire, and he waited for it to cook.

In the meantime, along the trail came some other creatures. They smelled the salmon. They sneaked up and saw Spilyáy roasting it. They wished him asleep, "Sleep, sleep, sleep Spilyáy." Soon Spilyáy was sound asleep. Later he woke up, "Uh! I'm all covered with grease." He looked at himself. He was all covered with grease on his coat and on his arms and down his legs. He looked around. "I couldn't have eaten this salmon. My stomach is still growling." He couldn't remember when he ate his salmon. Then he asked his wise sisters about what happened. Again they were reluctant to tell him. When they told him what happened, "Oh, that is exactly what I thought," said Spilyáy. Although they were disgusted with Spilyáy, they told him who ate his salmon. "It was the Wolf brothers."

Spilyáy continued on his journey because he was very, very hungry. Suddenly he smelled something. The wolves were roasting eggs in huge pits. They were gathering wood and cooking. He overheard them laughing, "I wonder if Spilyáy is awake yet! Ha, ha, ha. I wonder what he will do when he finds out we ate all his salmon!" Coyote was angry; he swore revenge on these people. Then he wished them to sleep. He exerted all his powers, "Sleep, sleep, slowly go to sleep, SLEEP!" He kept repeating over and over again as he looked down on them from the high cliff, while they busily roasted their eggs and stínstins (water chestnuts) mixed together. Finally one of the creatures walked over to a stump, lay back, and was sound asleep. Then another one walked over by the fire and lay down and went sound asleep. Soon they were all sound asleep lying around by the fire while their mounds of eggs and chestnuts steamed away, cooking and smelling delicious.

After these creatures were asleep, Spilyáy gathered some more wood and began to cook the eggs for himself. When they were cooked, he uncovered the leaves and dirt from the top, exposing the steaming food. Oh how his mouth watered as he feasted his eyes on this delicious looking food.

He took a stick, rolled the eggs out of the pit, and he grabbed the water chestnuts and ate and ate, until he was filled up. He saved all of the shells and the stems and skins from the water chestnuts and then he put all of this back into the pit and covered it all up with the cooking leaves and dirt. He put out the fires and walked away smiling happily. He paid back those creatures for stealing his salmon.

The creatures woke up from their deep sleep, hungry and refreshed. They began to uncover the pits of eggs thinking, "Oh my, we are going to have a delicious meal of eggs and water chestnuts." They were so surprised when they uncovered the eggs; they looked white and funny. They said, "The eggs must have had baby chicks inside of them when we baked them." (Spilyáy mixed some of his leavings with these shells.) "The babies in the eggs must have already had some feathers on them!" Actually these were the sticks and things that Spilyáy picked up while he was scavenging around when he couldn't find anything to eat.

The creatures were still wondering what happened, when the youngest creature came back from tracking the culprit. He told the others, "You have played tricks on a famous person. Now he paid you back. You are now eating his leavings." The creatures were ill, and they were remorseful because they had eaten Spilyáy's leavings.

In the meantime, Spilyáy was doing all sorts of things in his travels along the river. He would encounter a situation and then he would make predictions for those things. He created all kinds of landmarks along the river and in the mountains. Wherever he went something happened. He made rivers and streams for the fish to swim up, so that the people would have something to eat. He would tell the salmon, "Don't go up this stream because it's bad for you." Sometimes people would not treat him right and he would not allow the salmon or fish to go up that river. That's why you don't find salmon in some rivers.

Legend of the Lost Salmon

When the people ignored the direction of the Creator about caring for the salmon, the salmon disappeared. All of their attempts to bring the salmon back failed until Łpushayáy (Snake) used his powers to revive the salmon. The people were not fooled by Spilyáy's pretentious effort to revive the salmon.

THIS is a legend about the salmon, when it mysteriously disappeared—vanished! The story is about the red salmon, which we call the Chinook or King Salmon. This legend dates back to ancient times when our Creator first planted food, at the time of the animal world.

The Creator made the salmon. He planted the salmon upon this earth for the people. He taught them how to care for this food which was created especially for them. He said, "Do not neglect this food. Be careful that you don't break the rules in taking care of this salmon." He taught the people to observe certain regulations regarding this food. "Do not take more than you need. Never lay a salmon down on the ground with his head towards the river. Always place the salmon with his head away from the body of water." He told them if they observed these regulations, the salmon would multiply several times over as long as they lived.

At first the people diligently obeyed the rules, and they lived happily without problems. All along the river there were different bands of people living in their fishing villages. There were many, many people busy with catching and drying their supply of salmon. That was the way it was when the Creator made the salmon for the people. They had everything planted for them, the fish, game, plants for food, everything!

One day something strange happened. The people became careless and they neglected to follow the instructions made by the Creator. They became greedy. They did not take care of the salmon. They let it go to waste when they caught more than they needed for their families. They would not listen to the advice from those who were trying to follow the rules. Suddenly, the salmon disappeared.

When the salmon were no longer coming up the stream for the people to catch, everybody was frantically searching the rivers, but all in vain. There was not one salmon left to be found. Soon they became hungry; their little children were crying, and the old people were forced to beg for food.

One day, while they were searching the river, they found a dead salmon lying on the bank of the river. They stared down at it in disbelief when they realized what had happened. They began to cry out in shame and lament their mistakes, "If we are given one more chance, we will do better. If only we could awaken this salmon, the other salmon might come up the stream." The Announcer who would always announce important matters to the people went throughout the village to ask everyone to use all their powers to help revive this one dead salmon.

The people called a council, and they talked about how they should each use their spiritual powers to ask the good Guardian Spirit to give life back to the salmon.

In legendary times, those with supernatural powers could revive a lifeless creature by stepping over it five times. This is what the people tried to do. (At that time all of the creatures were not humans.) Finally, everyone had his turn except one called *Ɨpushayáy* (Grandfather), none other than Old Man Rattlesnake. He was a recluse. He never went anywhere, always staying off by himself. He was very ancient, and all the people called him "Grandfather" (Púsha).

One spokesman suggested, "Let us ask Ɨpushayáy to help us. He is a powerful man. Let him revive the salmon!" A messenger went to his house to get him, "Oh Grandfather, would you come and help us revive the salmon. Everybody has failed." Púsha listened and replied, "What makes you think I am capable of reviving this lone salmon after everyone else has failed? I am an old man. My skin is covered with scabs, my eyes are filled with matter, and my body is racked with dry coughing. How do you expect an old man like me to possess powers to do the impossible?!"

Everybody was disappointed. They all begged Ɨpushayáy to help them. "You are our last hope. Please help us, Púsha." Finally he agreed to do it.

Old Man Rattlesnake reviving the salmon

"All right, since you have so much confidence in my powers, I will come and try my best."

Łpushayáy was so old it was very painful for him to move fast. He moved ever so slowly as he prepared himself for the long journey. He crawled towards the place where the people were gathered around the dead salmon. It seemed such a long way to one so old, and it took quite a long time for him to reach this place.

While Łpushayáy was still on his way, Spilyáy was trying out his powers to revive the dead salmon. He was desperately using all his wily skills to convince the people he possessed supernatural powers. He was thinking to himself, "If I revive this salmon, I will be a very famous person." He stepped over it four times, and just as he was stepping over the fifth time, he pushed the salmon with the tip of his toe to make it appear as though it moved. He slyly pushed it and announced loudly, "O look, my people, I made the salmon come to life. Did you see it move?" But the people were wise to the ways of Spilyáy and they completely ignored him because nobody believed him.

Old Łpushayáy finally arrived. He was barely able to move along, laboring as if every inch was an effort which took all his strength. He crawled on top of the salmon four times. The fifth time he went right inside the salmon's spine. This is when the salmon woke up and came back to life!

Today, when you catch a salmon, and you are getting it ready to preserve or prepare for eating, when you break the spine you will find a white membrane inside this spine. That is the old Łpushayáy, who gave life back to the dead salmon.

This is how the Indian People exist on this earth. The Creator provided them with this food for their survival, salmon, the basic food of the Indians.

Tsiláan

(Deep Water)

Once there was more than enough game, plants, and fish of every kind for the people to eat. But they took their wealth for granted and were rude to Spilyáy when he offered them more food. Consequently, they lost almost everything they had.

SPILYÁY was the person that destroyed all things that were bad for the common people. There was a time that he was going around predestinating things. He knew the animals would be reduced in power. He was going around telling the animal world that there was going to be a change. This is what I am going to tell you about.

Spilyáy was determined to destroy all bad things that were destroying people. The animals were the people at that time. He told them, "We are going to be reduced in power. There are others coming who are going to be rulers over all of us, and over all this country."

This story happens after Spilyáy destroyed the dam the five sisters built at Celilo Falls. Spilyáy came up the river from Celilo Falls, and when he reached Chelan River he looked it over. (It is buried now and shallow.) He felt there was something he should do here. So he asked his "power" what he should do. The power or the counselors were his five sisters which he carried around inside of him. The sisters told him that there were no fish in the Chelan River, that he should fix it so the fish could go up the river. These were the fish that were liberated in Celilo.

The Chelan River was too swift, and the salmon could not go up the river. So he built steps with rocks for the salmon to swim up the river. There was also a deep gorge there that was not wide enough. He widened the gorge allowing the salmon to go through. In the back there was a deep water hole below the falls. He fixed it up so that this would be a place for the salmon to rest up before they swam up the Chelan River, because the river was too swift and the salmon became very tired.

When he came up to Mud Flats, Spilyáy found that the river was too shallow for the salmon to go up. So he built a place at the head of the shoreline, a high rocky cliff, and a rapids. Then on the north side where the dam is now, he made a little pocket which was like a trap. Here the fish rested as they swam up over the dam. This is where the Indians used to fish for salmon. They would spear and gaff salmon. Also, they would dip out the salmon from the fish trap built by Spilyáy, where the pocket was in the river. He fixed everything up for the people. (He made the falls and everything all the way up the lake clear to the Stehekin River, and on up to the Cascade Summit.) The dam is still there, but it has been covered over with high water. It won't wear down. Now it is like the rapids; you can still see the rocks in the bottom. When the water fills up it still remains wavy where the trap is. This represents the name of Spilyáy, and it will stay there for all time. I can't tell you how big it is, but it was big enough so that we could once catch all the fish we wanted during the run.

When Spilyáy was coming down the north side he made two dry lakes and Wapato Lake. Those were supposed to be the greatest small lake fishing places in the world. The dry lakes were about eight miles long and one and half miles wide. They were planned for small fish, but the lakes have dried up and turned into meadows. Now there are camas and other roots growing there. It is good fertile soil for roots.

When he was doing all this work, making the place for Indians, he camped near here. He drew up his birch bark canoe and made camp. After he finished his work, he had no more use for the canoe, so he turned it into stone. It is still there today, located at the corner of Madeline and Manson Roads on the shore of Lake Chelan. You can still see the seams on the bottom of the canoe where it is sewed together.

While Spilyáy was working on the northside, he fixed Stehekin River so the fish could spawn there. He came down and fixed other lakes, but there was another small lake, which he fixed for the Indians to fish. They would fish and spear and dip net there. There was deep water there. When the fish got in they couldn't get away, yet the Indians could not dip them out, because the water was so deep.

There were some places where there were numerous little pockets in the lakes where the fish would go when the water got too rough. There was a stretch in the water when the water got choppy and rough, when the waves came up. The waves got up to seventy feet high. When you took your canoe out in that water and tried to go through it, your canoe would fill right up with water. Spilyáy wasn't too worried, though, because he had a twenty-eight-foot canoe.

While he was working on Dry Lake, Spilyáy left his canoe on the shore. He had a motive for what he was doing. He saw a pretty girl, and he told the people, "I want the most beautiful princess you have in your village and I'll fix up a lot of places where you can catch a lot of fish. I'll even fix places where you can dry your own fish." But the people told him, "We don't need your fish. We will not give you our prettiest girl. We have enough game here to sustain us. We have mountain goats, mountain lion, game birds, quail, grouse, and turtle doves, and we have bear and deer. We don't need your fish." Then he started back and destroyed everything that he had done. He destroyed all of the fishing sites, drove out all the fish from the spawning grounds, and he made the water holes dry up. The stones he made for fish ladders stayed as they were because they were covered with water. That's when he left his canoe there. He didn't want anybody to get any use out of it, so he turned it into stone.

The Chelan River shoreline stayed that way all the time, but it remained under water. It never changed. It is always straight across.

That is when Spilyáy destroyed his fish trap. Some of it turned into sloughs with tules growing in it. He took back everything that was worthwhile. The lakes remained there but the salmon could not go in there. The only way they get fish anymore is by planting them in the lakes.

Spilyáy went down to the mouth of Chelan River and destroyed his fish ladder that was enabling the salmon to come up the steps to the lake. Now there is only the falls there and the fish can't come up. He destroyed the places he had fixed for the fish to stop and rest while they were migrating up into the lakes. They had no place to stop, and they couldn't come up.

The lakes that he had made became camas grounds for the fishermen. He destroyed all the lakes. When he came to Lake Wapato, he made a barrier there, so that the fish could not go into the lake. Wapato Lake began to grow water grass and lots of food was growing around it, but

is happening to me." His sisters told him, "Oh, if we tell you then you'll say, I knew it all along!" He replied, "All right, if you won't tell me, then I will ask the hail to come down and wash you into the ground." They became alarmed and begged him not to ask the hail to come, that they would tell him. They told him, "When you leave here and reach your destination and fall asleep, Sun comes up and carries you back to the beginning of your destination. Sun is the one who is playing tricks on you. She knows what you are up to."

Then Spilyáy said, "All right, I will take good care of you. You have done me a great favor. Now you must tell me what to do." His sisters told him, "You must find a place where the wind blows hardest from the west to the east. You will find a plant there, wáx̱tx̱t (thistle). The wind blows its thistledown to the east. And there is a syringa tree which has a heavy limb. You will change yourself into both of these things. When the wind blows hard say, 'I am now a shapyashápya (thistledown), I will travel like a spirit in the air.' The wind will pick you up and carry you into the sky. If you go too high, then you say, 'I am now a heavy limb,' and you will drop down again. This way you will reach your destination. You will be carried by the wind."

Spilyáy found the place where the wind blew hard and waited for it to come. Then he faced east and said, "I am no longer Spilyáy, I am now a thistledown man and I am going to the east. I am traveling spiritually to the land of my destination." He spoke thus five times. He blew up into the air like a light airy thistledown. Then he looked down and admired the land and how good it looked. He could see for miles and miles. He became so absorbed in what he was doing that he forgot how high he was flying. When all of a sudden he looked down, and found he was almost to the top of the universe, he became alarmed and hollered, "Oh! Now I am a limb man!" He fell down to the ground too swiftly, and then he had to holler, "I am a thistledown man!" He did this back and forth until he reached the east. He did not travel very long, almost as long as we fly in an airplane today. Spilyáy was the first one to travel in the air to the east. He set the first precedent for air travel. "Now I have landed for a short time from the west. This is the way the People will travel after the animal people are gone. They will travel far in a short time by air, and they will land at their destination stepping down wherever they want to travel!" This is what Spilyáy decreed at that time.

He landed at a place that looked like the place the informer had described, where tsúłɨm lived. He landed and planted his feet on the ground, looked around, and saw the buffalo wandering around together in flocks. Then he saw a tepee setting on the prairie, just as he was told. "This must be the teepee of the chief. My informer told me that a chief lived in the teepee with his five beautiful daughters. His teepee is full of beautifully beaded costumes and all sorts of war bonnets and porcupine decorated clothes."

Spilyáy was so proud that he was able to do the impossible and that he had outwitted the Sun. He could do anything because he was Spilyáy. He said, "Nobody can do anything to me. I am supernatural!"

He walked up to the teepee but could not get himself to go inside. He stood outside waiting quietly. The chief knew he was out there. He already knew about him, knew why he came, and that he came from the west.

He did this five times before he opened the door and peeked inside cautiously. He wondered if this chief actually had beautiful things, as it was rumored by his informers. The chief was watching him and said, "Yes, I knew you were coming a long time ago. You are the stranger from another part of the country. Why do you peek around at my belongings? Why don't you come inside and take a good look? The food is all ready for you; sit down and eat. We are all prepared for your visit!" Coyote thought, "Ah, I am truly immortal. They have already prepared my food." He was so proud of himself thinking that his powers had caused all this good fortune. Then he went inside and made himself comfortable.

Seated beside the chief was his wife, all decorated with beadwork made of porcupine quills. Hanging inside the teepee were the most beautiful costumes imaginable. The poles had hanging decorations around them, and on the beds were buffalo robes. Then he said to himself, "How powerful the chief is, how he surpasses everything on earth, even the People who are to come. That is how their costumes will be, all different kinds from different tribes. That is what I, Spilyáy, will decree to the hereafter for the People. They will go from west to east to exchange beautiful things. I have set the precedent and they will follow the law afterward."

The chief asked Spilyáy, "What is your mission?" Spilyáy told him, "I will eat first, then I will tell you." He ate dry buffalo meat, and after that he told the chief, "Yes, your part of the world is nice and flat. Where I came from, the land is different. In the west we have huge mountains, starting at a place called White—it is a mountain. There are several white mountains setting around. Those mountains I love with all my heart. Then far off to the south are Three Forks. They are three sisters, and they are small. That is the land I chose when I left for this country. When I came east I planned to go back to that part of the land to the three white peaks. There I will make my home forever. That is what I wanted to see you about, and now I have found you. Whatever I say will happen, that is how powerful I am. You have five daughters, do you not?"

The chief answered, "Yes, I have five daughters." Spilyáy told him, "I came after those five daughters. I will take them to where the three white mountain peaks rise from the ground. We will travel for five days to this place. When we arrive there, we will make our home." He described how the five daughters of the chief would stay there and raise their families and scatter all over the country. They would inhabit all of the mountain peaks. He told the chief, "They would also be the same as they are over in the east." He tried to convince the chief how wonderful it would be, to have buffaloes in the east and also in the west, all decorated alike. He flattered the chief, "Oh, how prominent you will become when you have grandchildren all over both east and west!" This was what he told Tsułɨmyáy, the buffalo man. This chief swelled with pride at the thought, not realizing Spilyáy was exchanging identities with him (páhaashtkniksha). Naturally the chief was flattered and agreed immediately saying, "All right, when you are comfortable, you can look around and see how we live. Then tomorrow the youngest daughter will lead the way, and the oldest will be last. You will follow them. You must never, never get ahead of them. When they step one way, you must step the same. When they go down to the river or spring to drink water, they must drink first. You must never, never drink or eat before they do. They must not become your wives until after the fifth day. You must observe this rule until you arrive at your place in the west."

Spilyáy became very excited when he saw the beautiful daughters. They came home from a trip to the prairie. He began to pick out the one he would take first to be his wife. He became impatient. The chief read his mind immediately and thought, "He will never be able to withstand the temptation for five days. His actions are already strange. We will have to wait and see how he comes out."

Spilyáy finally fell asleep towards morning, tossing nervously. In the morning they fed him, and they informed him they were ready to leave.

The chief said, "You must never look back after you leave. You are going one way, don't look back!" The chief made a strict rule for Spilyáy to follow because the chief observed Spilyáy's actions which appeared to be unreliable. He was shifty-eyed and nervous.

Spilyáy followed the five sisters and observed the regulations the first day. Every time the sisters went down to the river to drink he would wait until they were through drinking before he would take his turn.

In the evening he noticed a teepee setting in the meadow which was identical to the one that belonged to the chief. The sisters walked towards this teepee. Close up, it was the same teepee. It happened that the chief wished this teepee to be where it was. The girls ran into the teepee, like it was an everyday occurrence. Spilyáy also ran inside, and he observed that there was a Tule mat table with food spread on it, just like there was in the other teepee back east. Hanging inside the teepee were the same decorations he observed before. Then Spilyáy thought himself truly immortal because he assumed his personal powers had caused this to happen. He truly believed he had the powers to become a great chief.

Spilyáy spent the night with no problems. He tried to observe the rules. He did this for two days. But on the third day his tail twitched. He looked behind him and was surprised to see his tail had turned into a buffalo tail. His hind feet and toes had turned into hooves split like a buffalo's. "I have changed. Something is happening to me; I even feel like a buffalo." On the fourth day he went down to drink after the sisters had their drink. He looked at his reflection and was surprised at what he saw; his head and ears were that of a buffalo! "I am now a tsúłɨm! I am truly a chief now!" He became happy and he swelled with pride. After he drank water he felt so good he galloped around like the girls did when they finished drinking water. They would gallop and buck around twisting and turning, and this is what Spilyáy did. He felt just like a buffalo on the fourth day. The girls noticed this and they knew what he was thinking.

The oldest sister thought, "We must be nearly reaching our destination. I see the tops of the white mountains he spoke about, the three white mountain sisters. I don't want to stay here, and I don't want my sisters to live here!" She began to plot ways to make Spilyáy break the rules that were set down by their father. She chose to entice him with sex, to make him forget the regulations.

Coyote turning into a buffalo

That night they camped in the same teepee. There was food already prepared and waiting for them as before. Spilyáy was still galloping around. Afterward, when he came inside to go to bed he noticed the sisters were all asleep with their thighs showing, looking sexy. He thought, "What happened? All this time they were so modest, sleeping all curled up and hiding their female parts from me; now they sleep as if they were inviting me!"

In the meantime, the oldest sister had prepared all sorts of temptations for Spilyáy. She wished lots of light to show on the sisters as they slept with their thighs showing to entice Spilyáy. He thought, "It seems to me that I am ready to take over the duties as a tsúɫim, because my body is nearly all buffalo now. I believe I am ready to take these sisters as my wives. I could start with two tonight!" Just about that time one of the sisters turned over revealing more of her body to him and he could not contain himself. He crawled around all night looking at one, then another, but he controlled himself. Finally he fell asleep towards morning. The sisters woke up early in the morning. They knew that it would be easy to tempt him.

They began their journey again, but the girls were changed. They played more than ever; they were no longer serious as before. They were confident that they would be returning home soon. They did not find Spilyáy's country suitable for their future home. It was too confining, and they longed for the wide-open prairies from where they came.

On the fifth day, they ran into the teepee and found the same food there. By this time Spilyáy was all buffalo. He felt so excited he played and bucked with no effort. When it was time to retire he noticed the girls removed all their clothes. He could not believe it! Then he decided he would start with oldest girl. "I don't have to wait out the whole fifth day. I am all buffalo now! Why should I wait to take them for my wives? Besides they are inviting me. They want me just as bad as I want them." He debated all night and towards morning he could not wait any longer. He crawled towards the oldest girl and proceeded to make her his wife. She turned towards her sisters and said something in their own language. The youngest one jumped up tearing down the teepee. Two of the sisters kicked Spilyáy, throwing him into the fireplace, covering him with ashes. They took away all of his new clothing which made him into a buffalo. He was rolling around on the ground covered with ashes wearing his old Spilyáy clothes. He was turned back into a coyote. "Oh, what have I done? It is still not completely five days yet and I made my big mistake." He brushed off

Coyote and the Buffalo People

the ashes and he walked down to the river, stooped down to drink water and saw himself turned back into a coyote again. He realized his mistake. Then he let his five sisters out and asked them, "What shall I do?" But they told him, "You have made a big mistake. This was your last day and you would have reached your destination. You could have lived there as a buffalo forever, and you would have been a great chief. Your children would have been white buffaloes roaming all over this part of the country. They would not be brown like they are in the east! But you have made your mistake, now it will not be so." He asked if he could try again, but they said, "No! You only had one chance. You have lost a big stake for those People who are coming soon. Now they will not benefit from what could have been here in the west. They could have had the beautiful costumes they have in the east, and buffalo meat to eat."

That is how Spilyáy did not live up to his responsibility and lost something important for the People who came afterward. We could have had white buffalo roaming our plains and meadows, and we could have had beautiful costumes here like they do in the Plains Country where the Buffalo roam. Now we have to trade with those people for their costumes and hides or learn their trade in order to have nice things. That was because Spilyáy could not observe the law and control his personal feelings. Instead he broke the law and lost.

Wáx̱push

(Rattlesnake)

When Wáx̱push loses her temper and curses Kw'aykw'ayyáy (Mountain Wren) for refusing to give her all her food, Spilyáy becomes angry and makes her the kind of creature she is today—a mean, crabby poisonous snake, feared and disliked by everybody. In this story we also learn that it is a very bad thing to be greedy and lazy, and such people get what they deserve.

THERE was a woman called Kw'aykw'ayyáy (Mountain Wren) and she had many children, and they were all living together in this home. This woman had to go after water for quite a long way. Whenever she went after water, all of her children would follow behind her, in a single file running along to keep up with her.

Living next door to Kw'aykw'ayyáy was another woman named Wáx̱push (Rattlesnake). She also had many children, a very large family.

There was a season when all the animal creatures would dig their food and preserve it for future use. This Kw'aykw'ayyáy would go out and find this food and dig it up for her children. There were many places to go to dig different types of roots because they all don't grow in the same place.

Now this other woman, Wáx̱push, was a crabby woman. She would become stingy with the food growing around her home. She did not want the others to come and dig around her place. She would quarrel at them. This was her nature. Even when she went to dig someplace, she would quarrel at anybody that happened to be digging there too. Everybody was afraid of her because she was able to kill people, and most of all they were afraid of her bad nature. When they knew she was in a certain area, the mothers would warn their children, "Don't go near Wáx̱push, she is a twáti (medicine woman). She will harm you! Stay away from her." This went on for as long as the digging season lasted. Everybody was afraid of Wáx̱push.

As a matter of fact, Wáx̱push became so absorbed in her practice of quarreling at people that she neglected her duties in preserving enough food to feed her large family. She would go to the pyax̱í (bitterroot) digging place and guard it so nobody could dig the food. She became too busy guarding it. When the season was over she did not have enough food to feed her family. She did the same with the other roots that grew in various other areas.

When wintertime came around Wáx̱push did not have as much food as Kw'aykw'ayyáy. She sent her children over to tell her neighbor that because they were related it was proper to share some food because she did not have enough.

When the food was all eaten up, she would send her children over again saying, "Go tell my sister that we need some more food." The children went over to Kw'aykw'ayyáy's again and they told her what their mother said. Because Wáx̱push was a twáti, Kw'aykw'ayyáy was afraid to refuse. She would give the food to the little children to take back to their mother.

That was the way Wáx̱push and her children lived. They were begging for food from the neighbors. They got the food because everybody was afraid of her because she was a twáti, and too, they were afraid of her crabby nature.

Finally, when this happened too many times, Kw'aykw'ayyáy looked over her food storage and found she only had five more packages of food left. She was very worried because the starvation period was not over.

The little Wáx̱push children came over to ask for more food again. "Our mother sent us over because we are pitifully hungry." Kw'aykw'ayyáy became very irritated and she replied, "You are a nuisance! You have eaten all of our food. We make our food last all winter, but now it is nearly all gone. We don't have enough for ourselves. We can't give away any more food." Then she added, "Your mother is stingy with the roots all summer when we try to dig it for food. Why does she not put some away for her own family?!" She told the little children, "You should not follow the example of your mother. Because if you do, you will become like her. You should share the different places where food is growing, and not be stingy with it."

The little Wáx̱push children ran back to their home crying because they did not get anything to eat, and because Kw'aykw'ayyáy had reproached them for begging. When they reached home their mother asked them, "Where is the food?" Then they told her, "Our Aunt told us all kinds of bad things. She called us all kinds of names. She refused to share her food because she has only enough for her own family."

The children also told their mother that they saw Kw'aykw'ayyáy's food supply, and she was right. She only had a few more bundles of food left for her family. Then Wáx̱push said to her children, "Yes, all right, that will be the last time she will ever say bad things to me. My sister has offended me. I will have my revenge. I will put a bad omen upon her. If she is as brave as she pretends to be, she will be able to withstand this bad omen, and she will survive it."

When the day was over, Wáx̱push went over to Kw'aykw'ayyáy's home. She went inside secretly and found a bag of dried food. She took out one of her teeth and tucked it under the cover of the storage bag.

The next morning Kw'aykw'ayyáy awakened and prepared food for her children. She went to her storage place and picked up the bag of dried food. She took the strings off and lifted the cover from the storage bag. While she was taking off the cover, the tooth of Wáx̱push pricked her hand. Kw'aykw'ayyáy screamed with fright! The children woke up and asked her what was wrong, and she told them, "Something bad has happened. Somebody has put a bad omen upon me." Her hand began to turn blue and swollen. Her lung ached and she found it hard to breathe. She turned to her children and said, "Quickly go tell Wáx̱push. She is a medicine woman. Tell her to come and help me! Tell her I will pay her one bag of dried food." The little children ran frantically over to Wáx̱push's home. They told her, "Our mother had a bad omen put upon her. She is suffering, and she will surely die if you don't come and help her. She will give you one bag of food if you will help her." But Wáx̱push slyly replied, "Let her keep that one bag of food. She does not want to share it with anyone. Why does she feel so generous now? Let her keep it and tell her I cannot help her! Tell her not to annoy me anymore!" She sent the children away. The children ran back to their mother and told her, "She made us go away.

She said you value that one bag of food so much, you can keep it. She will not come help you." Kw'aykw'ayyáy told them to go back and ask her again. She promised to give Wáx̱push two bags of food if she would come and help her.

The Kw'aykw'ayyáy children ran back to Wáx̱push's home and delivered the message. "My mother sent us back. She wants to live. You are a strong medicine woman and can help her. She will give you two bags of roots if you will help her." They pleaded with Wáx̱push, but she said, "No! Your mother values food too much."

This happened four times. Wáx̱push still would not help. Each time more food was offered, but Wáx̱push would not help Kw'aykw'ayyáy, although it was apparent that· Kw'aykw'ayyáy was becoming very, very sick. She was beginning to swell up all over. She was so ill, in fact, that she could no longer take care of her own little children.

The fifth time she sent her children to beg Wáx̱push for help, she offered her last bag of food to Wáx̱push. The children said, "Our mother told us to tell you that she will offer you all of our food, five bags of dried roots, if you will help her." When they told her this, Wáx̱push finally agreed to help the mother Kw'aykw'ayyáy.

She went to Kw'aykw'ayyáy's home. The Wax̱púya, the medicine woman, performed the rituals that most medicine women do when they are helping a patient. All of the children were sitting quietly by, watching every move. They were so afraid of Wáx̱push woman and her strange ways. The medicine woman told the patient, "Somebody must have left a bad omen in your food. You touched it; that is why you are suffering." There was no way for Kw'aykw'ayyáy woman to know that it was Wáx̱push who did this to her. She performed her ritual, sang her medicine song, and pretended she did not know who left this tooth in the lid of the bag cover. She pulled it out and showed it to her patient. They thought she was truly a remarkable medicine woman! Wáx̱push took her pay and went home.

At the beginning, before this happened, Spilyáy heard about his relative Kw'aykw'ayyáy's illness. He was very concerned because it was his responsibility to keep track of all his relatives and to take care of their problems. He immediately journeyed towards where Kw'aykw'ayyáy was living to find out if he could help her.

When he came to Kw'aykw'ayyáy's home, he was informed by the Meadowlark what actually happened. Spilyáy was very angry. He was angry because Wáx̱push was lazy and was taking advantage of others with her reputation as a medicine woman and her bad temper. She frightened everybody into submission to her wishes. This was not the way it should be. He was angry, too, that there was stinginess involved. One should never refuse help to a neighbor in need.

When he had arrived where Wáx̱push was still helping Kw'aykw'ayyáy, he pretended he didn't know all the details about what actually happened. Spilyáy made himself available to be an interpreter for Wáx̱push. A medicine woman always has to have an interpreter.

After Wáx̱push took away Kw'aykw'ayyáy's food, Spilyáy made it clear that he already knew what happened. He said, "All right, I know what you sisters have been doing. I know that Wáx̱push deceived Kw'aykw'ayyáy, and I also know that the other sister refused help when it was needed. From this day, after the People come here to this country, Kw'aykw'ayyáy will live in the mountains. She will sing pretty songs and will remain there as long as she lives. Wáx̱push will retain that bad temper. She will still grumble around, frowning and acting crabby. You will be angry at everybody, making hissing and rattling noises; the people will be afraid of you. They will hear you and say, 'Listen, Wáx̱push must be around.' Sometimes they will see you. But you will no longer be a threat to people. You will carry your protection, but you will use it only when you need it." This is what Spilyáy predicted for Wáx̱push and Kw'aykw'ayyáy. It has been that way since that time.

Legend about the Sun and Moon

In the beginning there was no day and night. This story tells how day and night came to be. It also admonishes the people not to gossip, be vain, or insult others.

ONCE there was a time when we had no day or night. The people at Winátsha decided to have a time for rest at night and time to hunt and do other things in the daylight.

About this time two friends were traveling together around the country and they happened to come to Winátsha just at the time the creatures were trying out for day and night. These two brothers were named Sun and Moon.

The first one to try out was a yellow bird. He went up in the sky, but he was too bright and the people did not like it. So they told him, "Oh, come on down." Even Spilyáy said, "I will go up and be the light." Then he went up, but he was telling on everybody. He became a nuisance and the people did not think he was fit to be the light, "We don't want him for our light." They brought him back down.

The brothers Sun and Moon were coming up the Columbia River near Ribbon Cliff and they saw a bird on the top of the cliff. There was a blind dog lying at the foot of the cliff. His lookout was a bird and anytime something came up the river the bird would warn him. The dog would ask, "Which way is the canoe coming up the river?" and the bird would describe to the blind dog where the canoe was located. "It is downriver" or "Up the river." This big dog would inform a monster living at the bottom of the river, and he would open his mouth and swallow whoever was coming up or down the river.

The two brothers went down the river and found Sandpiper, who was the watchman for the monster. To distract this sandpiper, they told her, "We will do you a favor." They brought out some Indian paint and told her, "We will paint you real pretty if you don't tell on us," but the sandpiper wanted to remain faithful to the monster and she screeched real loud, "Yiit!" The dog heard her and asked, "Up the river or down the river?" The Sun grabbed her by the throat threateningly, and she said, "No, I must have dozed off and nearly fell off my perch. That is why I made that noise." The dog said, "Oh," and he relaxed and went back to sleep. The Moon and the Sun painted Sandpiper all up. They painted her feathers on her wings and around her eyes and she admired herself in the water reflection. Then they told her to fly away. She flew away admiring herself in the reflection, forgetting her duty as a watchman.

The brothers sneaked up on the dog as he slept, but they made a little noise and he became suspicious, although the Sandpiper had not warned him. He sensed something was wrong. He jumped up and ran away. The Moon and Sun grabbed big sticks and they hit him over and over until he bled. The dog tried his best to get away, but because he was blind and could not see, he ran zigzagging up and down the hill bleeding all the while. That is why you see streaks of blood there at Ribbon Cliff near Entiat. Finally he jumped into the Columbia River and got away from them. They did not pursue him any longer. They let him go.

The brothers continued on to Winátsha. When they reached that place they saw a lot of people camped there. They were sauntering around looking at everything and visiting. All this time the maiden Frog was admiring the Sun. She fell in love with him. The Sun was a handsome youth, tall and bronze with long black hair.

The brothers were given a place to stay, and after they had retired, the Frog bundled her belongings and came into their camp. She asked, "Where can I make my bed?" The Moon thought this was funny and he jokingly told her, "Right here!" He put his finger up to his eye and pulled the lower lid down (as if to ask her to jump into his eye). She jumped straight into his eye and held on tightly. He hollered and tried to pull her off but she hung on more tightly. Everybody was soon involved in trying to pry her loose, but they could not get her off his eye. That is why the Moon has one black eye. That is the frog. The Elders criticized the Moon for making fun of her and he said he didn't think she would do that.

Moon with Frog in his eye

The brothers were selected for determining who would be day and night. The Moon was ashamed because he had this frog in his eye, and he said, "My brother can work in the daytime, and I will work the night." That is how the people then had daylight and nightlight. It was decided by Moon that he would work the night because he was foolish enough to insult the Frog.

Mourning Dove and His Grandmother

When young Dove learned that his grandmother was breaking sex taboos and food taboos, he was forced to kill her. But it made him sad and he cries, "Woo, whooo, woo, woo, woo!" to this day.

ONCE there lived a Dove and his grandmother. They were very poor. They were starving because there was nobody to give them food to eat. One day Dove decided he would make a bow and arrow so that he could shoot some game for food—deer, bear—anything that is edible.

He went out to hunt. He came home very happy and he told his grandmother, "I shot a big deer. Let us prepare to go pack it home." So they went to the place where he had shot the deer. They skinned it and cut it into sections to pack on their backs. Then he asked his grandmother, "What do you want to pack, the shoulder?" She said, "No, it might shoulder, shoulder me." He looked over the pile and said, "Here, do you want to pack the thigh?" She said, "No, it might thigh, thigh me." "How about the ribs?" he asked his grandmother. She said, "No, it might rib, rib me." Then he pulled out the leg. "Would you like to carry the leg?" "No, it might leg, leg me," the old lady said. He looked around some more until he found the rump. "Do you want to pack the rump?" She shook her head, "No, it might rump, rump me!" He was almost losing his patience. "Here is a hip, do you want to pack the hip?" Again she said, "No, it might hip, hip me." Then he found the head. "Here is the head. Would you like to carry it?" She said, "No, it might head, head me." He looked around some more, then he said, "All that is left are the male parts. Do you want to carry that?" She said, "Yes, I can carry that!" So he prepared it into a bundle and put it on her back. The old lady went on ahead towards home with her pack while he stayed behind to reassemble the pack so that he could carry it home.

The grandmother hurried home, but instead of going to their home, she took her pack into the sweathouse.

The boy was nearing his home with the pack on his back, when he heard strange sounds coming from the sweathouse. A male voice was laughing softly, "Ho, ho, ho, ho!" while his grandmother was giggling, "He, he, he, he!" Dove became very remorseful, because he knew immediately that his grandmother had broken the strict law of the land. She was desecrating their food.

He knew what he had to do. He killed his grandmother in the sweathouse. It made him very sad, and he vowed that to the end of the world he would mourn his grandmother and mourn the fact that she had broken the strict code by desecrating their life-giving food. To this day you will hear the Mourning Dove crying in the woods, "Woo, whoooo, woo, woo, woo!"

When the People came to inhabit this earth, they too had to observe the law of the land by observing this strict code of food preservation. They are to use it only for food. They can preserve it in any method they choose—drying, pulverizing, but they are never to use it like the old lady did in the sweathouse.

Origin of Basket Weaving

It isn't easy to learn to do things right the first time, as a Łátax̱at (Klikitat) girl learns. But by following the instructions of others and observing things carefully, the girl learns to weave baskets with beautiful designs taken from nature.

One time in the animal world there lived a young woman at White Salmon River. She was Sɨnmí (Squirrel) and she carried food in a pouch inside her mouth. White Salmon is where some people live and they are called Łátax̱at (Klikitat). But animal people lived there before the People came.

A long time ago everything was human. All the animals, plants, and creatures were like people are today. They were able to talk and walk like we do. This young woman lived at White Salmon River. She didn't know how to do things right like the other girls. She was slow and her fingers were clumsy, so she was avoided by the other people. This girl lived all by herself near a huge tree. Underneath this huge nank (cedar tree) she would sit and dream in the shade because she did not have anything else to do.

This tree would watch this girl and he worried about her. He was sorry for her because nobody wanted to help her. "That poor girl. She does not know all the things a young girl should know." One day he talked to the girl, "Áana, my little sister. I cannot allow you to grow up like this, not knowing anything. You must learn to do something to help yourself. I will teach you. You go to the mountains and find this kind of grass; it is called yaay (bear grass). That grass is used for decoration for what I want to teach you. Pick this grass by pulling it out by the roots. Dry it in the sun and bundle it up neatly. Then you can pick berries and plants for coloring.

After you have done this, come back here and dig up my tenderest roots. Split them into thin straight splices and dry them in the sun. You must do as I say and follow my instructions accurately. Some day you will be famous for your work."

This young woman prepared for the journey. She packed her root digger, flint knife, and everything else she needed; then she walked towards the mountains. When she reached that place she found the plants were all there as Nank had told her. She began to dig all the yaay and she separated them and laid them out in the sun to dry. Then she sized them all up and tied them into neat little bundles and packed them away. Then she searched for the coloring plants he told her to find. When she was finished, she went home.

The young woman took the bundle to Cedar Tree and she showed him what she had done. "I did as you asked. Here are the things you wanted me to get." Cedar Tree said, "Yes, you have followed my instructions correctly. Now you must dig my tender roots and slice them into long strips and dry them in the sun."

The maiden worked and worked all day. When she would get discouraged and tired, she would think it over and say to herself, "I have worked this long and I must continue on. I will follow his instructions and find out what I am supposed to learn." She kept on working until she completed her task.

When she was through, she laid out a blanket and spread out all those things she had gathered for her project. She showed it to Cedar Tree, and he was very pleased. "All right, now you must do this with it," and he showed her how to weave a basket. "You are to make a cedar basket, like this."

The girl selected all the material she was supposed to use and she began to weave it into a basket. She worked all day and far into the night. Finally she finished one basket. She couldn't believe it. "I did this all by myself!" She told Cedar Tree, "This is the first time I have been able to weave a basket all by myself." Cedar Tree was very proud of her. The girl exclaimed, "I watched those other girls doing things like this, but I never had anybody show me how to weave a basket." The girl was extremely proud of herself.

Cedar Tree told her, "Don't get too conceited. You still have to pass a test. You must take this basket and dip it into the water. If the water does not drip out of it, then you have accomplished your goal."

Girl sitting under a cedar tree

The girl took the basket and she carried it down to the lake and she dipped out some water. The water ran right through the basket. She went home dragging her feet.

She told Cedar Tree what happened. Then she sat down and cried. Nank told her, "Don't feel sorry for yourself. You are just beginning to accomplish something. Soon you will be very talented. You have to practice and practice until you are perfect. Now you must go out in the woods and find some designs. Seek out the things of nature and bring them back pictured in your mind. That is when you will be able to make beautiful things."

When he encouraged her like this, she could not resist becoming more determined to succeed. "He has so much confidence in me, perhaps I will someday make beautiful baskets."

She walked for many days looking at everything. She became confused because she did not know what she was seeking. She was walking down the trail one day when a rattlesnake crossed her path. He spoke to her, "See the designs on my back? Use them to design the edging on your baskets." She was grateful to the rattlesnake, but she was thinking, "I can't put just edgings on my baskets."

She continued walking down the trail until she saw Pátu (Mountain). He spoke to her, "Look at me very closely; this is the way I am, like a design. The outlines of my peaks are like designs." She looked at his peaks and thought, "Truly, the peaks look like designs. It would be beautiful in a basket design." She was grateful to Pátu and journeyed on.

Farther down the trail Grouse ran across her path. She stopped, and he spoke to her, "See my tracks? You may copy my footprints for your designs." The girl looked at Grouse's footprints and thought, "Yes indeed, those tracks look just like designs." She was grateful to Grouse and went on.

Several days later it was getting dark when she decided it was time to return home. She came to a brook and decided to have a drink. She knelt down on her knees by this brook, and he spoke to her, "Look at me. See the reflections and the designs with waves of water. You can make designs like this on your baskets." She looked down into the water and she saw the beautiful things in the water reflected like pictures. She thought what beautiful designs these would make on her baskets, especially the reflection of the evening star.

The next day she took a blanket and spread it out under the cedar tree. She told Cedar all about the designs she found in the forest. "Now that I have seen nature and the beautiful things in it, I feel much wiser and more capable of doing what you have been trying to teach me. I believe I can do it now."

The girl sat down and began to weave her basket. She was so engrossed in what she was doing she forgot what time of day it was. She wove all the designs she was given in the forest. She completed one beautiful basket. It was the most beautiful basket anyone ever saw. It had the diamond back rattlesnake designs around the edges, and the mountain design, and many other designs. She showed it to Nank. He told her, "You still have to pass the test. You must take this basket to the river and find out if it will hold the water."

She took the basket down to the Columbia River and she dipped it in. It did not leak. She had succeeded in making a water-tight cedar basket! She was so proud of her work. Cedar Tree was also very proud of her.

Cedar Tree said to the young woman, "Take the first perfect basket with the beautiful designs behind the bushes and sacrifice it as an offering. This will teach you to be thankful. Then make five small baskets and give them away to the oldest women members in the village." (This is still practiced by the Klikitat people.) The young woman was reluctant to do this. She selfishly wanted to keep all the baskets. Cedar Tree patiently told her if she didn't give away the baskets she would never be an accomplished basket weaver.

Spilyáy happened to be coming down the Columbia River at that time and he found out from Blue Jay what was going on at White Salmon River. He talked to Cedar Tree and the girl and he inspected the beautiful cedar basket. He was very impressed. "Not far from now, there are People coming to this part of the land. They are so close you can hear their footsteps. From this day forward this land called Łátax̱at will be famous for their cedar baskets." This is the reason the people who are called Klikitats are famous for basket weaving. They are known for their famous cedar baskets. People travel for hundreds of miles to trade with these people for their baskets.

This is the old Indian tradition taught by the Elders. They must sacrifice their first accomplishments by giving them away to the oldest person of their village or tribe. For example, the first deer a young brave shoots is given away. The father of the brave and his family give a big dinner to

Girl weaving cedar baskets

honor this occasion. At this dinner the father gives the weapon that the brave killed the deer with to the oldest hunter.

When a girl picks her first berry or digs her first roots, they are also given away to the oldest women members of the village or tribe. The girl's berry basket and root digger are also given away at a dinner ceremony too. This ceremony is still held for all the first accomplishments in adult world functions for both young men and young women.

Spilyáy and Shɨ́shaash

(Porcupine)

The only reason porcupines still roam the hills today is because little Shɨ́shaash was quick thinking when Spilyáy was after her.

ONCE Spilyáy was looking for food and he came upon a creek and took a drink of water. Suddenly he saw a movement farther down the road and he sneaked up to investigate and found it was Shɨ́shaash (Porcupine) walking down the trail. Spilyáy thought, "Oh, that is a fat one. I can already taste that nice fat meat!" However, when he got closer to Shɨ́shaash, she did not look alive! He sneaked up a little closer and stared at Shɨ́shaash, and now she looked like she had been dead a long time. Spilyáy began to worry. He was sure he saw Shɨ́shaash walking down the trail a little while ago. He came closer to get a better look, and he saw a bunch of long hair and quills, with the skin all dried up and worms crawling all over the dead body. Spilyáy did not know what to think! Then he joked, "I'm not afraid of anything! There is only one thing that frightens me and that's a Kwikwɬá (Whistling Marmot)." When the Shɨ́shaash heard this she was very relieved because she was beginning to think she was really a dead porcupine.

Shɨ́shaash had wished herself dead and made herself look decayed so Spilyáy would not eat her. She also made those worms crawl all over her body to make her carcass look dead and dried up.

Spilyáy picked up Shɨ́shaash, stuffed her into his pack, and he walked down the trail looking for a good place to stop and eat his lunch. All of a sudden there was a soft whistle. Spilyáy broke into a fast run. He ran and ran down the trail until he was all out of breath, then he slowed down to a trot to catch his breath. All of a sudden there was another, louder "Kwíkw!" Spilyáy thought, "Oh, the Whistler is catching up with me!" He stretched his legs into a fast gallop and scrambled up the hill. He found a place thick with wild rose bushes. He ran underneath the bushes to hide himself. When he ducked under the bushes the pack on his back came off, and Shɨ́shaash was free from Spilyáy's back. She scrambled away as fast as she could go, glad to be alive again. This is the way Shɨ́shaash outwitted Spilyáy by frightening him into thinking that Kwikwłá was after him. That is the reason porcupines still roam the hills and the reason coyotes are deathly afraid of marmots.

Duck and His Wife

In this legend we learn how the male and female mallard ducks got their beautiful markings. We see that the medicine dance should always be taken seriously. Spilyáy's (Coyote's) attempt to impress the people with his fake medicine dance almost brings disaster on everyone.

THIS is the legend that tells how the Mallard Duck got those beautiful decorations on his body, for example, the necklace he wears today. It also shows how Mrs. Duck got that beautiful brown robe decorated with blue and white colors with polka dots all over it.

One time in the winter season the weather became so cold all of the animals and birds and other creatures suffered. There was snow covering all of the food and even the drinking water was frozen over. Everything was starving to death. The snow kept coming down, down, down, until everything was all covered and white. The people (animal people) became so desperate they tried everything to stop this snow from coming down and the cold from freezing everything. They used all the powers they could think of, witchcraft and other supernatural powers that people have to fight bad things in this world.

They decided the best method of stopping the cold weather, which had been successful in the past, would be the medicine dance where they sing their guardian spirit song and exert the powers that were given along with it. When they sing their songs they dance and drive the bad things away. They were sure this was the only way to drive away the cold weather and bring on the warm weather again so that the food would grow and the water would thaw out and the brooks would begin to sing again.

Raven was the biggest medicine man of that time. The people went to him and they all agreed this is what they should do. "We must have a medicine dance to drive away the cold weather before we all perish." Raven told them, "We must build a Longhouse for this dance." So everybody got together and they built a Longhouse.

Raven was the host as well as the strongest medicine man, so he was the first to sing. Raven has long legs with knobby knees, so when he sang his song he kept time to the music with his knees, and his knees made a beating sound, "Yaw, yaw, yaw, yaw, yaw!" The people would hear this and would say, "Raven is going to drive away the cold weather." But instead of getting warm it became colder. The north wind blew stronger and colder, "Whuu!" freezing everything. All of the other creatures took their turn singing their song and calling on their power to make the cold weather go away. Still it became colder and colder until they became desperate, because they all tried and failed.

One old man spoke up during the resting period, "We have all failed. I wonder how Típikat and his wife are getting along. (Típikat is the legendary name for Mallard Duck.) Not one of us has brought results, and the wind is still blowing cold. The winááwa (warm wind) is still quiet. We should ask Típikat and his wife to come try their powers." Old Spilyáy was sitting by the door at the Longhouse and he spoke up, "Ah, how can they do anything? Even I, Spilyáy, failed to make it warmer." They all ignored Spilyáy and sent Meadowlark, the informer, to Mallard Duck's house. He found them lying down all covered up trying to keep warm. Meadowlark told them, "You are asked to come to the Longhouse to sing for warm weather. Raven, the medicine man, is asking you to come." Mrs. Duck answered, "Oh, that poor man. How can we help when all of the more capable ones failed? My husband has trouble walking, and so do I. How can we travel that far just to fail like the rest of them?" Meadowlark insisted because he was sure they had the power to succeed. He finally convinced them and they consented to go, especially when he told them they did not have to give anything away as is customary when the medicine men sing their songs and dance. Each singer must give something away and hang it on a lodge pole hanging from the ceiling. These things are given away after the ceremony is over.

Mr. and Mrs. Duck prepared to travel with Meadowlark to Raven's Longhouse. They were both crippled and they walked with a limp rocking back and forth together. They were fat and they had very short legs. When they arrived at the Longhouse they hesitated near the door where Spilyáy was sitting. They found an open spot there and sat down.

Raven was at the west end of the Longhouse all decorated up like medicine men decorate themselves when they sing. He was glad to see Duck and his wife. "I have asked you to come, my brother, to ask you for help. You must have great powers because you are mature and must have found your guardian spirit. I am asking you to sing your song and help us to bring the warm winds. Something might hear you and respond. Our relatives are dying and some are having a hard time staying alive. We must find a way to help these poor creatures. I am sure you can make it warmer." Mallard Duck sat there quietly for a while, and then he answered, "Áana, it's too bad. I'm sorry you feel that way. I look around and see all of the powerful medicine men and women sitting around here who failed to bring warm winds. How can I, a poor humble man, succeed in persuading the angry cold wind brother to leave?" Duck sat down again and bowed his head. He was wearing a vest and he pulled it up tighter to his chest to keep warm.

Chief Raven stood up and made this offer, "I will reward you generously. I will give you a beautiful robe and a beautiful hat. You will have any design you want on this robe." Duck was quite impressed, "All right, I always wanted a robe like that with a hat attached to it. I want white designs on the ends with blues and greens and silver with some yellow casts on it. This will make a big impression when I attend other medicine dances." Chief Raven said, "All right, we will do that for you." Spilyáy was jealous. He said, "Ii, why do you not offer to make a robe like that for me? I have strong powers too."

Mallard Duck turned to his wife and asked her, "Where is your medicine? Throw it into the fire." Old Lady Duck waddled out to the fire, threw something into it, then she blew into the air, "Puh, puh, puh, puh!" There were five fires, and she did this at each fire. When she finished, the Old Man Duck sang his medicine song. "Whence-so-ever is it that my sister and I float on top of the muddy waters. "X̱aat! X̱aat, x̱aat, x̱aat, x̱aat! X̱aat, x̱aat, x̱aat." That's the way Mr. Duck sang his song. He waddled from one end of the Longhouse to the other, his wife following behind waddling in his steps. All of a sudden there was a heavy gust of wind, "Shux," blowing around the Longhouse, changing from cold to warm and back again to warm and cold. Mr. Duck finished his song and waddled back to his seat.

As soon as Duck sat down Spilyáy sauntered out casually, rubbing his hands together, "That exhibition aroused something hot in my soul. I didn't bring my herbs to burn; that's why I didn't perform that ceremony. Nevertheless I'll sing my spirit song." Then he sang his song, "When I came, I came from far away . . . it . . . must have been my destiny . . . to sing here . . . ih, hi, hi, hi, hi; ih, hi, hi, hi, hi." He walked down to the other end of the Longhouse and he sang the same song and words, "when I came, I came from far away . . . it . . . must have been my destiny . . . to sing here . . . ih, hi, hi, hi, hi; ih, hi, hi, hi, hi."

He did this five times, walking back and forth singing. After that he asked everybody to stand up and dance for him. "When you dance lively, the warm wind will blow extra hard!" Then he instructed all of the creatures to line up side by side and dance up and down standing in place. Then he changed his song, "At the time . . . I began my journey here; that's the time . . . I uncovered the cold!" He waved his hands towards the young maidens dancing on the side saying, "All you virgin maidens come out and dance this special dance while I sing. This will add extra magic to my power!" The maidens stepped out and danced jumping high and rhythmically to the music. Then Spilyáy turned towards the door, "Go out and see if it stopped snowing, or if it's beginning to melt." One person ran out there and felt the snow, "The snow seems to be melting." He brought a handful to Spilyáy to show him.

There were five fires burning in the middle of the Longhouse. Spilyáy sang one verse at each fire, making everybody dance to the rhythm of his song. Then he changed the words to, "When I came to the turn of the mountain . . . that's where I fell down and cracked my shins." As soon as he said that, the wind began to howl like a hurricane, freezing cold, "Kaw!" It was colder than ever. He reversed all of Mr. Duck's magical effect on the cold wind. Raven saw what happened and he pulled Spilyáy off the floor, making him stop. "Stop singing! You had better sit down. The cold wind is blowing again more than ever." Spilyáy tried to argue, "No, that's just for a little while; the warm wind will overcome the cold very soon!" Instead the wind blew stronger than ever.

Mr. and Mrs. Duck had gone home while this was going on. They were at home asleep when Meadowlark came after them again. "The Raven wants you to come back and sing again. Something happened to change your power. Spilyáy sang carelessly and caused it to turn cold again!"

Duck replied, "Oh, I can't help any more than I am capable of doing. However, if you really believe in us, we will sing all night without stopping. We may not dance hard, maybe we will just walk up and down the Longhouse, but we will sing all night long. Then you will find out what will happen." When Meadowlark delivered the message, some of the participants did not want to dance all night. They were very tired, having danced hard for Spilyáy. But Raven consented to let Duck sing all night.

Duck told his wife, "Bring everything we have with you, all of our medicines we have put away." Duck prepared, carefully brushing up his new coat and hat. He painted himself all green around his neck and head, trimming it off with black and white colors. He told his wife to do the same, although she dressed plainly. When he got there he wanted to start right away. The people were tired from dancing and they were resting. He said, "I don't want to delay any longer. I must start right away. When I finish I will return home immediately." This time they were indifferent because they had experienced some comfort while the warm wind was blowing and they were not so cold. They told Duck, "We should wait until everybody is here; some have gone home to rest. We are all tired from dancing for Spilyáy."

Duck waited and waited until he became tired, falling asleep with his head tucked inside his wing. His wife woke him up saying, "I guess they didn't really want us to come. Let's go home, I'm very tired." They slipped away unnoticed and went home. When they arrived there they lay down across from one another and were soon sound asleep.

They didn't sleep long before Meadowlark was at their door asking them to come back. Duck told him, "No, we waited long enough. We are tired and have decided to stay home and rest." Another bird came along and asked them to come to the Longhouse to complete their work, but Duck still resisted. Five people finally came to their house to ask them to return. His wife told Duck to get ready that they would not be able to get any rest if this continued much longer. He reluctantly agreed, but he waited a little longer.

Meanwhile at the Longhouse Spilyáy was still walking up and down singing his song. The wind blew more than ever making it colder. Raven's horse died and other creatures began to fall over dying. Even Raven was singing, beating time with his knees, "Kaw, kaw, kaw, kaw." Still it began to get colder.

Mallard Duck receiving his reward

Now, Raven's wife was a sister to Mrs. Duck, who was the older of the two. Raven's wife became desperate and she paid a visit to Mr. and Mrs. Duck. "I will make you (Mr. Duck) a beautiful necklace and put it around your neck. And I will give you a pair of beautiful earrings. These are the last and only possessions that I own. I am begging you to come and sing for good weather." She had confidence in Duck because she knew of his powers through her sister. He still tried to refuse, saying, "Áana, what can I do when Spilyáy, your leader, failed to make it warmer? He interfered with my powers before. Let him do the work." Mrs. Raven came to his house five times to ask Duck for help. "Those are my last possessions—everything else is gone. I am offering that to you for payment. Raven also gave you his prize possession the first time." At last Duck consented to try again.

When they arrived at the Longhouse they were treated royally. They were given the best seat at the west side of the Longhouse, which is the most honorary seat. Raven told him, "This floor is all yours; you may do anything you wish with no interference from anyone. You may sing as long as you like." Duck put on his new robe again, then Mrs. Raven walked up to him and she put the necklace around his neck. She took the Mother of Pearl earrings from Duck's ears and put her own white ones on him. She fixed him all up into a handsome person, just like Mallard Duck looks today. Then she turned towards Mrs. Duck and gave her a beautiful robe of brown buckskin, decorated at the sleeves in blue designs and white shiny embroidery and a robe beaded with dark brown shells all over. She gave up all her most prized possessions and then the Raven and his wife had nothing more to give.

Duck sang his song again, "Whence-so-ever is it that my sister and I . . . float on top of the muddy waters. X̱aat! X̱aat, x̱aat, x̱aat, x̱aat! X̱aat, x̱aat, x̱aat," singing as he waddled out to the middle of the floor with his wife following behind keeping time with the music. Mrs. Duck poured the herbs into the first fire, then a few into each one on down to the fifth one. Duck kept singing his song until he sang five verses walking up and down to the east and then to the west. All of a sudden the wind changed direction and began to blow, "Shux!" The warm wind began to melt the snow outside. He called out loudly, "Everybody stay in your place. Nobody must go outside." Although Spilyáy was desperately trying to get past the doorkeeper to see if the snow was really melting, they wouldn't let him pass. Soon the wind blew so hard the Raven's Longhouse nearly blew over. The next day when they rose from their beds, there was a flood from the melted snow. In spite of all the warnings, Spilyáy was still faking around singing his phony song, claiming he made it warm.

Duck and his wife walked right into the water and floated on top and went home. They swam away just the way he sang the lyrics in his medicine song. That's how Duck saved the world and the creatures from freezing. Raven's stock and all his food were freezing, and they were only eating what they could find, which was not very much. Everybody else was the same, starving to death, until Duck sang his powerful song. That's why Mallard Duck has that beautiful robe, necklace, and earrings, and his wife has that beautiful brownish robe decorated at the sleeves with those blue-green and white colors and the shells dotting her robe all over. Someday when you visit the pond where there are ducks swimming around you will find Mr. and Mrs. Duck swimming around wearing these clothes, singing, "X̱aat! X̱aat! X̱aat! X̱aat!"

The Scavenger

It is unwise to try to deceive others into thinking you are important, as Spilyáy (Coyote) discovered when he met a mythical being, Deer Tick.

ÁWACHA NAY! There was a time when Spilyáy (Coyote) was extremely hungry. He was unable to find food anywhere and so he started out to travel to unknown territories to scavenge for food. He was loping along, nose to the ground, when he smelled smoke and looked up to see it curling up into the sky. He thought, "There must be people there. Now is my chance to get a free meal." He sauntered over towards the smoke and found a small hut that looked like a sweathouse. He thought somebody was taking a sweatbath. He called out a greeting to whoever was inside, "Whoooo are you? I am stopping by as a guest. Is it all right if I take a sweatbath with you? We can catch up on some news. I am a traveling man and I attend many important councils throughout the world. I can tell you many things." There was complete silence. He called out five times until finally a voice spoke from inside, "All right, apparently you refuse to give up. I am not an ordinary person. This is my home. It is not a sweathouse." Spilyáy cheerfully replied, "Oh, this is the way I live too. I have a small place and it is full of wealth which I accumulated in my travels. I left it to come over here. Wherever I go people look after me! I am a born leader and am respected by everybody." The voice said, "All right, you may come inside since you are an important person, but my home is a humble place for one so important." (He already knew who Spilyáy was—a trickster—always wanting to deceive people.) The man inside knew Spilyáy wanted something from him. He told Spilyáy to come inside.

Spilyáy wanted to remove all his clothing before he went inside. He took a bath first. The small hut was crowded and there was a small place prepared for him already. The man invited Spilyáy to sit down and Coyote said, "So this is the way you live. My home is just the same, all crowded with my belongings." He kept on chattering away, but the man would not answer him. He just lay on his bed on his side, listening. In spite of Spilyáy's tactics to get some kind of response, he was unsuccessful. The man just lay there silently listening. Spilyáy reached over towards the man to make sure he was there, shook him and asked, "Are you still there? I might be talking to myself!" Finally Spilyáy said, "I am getting tired. My backside is sore from sitting down. I am not used to sitting so long. Usually I sit on something soft. I will dig around and pile up some soft dirt for me to lie upon. This will also enlarge your little house." Spilyáy was getting hot, his tongue was beginning to hang out, and he began to pant. He kept up the chatter but the host still refused to talk. Coyote dug around, piled up a mound of dirt, and moved over on top of it commenting, "That feels good, this is how I usually rest." He looked over at the man dressed all in red, quietly lying there as he ignored Spilyáy's chatter.

There were strips of meat and entrails hanging down from the ceiling dripping grease. Spilyáy began to hungrily slurp it up as it dripped down around him and lick it off his arms as it slid down. Gradually, he worked his way up to the meat, snitching small pieces, quickly popping them into his mouth at first, and finally openly helping himself. He was thinking what an easy life he would have if he could move in with this man and help him eat his food supply. He decided to spend the winter there. The man knew Spilyáy's thoughts and he knew Spilyáy wanted him to take care of him all winter.

Spilyáy said, "Why can't we have some water to pour on the hot rocks? We might as well sweat while we sit around. It's hot enough for a sweathouse and a shame to waste this opportunity. We need the moisture; my skin is drying out." He asked five times and the man finally told him, "All right, I will give you some water," and he gave Spilyáy five containers of water. Spilyáy poured the water on the hot rocks time and again, even burning himself, but the man continued to lie there quietly. The heat became so hot it melted the grease on the meat and entrails hanging in the ceiling and the grease dripped all over Spilyáy.

He tried again to make conversation with the quiet man but still he didn't get a reply. Soon he became more reckless and he poured more and more water on the stones, talking to the fire as if he were taking a sweat-bath. He did this four times, still no response, then he did it five times. Five times again, until he did it four times five. When he was ready to pour it for the fifth time, he said, "Ilíi, your water bucket is so small. If you would bring a larger container we can really sweat in earnest. We can talk to the 'Old Man.'"

Suddenly the man hollered, "Run away! RUN AWAY!" He did this five times. Then he pushed the door open, burst out like the wind, and was gone. Spilyáy chuckled, "Aah; run away," he mocked. "I'll bet you thought you wouldn't burn." Then Spilyáy crawled out too, and he saw a big cloud of dust, deer, elk, running away in herds. He sat there all blistered and scorched. Some of his hair was burned off.

Spilyáy looked inside the hut and found everything was gone. All of the entrails, deer fat, and meat were gone. There he sat with his stomach making growling sounds. He got up and brushed the ashes off his coat and began to walk down the trail. Then he noticed there wasn't a sound in the woods. It was very still. He remembered when he first came down this trail everything was alive and making all sorts of sounds. The birds were singing, the brook was making bubbling sounds, the deer was leaping into the brush, but now everything was still. Spilyáy was alarmed, "What did I do?"

It was time to consult his five sisters that he carried around inside of him. He let them out and asked them what happened. They responded reluctantly, "We don't want to tell you because you always say, 'I knew it all along,' after you find out." Spilyáy was disgusted with his sisters and he blew upward into the sky, "Puh, puh! Puh, puh! Puh, puh! Puh, puh! Rain, come down and beat these ungrateful things into the ground." He did this until they finally decided to tell him. "That man you thought you were taking a sweatbath with is a mythical being. He owns all of the wild game. He wears a red garb. You have offended him. You caused him to take everything away from you. You will starve. He took all the game." This would not discourage Spilyáy. He told his sisters, "I can create food. I won't starve. I'm immortal too, and able to find my own food."

He walked down the trail until he found a knoll. He sat up on top of this little hill and howled, "Wah wah wah wah, ow ow ow ow ow!" The sound echoed all around and sounded like a whole flock of coyotes. This sound was coming from inside of Spilyáy. (The sound was coming from inside his anus.) Right at that time the full moon was peeking over the hill and it was dusk. Right away a whole flock of wolves answered Spilyáy. They were all around him; one was on top of a hill, another down the canyon, and one nearly right behind him.

Spilyáy jumped up and ran down the hill as fast as he could go. He thought, "They are after me!" They followed along behind him, loping with their noses to the ground. They were not chasing Spilyáy. They were on their way to the east. But Coyote thought they were going to eat him.

This is the way wolves travel. They travel in packs and they will kill anything that crosses their path. That's their way. They are five brothers, and their oldest brother's name is Lalawísh (Devil Wolf). All the Indians know him by that legendary name.

This went on for quite a distance; Spilyáy running with all his might and the wolves loping alongside of him. When Spilyáy could not keep up the pace, he began to weaken and finally fell down on the ground. The wolves ran right past him without as much as a glance towards him. Spilyáy said, to nobody in particular, "Ay, I am immortal. My powers overcame those ferocious creatures and I outwitted them! I am REALLY immortal." He dusted himself off and walked down the trail again.

T’at’ałíya

(The Witch Woman)

T’at’ałíya (Witch Woman), after tangling with Spilyáy, becomes a way of scaring little children when they misbehave. Parents say, “If you don’t behave, T’at’ałíya will come and take you away!”

ONE day when the day was clear and beautiful, Spilyáy took a walk up the canyon. On this day he decided to bring his pet dog which was tied to a leash. His dog’s name was Túlulkin. The dog was an unusual dog. There was not another dog like it, because Spilyáy had created this dog all by himself. This unusual dog had a sharp horn in the middle of his forehead.

Spilyáy, in keeping with his character, was planning ahead for the future. That was the reason he tied freshwater clams around his knees. When Spilyáy walked he made a loud sound, “Shay, shay, shay, shay,” like chimes. It was all planned.

There is a law that when your brother dies the next of kin will marry the widow (awít). Now T’at’ałíya (Witch Woman) was Spilyáy’s awít. The thought of marrying Witch Woman was distasteful to Spilyáy and he had already planned ahead how to avoid this.

On this day, when he took this particular walk, he eventually met T’at’ałíya. She was very impressed with Spilyáy’s decorations around his knees and the beautiful sounds they made. She said, “Ilii! I think the sounds you make when you walk are wonderful. They are so beautiful.” Spilyáy replied, “That’s not so hard. It’s easy to make these sounds if you know how! You can learn to walk musically too! All you have to do is find a large flat rock and lay your leg on it and pound your leg with a rock.

Make sure you pound your leg thoroughly, then you will get the same results and you will be able to walk musically like I do."

The old Witch Woman believed Spilyáy, and she did as he instructed. She found a large flat rock and pounded her leg flat. But when she tried to walk, her legs wobbled and would not support her. She fell this way and that way. When she finally realized Spilyáy had tricked her, she became very angry! She became so angry, in fact, she made her legs carry her, even though they were pounded flat.

Spilyáy saw her coming and he ran up the canyon as fast as he could run, dragging his dog behind on a leash. Spilyáy began to plan how he was going to get away from this old Witch Woman. He wanted to live! "Which way shall I run?! When that old woman catches up with me, she will eat me!"

The old Witch Woman was catching up to Spilyáy when he happened to see an old rabbit hole (den). He ran fast trying to reach that den before the witch could catch him. He scrambled inside the den before she could grab him; he made his escape. Old Witch Woman sat down on top of the opening of the den and she said, "Now I have you trapped, Spilyáy."

Although it looked hopeless for Spilyáy, everything was turning out as he planned, except he forgot to bring something to eat. Eventually, Spilyáy became hungry and he grew thirsty. As the days passed he grew weaker and thinner. Finally he became so skinny he was like a skeleton. When he turned his body over to change positions he would make this sound, "Yaw-yaw! Yaw-yaw!" That was how things were becoming when, at last, he began to make serious plans for his survival. All at once he remembered, "I have my eyes! I will take out my eye and hold it in my mouth, then I will not be hungry. The juice in my saliva will keep me alive!" That's what Spilyáy did. But he concentrated so much on the flavor, he swallowed his eye. Then he took out his other eye and put it in his mouth. This time he told himself, "Don't forget, Spilyáy, don't swallow your eye! Just swallow the saliva!" But again, Spilyáy swallowed his other eye! Now Spilyáy had no eyes! He was totally blind.

Spilyáy was still very hungry, and his mind was racing desperately to think of a plan to keep alive. He took an inventory of his body. He wondered what other part of his body he could use to stay alive. Then he felt his balls. "They will keep me alive until I am able to get out of this den!" Then he took one out and put it in his mouth to hold there, as he did with his eyes. The same thing happened again. He forgot and swallowed both of them! Poor Spilyáy became weaker and weaker, even to the point of dying.

All this time that Spilyáy was suffering inside this den, T'at'ałíya was sitting on top of the opening to keep Spilyáy from escaping. She sat there so long grass began to grow into her clothes. She finally decided he was not worth all this trouble. She said, "I can find him another time and catch him." Then she stood up and tearing loose from the grass growing into her clothing, she walked away from the den where Spilyáy was held captive. Poor Spilyáy. He was practically a skeleton, and besides that, he was sterile and blind!

Spilyáy was curled up in a corner of the den, when suddenly he felt some breeze on his face. The breeze was blowing on his poor bony body. "Uh! T'at'ałíya must have gone away! The warm breeze is blowing on my body." Then Spilyáy barely crawled out of the den, feeling his way because he was blind. He was desperately trying to think of something he should do to get his sight back. "There must be something I can substitute for my eyes," he thought. He was crawling around on the ground, feeling around, when his hands found a flower (what we call Coyote Eyes). He broke one off and stuck it in the socket where his eye had been; then he broke off another and did the same with the other socket. All of a sudden he was able to see. "Ei, ii, ii, ii! What remarkable eyes!" I can look clear across the canyon and see a herd of deer grazing in the meadow!" There was one problem, however. When the flower wilted, Spilyáy's eyesight would gradually weaken until he became totally blind again.

Spilyáy finally decided, "I must find somebody with good eyes and trick him out of them." With this plan in mind he began to travel away from this den, and he happened to meet a small bird. He heard this little wren warbling prettily in the brush. He approached it and said, "You should see my remarkable eyes. It's so clear, I can look across the canyon and see the deer over on the other mountain grazing in the meadow!" The little wren did not trust him, and she said, "Waaah! I don't believe you. Nobody has eyes like that." But Spilyáy slyly replied, "Try it! Then you'll believe me." Little Wren thought, "I might as well try it and see for myself." Wren took one of her eyes out and laid it down on the ground. Then she took her other eye and laid it down beside the other and reached out and took the yellow flowers from Spilyáy and put them inside her eye sockets. "My, what remarkable eyes! It's true, I can see those deer grazing in the meadow clear across the canyon!" Little Wren was so busy gazing around that she forgot about Spilyáy. He grabbed her eyes from the ground, stuck them in his eye sockets, and ran away as fast as he could run, clear out of sight.

Several days later, when he felt safe, Spilyáy decided he must kill T'at'ał́íya because he did not want to marry her. There were five sisters, and one of them had married his cousin who died. This sister was the one who wanted to trap him and made him lose his eyes. Spilyáy wanted revenge, and he made a plan.

At this time, the T'at'ałíya sisters planned a medicine dance. They invited all the creatures to this big event. "Everybody come. We are going to have a medicine dance."

All the creatures went—the Ants, the Crickets—they all participated. Even Spilyáy was there. They, of course, were especially glad to see Spilyáy. So, his awít provided him with the best seat in the house, and she set a basket full of lice in front of him. There were millions of lice (considered a delicacy there) rippling in waves inside of this basket, and Spilyáy was offered this to show he was an honored guest. He looked down inside this basket, but when he saw waves and waves of lice, he lost his appetite. This was not his kind of food. He knew that if he did not eat it though, T'at'ałíya would kill him. So he pretended to eat them. He would grab a handful of lice and pretend to throw it in his mouth, but when they weren't looking he would throw them out of sight behind him. Then when he threw them all away, he pretended he finished his meal; he wiped his mouth, making smacking noises to show his enjoyment.

As the evening progressed he prepared to sing and show his supernatural powers. He had a pile of pitch outside the house of T'at'ałíya and before the singing began, he brought the pitch inside and distributed it all around the room. While he was scattering this around, he whispered to his friends to prepare to run away because he planned to kill the Witch Women. He planned to kill all of the sisters. He said, "When I give the signal, run away with all your might. Save yourself, because if you don't you will surely die!" Then he looked down at his cousin Skɨlwisá (Ant). He thought, "How is this little ant going to run fast enough to save himself? He is so clumsy and small." But Skɨlwisá read his thoughts with his antennae, and he told Spilyáy, "Don't worry about me, I am capable of taking

Witch Woman gathering little children

care of myself. When you give the signal I will escape; I will not burn. Don't worry about me. I will escape underground by tunneling my way out!"

The T'at'ałíya sisters prepared to start the singing. Each one took her turn, and afterward the guests followed suit. There was X̱atx̱áatya (Duck), Wilaalikyáy (Jack Rabbit), Skɨlwisayáy (Ant), all of whom took turns singing their medicine songs. Spilyáy was the last one to sing. When he completed his song he hollered, "Aw!" (Now!), and then he set fire to the pitch which exploded into an inferno of hot blazing fire, catching the witches unprepared. Spilyáy raced for the doorway where his friends were already waiting with a huge boulder. They pushed this boulder in front of the doorway to block it off, and the poor Witch Women burned to death in their own home. Little Ant tunneled his way to safety as he promised.

Afterward, Spilyáy predicted the future for the T'at'ałíya (Witch Women). He said, "Hereafter, you will only be a myth. When a human child disobeys, or he refuses to listen to parents, they will frighten him by telling the child, 'If you don't behave, T'at'ałíya will come and take you away. She will eat you if you don't behave!' The People are coming closer; they are almost here. You can almost hear their footsteps. This will be your punishment, to them you will only be a myth!"

Legend about Fire

There was a time when the creatures of earth had no fire because T'at'ałíya (Witch Woman) kept it all for herself. This legend tells how T'at'ałíya fell for Spilyáy's (Coyote's) flattery and lost the fire to him and the creatures. It explains how the coyote, wolf, squirrel, and other animals got their markings, and it stresses how important fire is in everyday life.

MANY ages ago, the Creator made the fire and he put it on earth. But, somehow, T'at'ałíya (Witch Woman) happened to be there when it was put on earth, and she grabbed it and kept it to herself. She did not want to share it with the other creatures. She was afraid they would use it against her and become more powerful than she.

T'at'ałíya kept this fire deep down inside a cave, miles and miles inside the ground, selfishly guarding it. Nobody was allowed to come inside this cave. She was the only one who used this fire to keep warm. While she was comfortable and warm inside the cave, all of the other creatures were freezing outside. Everything was freezing. Some were dying from exposure and hunger. Everybody was suffering.

One day the creatures decided something must be done about it. Spilyáy (Coyote) called a meeting sending the birds who fly a long way to distribute the message. "How can we plan to take that fire away from the old witch?" They all came—the creatures of the forest, the river, and mountains. Everything on this earth came in response to the message distributed by Robin, Eagle, Dove and Meadowlark—the gossip of all birds spread the word all over to the four corners of this earth. They came by the hundreds; all the people (animal people) came.

All of the leaders sat down in council. They chose Spilyáy, "We want you, Spilyáy, to pay a visit to T'at'ałíya because you are well known for your persuasiveness and crafty methods."

Spilyáy told them, "I can't do this all by myself. She is a very strong-willed person, and she has great powers. She can use these powers well. I will need the assistance of some others." He named Wolf, his cousin, "You will wait at the doorway of the cave, because by the time I reach there she will be catching up with me." He was sure he would be all tired out because the passage to the door from the bottom of the cave was a steep climb and it was quite far.

He named Sɨnmí (Squirrel). "You will wait for brother Wolf to bring the fire to you. He will be very tired because the old Witch can run fast and she will be catching up with him about that time." He named Aluḵ'át (Bull Frog). "You are to wait near the lake for Squirrel because she will be more angry by then and will be desperate. She will run like the wind to catch brother squirrel." That was the strategy they planned against T'at'ałíya, guardian of the fire.

On this day Spilyáy quietly sneaked down inside the cave to where Old Lady Witch was sitting by the fire half snoozing away. She didn't dare fall asleep, so she would keep herself awake by thinking to herself, "They want to steal my fire; I must not fall asleep."

Spilyáy watched her for a while, then he spoke up, "Oh, my relative, you are making yourself tired. Why don't you let me sit with the fire for you while you rest?" Old Lady Witch flared up at him, "No! No! I don't want you near me. Stay away! Leave this place and leave me alone! You have no right to be here. You are an outside creature, so stay outside. Who let you inside?"

He walked away behind a boulder and planned what he should do. Then he crawled towards her humbly and said, "Oh my brother's widow. I have admired you for a long time, although I am plagued by all those beautiful maidens asking me to marry them. I think about you and wait around for some sign from you." He flattered her, "You are so mature and wise in your ways. That's the reason I always remember you when the younger ones approach me. If they were as wise as you, perhaps I would consider marrying them. Some are beautiful, that's true, but they are so immature." Old Lady Witch softened, and Spilyáy went on, "You have the most interesting looking eyes. When you look at me I forget everything!"

Old Lady Witch was flattered, and she began to simper and smooth her bushy hair. She would spit on the palms of her hands and smooth her hair down with it. Spilyáy began to talk to her in a monotone voice and he began to crawl a little closer and closer. He spoke to her five times. Each time he would talk a little softer and smoother. Then he wished her to get sleepy. Combined with the smooth talk and the wish for her to get sleepy, Old Lady Witch was soon sound asleep.

All of a sudden Spilyáy jumped out at her, grabbed the fire stick and ran away with it. He put all of his strength into the first jump making the flame flare up. It covered the entire back of Spilyáy and singed his fur coat. That's why the Coyote has a burned look on his coat. It's yellow on the sides which gives it the smoked appearance. His back is all burned black from that time.

He climbed up out of the cave as fast as he could go to where Wolf was waiting at the entrance. Old Lady Witch was nearly catching Spilyáy, and he was glad to see Wolf. He handed the fire branch to Wolf and veered off to the side, away from Witch. She charged past him after brother Wolf.

Wolf jumped away with all his strength leaving Old Lady Witch behind. But it wasn't long until she was catching up with him. She reached out and tried to grab him while he desperately jumped away from her.

Wolf reached Sɨnmí (Squirrel) just in time to hand him the fire branch and then he jumped out of the way, crawling off to suffer from the burns on his back.

Squirrel grabbed the fire and ran away jumping up into a tree and running as fast as he could. Squirrel began to burn on his back too. He also has the yellow sides which resemble smoke stains, and his coat burned dark grey. Before this he must have been a different color. Witch nearly caught Squirrel. He barely made it in time to hand the fire branch to Bull Frog who waited a little way from the lake.

Bull Frog grabbed the fire and he leaped away about five times, blistering his back all up. That's why, when you see a bull frog in the mountains, he has huge blisters on his back. He got those when the fire blistered the skin on his back. Bull Frog reached the lake just in time as Witch was grabbing for him. He dove in, swimming underwater to the opposite side of the lake, out of sight. He came up beneath a dead dried up Nank (Cedar Tree). He swam up beneath this tree into the roots. That's where he deposited the fire.

T'at'ałíya scrambled around looking for Bull Frog, but she could not find him. She was not used to the cold outside weather and she soon became chilled. It wasn't long before she began to freeze like everybody else, and she fell over frozen to death.

Spilyáy approached her cautiously peering down at her, "Ah . . . so this is the ferocious old witch that everybody is afraid of. See, this is the way you are, just another creature capable of dying like everybody else!" He stepped all over her, breaking her into little pieces and throwing them in different directions.

He went to get the fire from where it was deposited by Bull Frog. He called everybody together to watch. The Old Man Cedar Tree was taking care of the fire inside of his body. They cut away a piece of Old Man Cedar and made a flat piece to lay on the ground and another sharp-pointed piece to fit in the center of it. Then they twisted it into the flat piece causing a friction that made a fire blaze up. This was the first time that Spilyáy built a fire in this manner.

Then he called all of the visitors who came to the meeting and he distributed the wood to everybody to take home. He instructed them all how to build a fire.

Since that time we have had fire to keep us warm. Now we use it for everything. We have benefited from Spilyáy's fire up to this day, and from the time they got together and stole the fire away from T'at'ałíya.

Yellow Bell is late!

Lazy Yellow Bell still asleep

Flowers blooming in the spring

doesn't get up and prepare her clothes." They shook their heads sadly. But the girl kept on sleeping. She did not awaken even when Grizzly Bear turned over on her bed in the next house. When Grizzly turns over on her bed it's like an earthquake shaking the mountains.

Pretty soon Chinook Wind came by and announced his arrival, "Come out little sisters, it's time for you to brighten up the world!" Then he raced on to announce his coming to other creatures.

The girls scrambled around putting on their costumes, straightening up their hats and lacing their moccasins. Violet ran over and shook the girl vigorously, "Wake up! Wake! The Chinook Wind is here! It's time to go out!" The girl scrambled out of bed, put on her moccasins that needed mending, and she tried to run her fingers through her hair to straighten it. Her costume was hanging limply on a branch and she vainly tried to splash some leftover paint on the skirt and the leaves, but it was not too effective. Her hat was faded and hanging over on the side.

The girls were all lined up at the door ready to go out, and this lazy girl was still trying to put on her clothes and her hat. The others were begging her, "Hurry, you'll make us late, get in line." They began to march out and she was the last one to come out, all rumpled and unprepared.

The Violet was beautifully attired in purple and green, smelling sweet. The Yellow Violet was brilliantly glowing with health, and the Bitter Root was all pink and feminine. But, alas, the girl who would not get up and prepare her clothing, all ragged and faded, with her hat hanging crooked on her head, was the Yellow Bell. This is the reason all of the spring flowers come out as soon as the Chinook Wind blows cozy and warm. They are wearing brilliantly colored costumes, their hats open and prettily perched on their heads, while the Yellow Bell never opens her hat into full bloom, and it is usually perched on the side of her head and crooked. She is not usually adorned in bright colors, but a dull mustard yellow color.

The Boulder

By using his wit and craftiness, Spilyáy conquers a monster boulder and turns it into a harmless legendary stone. He therefore makes the world a little safer for the People who are to come.

One day Spilyáy was nosing around looking for food. He loped down the trail and found some deer tracks faintly outlined in the dirt. They looked like they were months old. He found some dried manure and ate it because there was nothing else to eat.

He traveled through sagebrush, meadows, and flat lands until he came to a wooded area. There was a big trail there used regularly by the animal people. Later it was used by the People. When he approached this trail he saw a huge boulder lying at the top of the hill. This stone was perfectly round and it was light colored. He admired it and walked around and around looking it over and feeling the surface.

The stone lay in the middle of all kinds of ancient Indian things. There were beaded costumes, beads, shells, and just about everything you can think of. Spilyáy began to pick out the things he would like to own. He was already planning to take these things away from the stone. Whenever he thought, "I like that, and that," the stone would move back and forth making sounds like, "Yik̲', yik̲', yik̲', yik̲', yik̲'!" Spilyáy's ears would perk straight up and his eyes would dart wildly around, "It certainly looks like that stone is moving!"

It didn't take Spilyáy very long to decide which things he would take. He greedily began to pull them away from the stone, "I want this one and that one." He grabbed a beautifully beaded peace pipe, wampum beads, a bone breast plate, and other things. Soon he was having so much fun, "Heh, heh, heh, wait until the maidens see me dressed up in all this finery!" When the stone objected, he told him, "Ah come on friend, let me dress up in these fine costumes. It's only lying around on the ground anyway. How can you dress up in it? I want to wear these clothes at the next council meeting."

Spilyáy dressed himself all up and trotted down the trail again. Just as he was beginning to climb up the next mountain he heard this strange sound, "Tuh, tuh, tuh, tuh," along with a sound as if something was crashing into trees and mountains. When he turned around to see what it was, he saw this huge stone rolling after him. It surprised him at first; then he shrugged it off, "Hm, I have that stone's things. He can't climb up this steep hill anyway, so why should I worry."

Spilyáy ran straight up the hill, ran along the length of a huge fallen log, and then he climbed up the side of a steep cliff. When he reached the top he turned around and looked down. He was amazed to see the stone rolling up the hill after him. He ran straight down the hill as fast as he could run. Then he ran straight up another hill. He did this three times, and each time the stone kept rolling after him, getting closer and closer each time. "That stone is catching up with me. I must do something."

They reached an area where the mountains were bigger and harder to climb. When they finished climbing those, they came to flat land, and Spilyáy began to run faster and faster. The stone began to roll faster and faster too. At last he saw a big rock and fell down alongside it as the stone rolled right past him, rolling over his tail. "Oh, ho! He can't control his directions. Now is my chance to get away." He turned towards a big knoll running real fast. "Now I can hide and he will never find me." He ducked behind it, and when he peeked over the hill he saw the stone, "Iii! He's coming closer than ever!"

Spilyáy was frantic now, and he ran away with all his might. The stone kept right on following him. It caught up with him and rolled right over Spilyáy, flattening him right into the ground.

The stone gathered up all the belongings that Spilyáy had taken from him. He found five strange things scattered around on the ground and he picked them up and carried them away. They were the five wise sisters of Spilyáy who counseled him when he was in trouble. So he took the wisdom of Spilyáy away with him. He carried them for a way until they became too heavy and he threw them away. "They are too heavy to carry around, and I don't need them."

Spilyáy lay in that meadow, all flattened out, for five years. Soon he was stuck to the earth and the grass began to grow through his body. One day the Raven was hopping around on the ground looking for food. He happened to see this skeleton lying there. "My, that looks like my old friend Spilyáy. Somebody must have killed him." Raven found Spilyáy's eyes and began to tap them with the tip of his bill to see if they were fit to eat. Before he could eat the eyes, Spilyáy woke up. "Ay, what is happening? Who is poking at my eyes?" said Spilyáy, as he sat up. He was stuck to the grass and he had a hard time pulling his bones loose. He got up and began to gather up his scattered bones and put them back together again. Then he walked down the trail again, a skeleton with no flesh on his body. He tried all his old tricks but nothing happened because he did not have his wise sisters. "How can I find out what happened to me without my wise sisters. Why should I live like this?"

Just as he was passing a certain place, he sensed something strange and he looked down on the ground. He found five dried up objects lying on the ground. He picked them up and popped them into his mouth, swallowed them, and went on. He had to swallow five times to get them down. He thought it was food, not knowing they were his sisters that the stone had flung to the ground. He tried another trick, and this time his sisters spoke to him. "You are a Spilyáy, you are always spilyáywisha (pulling Coyote tricks). You tried to rob a powerful person. That stone never lets anybody pass him without paying a toll. Sometimes they even give him horses and other big valuables. That was what you tried to steal from him. If you want to make amends for what you did, you must help the People who are coming, by getting rid of this monster. You must make plans to get rid of him by planning a road. Plan a route towards a big lake with no bottom so that he will drop in and never come back up again. Find a place like that, lead him to it, make him fall in, and tell him, 'You will stay there forever. You cannot kill people because they don't give you gifts. The People are coming. Soon there will be lots of people on this earth. You can hear their footsteps. You cannot kill those people!'" His sisters told Spilyáy, "You must make that stone understand that the People who are coming are planned by the Higher Spirit. That's why they are coming after we have passed to other planes. This is what you are to tell that stone."

Spilyáy followed their instructions. He found a giant lake with no bottom, and he mapped a trail to it. His sisters told him that a young chief's daughter was held captive by the Boulder. "She was kidnapped. She has a horse which is tied nearby, but she is not allowed to go anywhere." He was instructed further to get a message to her somehow. "Tell her to run away as soon as she can because her horse is turning into stone. If she waits any longer, she too will turn to stone."

Spilyáy was willing, but he was also reluctant. "How can I do anything with my body the way it is? I am only a skeleton!" His sisters only laughed at him, "You are the famous Spilyáy. You will find a way."

The taunting voices of his sisters made Spilyáy determined to succeed. He began to exercise. He ran and jumped, exercising to develop his body again. He would run straight up the hill to see how fast he could run. He did this for days and days until he was satisfied that he could outrun the stone.

He had already picked out a deep lake, as his wise sisters suggested. It is not recorded which lake this might be, although some say it was that big lake called Crater Lake. He had his route all planned, and he was ready to begin. He went down to the lake and looked it over. It was angry and had huge whirlpools in the middle of it. He was satisfied that the stone could not survive this angry lake. He threw a piece of stick into it and it immediately disappeared, swallowed up by the water.

Then he walked up the trail to where this stone was lying in the sun. "Ay, here I am again! Take pity on me and don't be too angry until I explain. The reason I came is to admire your beautiful costumes. I am an old man and no longer able to earn such beautiful things. You are still a young man and capable of accumulating nice things. People bring you things too, but they don't do that for me. You have nothing to fear from me. You are a majestic person, respected by everybody, while I am only a poor old Coyote." He began to call upon all his powers to help him. Finally, Spilyáy grew more confident and he kept talking softly until he had the stone practically hypnotized.

While he talked, Spilyáy was putting on the costumes. Then he sneaked over to where the young woman was tied and he untied her. He had a hard time prying her loose from the tying post because she was already turning into stone and the wood was becoming petrified. Then he went on over and began to release the horse. He hurriedly put her on the horse, "Hurry, go straight down that way." Then she galloped away, her horse running as fast as he could go.

The Stone finally realized what happened and he became furious. He tore himself from his perch, and he chased after Spilyáy and the girl. This time Spilyáy did not wait for the Stone, like he did the first time. He just ran straight ahead as fast as he could run. So did the girl. When the girl separated from the Stone, her body softened up and she became a normal girl again. The same thing happened to her horse.

They ran and ran until they came to the place that Spilyáy had picked. Just as the Stone was ready to pounce on them, they both swerved to one side and the Stone fell right in the big lake. As it was swallowed up by the water in the lake, Spilyáy predicted, "You will no longer dominate anybody. Soon there will be People coming. You can hear their footsteps. There will be lots of them here soon. They will be backpacking into all of these trails, but you will no longer kill them because they do not pay you with their wealth. Oh, they will remember you, all right. They will say there is a legendary stone here, and they will throw things in the water—not their entire wealth, but just small trinkets. But you will remain there in that lake for the rest of eternity." That's where that stone is today.

When Spilyáy returned the Chief's daughter, her father wanted to make Spilyáy a chief. But Spilyáy refused. He did not want to be tied down where he could not help people.

Spilyáy was a trouble solver. He would go where there was trouble and he would help the people get rid of any monsters that killed them. Then he would predict the future for those monsters. This is the reason we have certain landmarks from each legend showing where certain things happened. Then Spilyáy would make the monsters into harmless creatures, or he would turn them into mountains, wishing wells or sometimes rocks.

This is the reason Spilyáy did not want to be a chief. He would not have the time to travel around looking for troublemakers.

Wawayáy

(Cannibal Mosquito)

A cannibal mosquito is so taken in by the flattering remarks of Spilyáy and his five sisters that he forgets to be cautious of strangers and is killed. That is why mosquitoes can no longer harm today.

ÁWACHA NAY! In legendary days there lived two evil men. They were cannibal mosquitoes and were eating all of the people. They would bite them and suck out all of the blood from these people. Soon there were scarcely any more people to kill.

A long, long time ago there was a big lake created by the Creator. This lake soon filled up and ran over and that is why we have the rivers—the Clearwater, the Yakima, the Columbia and all of the other rivers you hear about. That is where the cannibal brothers made their home, in the big lake.

One day the older Mosquito brother decided to go in search of other places where there might be people. He told his younger brother (Wawayáy) he was going away for a while and would soon return. The older brother came down the river and he saw lots and lots of people all up and down the Columbia River. The people were all busy catching salmon in the springtime when the fishing season first begins. He looked all around, and he thought, "My brother would certainly have enough to eat around here! Look at all of those people!" He went around tasting the people. They were delicious!

He decided to go home and tell his brother the good news! When he reached home, he said, "My brother, there are a l-o-t of people down the river. You go down there and watch them while I stay here at the lake. I can find some leftovers here and manage to live. You will have plenty to eat down there!" Then he continued, "If you should have some problems, like running out of people to eat, come back and I will help you find another place." Evidently, the younger cannibal was unable to take care of himself.

The older brother prepared his younger brother for the journey. He dressed him all up, painted him with Indian paint, combed his hair, and gave him some food to pack for the trip. The older brother had saved these things for this journey. These were special clothes put away for traveling and supplies. Then they built a raft and loaded these things on the raft. The older brother pushed the raft out in the middle of the Snake River and let him float down.

The younger cannibal brother had never been away from home, and he soon began to get lonely and cry, "Hi, ii, ii, ii, ii, ii, ii, ii! Hi, yii, yii, yii, yii, yii! Hi, yii, yii, yii, yii." He was so afraid.

In the daytime he would lie down on his back on his raft, and he would sing, "I am a stranger from a far-off land! Somebody take pity upon me! Somebody take pity upon me!" When the people heard him, they would invite him into their homes, and then he would eat them.

Every place he stopped, he would cache some of his food left over from the last meal. It was blood from the people he killed. He would release this material, and they would hatch into little baby cannibal mosquitoes. They began to multiply into hundreds all along the Columbia River. Soon, you could hear them making this loud sound, "Shay, shay, shay!"

This cannibal was all dressed up in white buckskin which was all decorated and everything he wore was beautifully beaded. He was an impressive looking person, and he had a magnificent voice. He would eat the four-legged creatures, the feathered creatures and anything that had blood in its body. He would drink their blood and eat them. Soon his stomach began to bulge out in front. Then he would crawl into bushes and he would let this blood out leaving tiny cannibals.

One day Spilyáy was coming down the point, along the Columbia River, scavenging for food. He was sitting on top of a hill crying from hunger, "Ow! Ow! Ow!" He happened to look down and he saw a raft floating by on the river. He said to himself, "What can that be floating down the river?" He heard the creature on the raft singing this song in the Nez Perce language, "Hi, yi, yi! Hi, yi, yi, yi! I am a bloodthirsty man. I can drink the blood soup of anybody, and I can drink more blood than

Cannibal Mosquito preparing his young brother for a journey

anybody! Hi, yi, yi, yi!" The song echoed and re-echoed up and down the river canyon, hitting the rocks and shaking the treetops. "I wish I could find some blood soup. If somebody would only make some blood soup, I would drink it all! I would drink it all! I would drink it all!"

Spilyáy watched this creature floating downriver on a raft. When he heard the words in his song, he thought, "This is no ordinary creature. I must deal with him carefully." He ran ahead, as fast as he could go to the village at McCredie where all of his relatives lived. He wanted to protect all of his relatives. When he reached them, he warned them of the stranger floating down the river who was planning to drink their blood. They called a council on how to deal with this stranger.

In the meantime, there were five sisters living in this village. They were wise women and they wanted to help Spilyáy protect their village. They told him, "You are the immortal one, you summon forth your powers and we will do the rest." Spilyáy let his sisters out and asked for their advice. He insisted on knowing what they knew and they refused to tell him five times, because he never gave them any credit for what they did. When he asked the sky to send down his hail and beat them all to pieces, the sisters said, "All right, All right! We will tell you!" Then they told him what to do. They told him, "If you would dig a tunnel with five doorways, the last doorway facing west, and invite this stranger to come inside, we would help you to outwit this stranger!"

Spilyáy used his immortal powers and made the long tunnel with five doorways facing west. The five wise women of the village were also preparing their help to protect the people. They gathered all of the thorns they could find, the thistle, cactus, and other thorny bushes to put around the doorway of the fifth tunnel door which Spilyáy made. When this was finished, they waited.

Soon they saw this man floating down the Columbia River on a raft. He was all dressed up in a beaded outfit. His hair was wrapped in ermine, and he was painted up with yellow and red paint, and he wore a red blanket wrapped around his white buckskin suit. He was lying down on a bed of robes and skins, and there were baskets piled beside him. He was singing his song, "Hi, yi, yi, yi! Hi, yi, yi, yi! I am a bloodthirsty man . . ." Although he knew he was being watched, he acted as if he was not aware of it.

The five sisters went out to greet the stranger, "We hear your song! You must be very hungry, and you must have traveled far. We are making

Mosquito floating down the river

you will not kill. The People are coming soon, and you will not be a threat to them." To this day the mosquitoes live in marshes and damp places. Spilyáy even threw a piece of Mosquito towards the ocean, where Wawayáy was journeying in the first place. If he hadn't been detained by the Thorn sisters, their grandmother Cactus, and Spilyáy, Wawayáy would have reached the ocean and he would have remained a giant and he would still be killing and eating people. The other giant mosquito brother died of starvation, so he was no longer a threat to anything or anybody.

CHAPTER II

Legends and Stories with a Lesson

The Yakama storyteller knew that telling a tale was one of the best ways of teaching a lesson. The following group of legends includes stories which are exciting, funny, or even frightening, but they all instruct the listener in some moral or practical manner. In "The Chipmunk and Witch," for example, a boy is told by his grandmother never to go too far away from home while he is playing. He ignores this advice and is almost killed by an old witch. A beautiful and conceited girl in "Legend about Wormface" nearly dies because she thinks she is better than other people.

Lessons of a practical nature can also be found in this group of tales. In "K'aláasya" we learn how acorns can be pickled, and "Legend about the Thunder and Rain" includes information on building an eagle trap. More subtle lessons on trickery and shrewdness are found in "Story about Chakyáy" and [chapter three's] "Twit'áaya."

When we consider the wealth of teachings included in these tales we understand why the Yakama storyteller often said, "When you listen to a legend, my children, take it into your heart and remember the lessons you learn from it."

X̱líipx̱liip

A young man learns that one should always listen to the wise counsel of his family, but the young girl X̱líipx̱liip (Open and Shut) never seems to learn to groom herself and sit properly. People also get angry at her because she eavesdrops on other people's conversations.

A LONG time ago there lived a young man and his grandmother. He was an orphan and his grandmother raised him. She was proud of her grandson as he matured under her strict tutorship. One day he informed her he was ready to take a wife.

His grandmother agreed readily, but she was disappointed that there were no young girls in the village whom she felt were suited to be a wife for her grandson. The young man agreed. There wasn't a single girl around who interested him. "There is a man living in the east named X̱aslú (Star). He has five young daughters. The youngest one is called X̱líipx̱liip (Open and Shut)." His grandmother understood, and she prepared him for a long journey.

When he was ready, the young man turned towards the east where X̱aslú lived, and he began his quest to seek a wife. Upon his arrival he was received cordially, invited inside the home, made comfortable, and X̱aslú said to his daughters, "Hurry up! Prepare food for this young man. He has come a long way to see me!" The young women scurried around preparing food while X̱aslú and the young man exchanged stories about the east and the west. After a while the food was served, and while he was eating, the young man did not waste any more time. He immediately told X̱aslú the purpose of his visit. "I would like to ask for your eldest daughter for my wife." (The negotiations are usually made by the grandparent, but in this case the grandmother was too old to travel this distance and he had to bargain for himself.) X̱aslú listened seriously and gave his consent to let his eldest daughter marry this young man.

When the sisters heard about what had happened, they accused the oldest sister of being selfish. They were angry with her and quarreled at her. The older sister said, "I have no choice in the matter. Our father made this decision." One sister asked, "Why don't you appeal to our father to let all of us become this young man's wives, and you will be the head wife. We can all help each other in whatever we have to do!" The elder sister listened and she was confused, even X̱líipx̱liip was pleading to be included as one of the wives. When the young man heard this he was annoyed because he did not want X̱líipx̱liip to be his wife. She was too curious, always eavesdropping on the conversation between X̱aslú and the young man. She was not groomed to be a wife. When she sat down she did it carelessly, exposing herself to everyone. However, the elder sister agreed to this arrangement, so the matter was settled.

X̱aslú and his daughters lived in two homes. One was an outdoor type ánutaash (living quarters), and then there was a cellar-type living quarters when the weather was cold. The young man wanted to help and he would go out to hunt every day, morning and night. He would go to the cold country and he would go to the warm weather country, but he could not find anything to shoot. He would see many deer tracks pointing towards the west, but he never saw any deer. His new wife told him never to go towards the west. She made him listen when she said, "Never, never go towards the west when you are hunting. You must pay heed to what I say. You might get killed if you go there!"

One day he was out hunting and he saw a huge deer. He tried to shoot it but he missed. The deer ran away from him, running towards the west. He chased it thinking, "You will never escape me!" He chased it toward the mountains. The mountains looked black and mysterious. When it turned dark and he thought it was time to make preparations to spend the night, he gathered some wood, built a fire, made a bed of boughs, and sat down to keep warm beside the fire. Then all of a sudden he remembered his wife's warning never to go west in the evening.

While he was thinking about his wife's warning and preparing to sleep, he heard a strange sound surrounding his camp. He saw dark shadows prowling around. They looked like huge wolves, but they were not. They had long sharp teeth, and they chased him around. He saw a tall tree, and he climbed up to get away from those strange creatures. They would grab the tree and throw it to the ground, but he would jump off before it landed on the ground and run to another tree. This happened four times. The fifth time he climbed up a pitch tree. The creatures could not sink their teeth into this tree because their teeth would stick to the pitch and they could not bite into it. Gradually as the night wore on, the creatures began to act strangely because they did not stay out in the daytime. (They slept all day.) When it began to turn daylight, they fell over and were sound asleep. Then the young man quietly climbed down the tree, tiptoed around the creatures as they lay on the ground, and finally walked away from them.

While the young man was away, his wife was very worried. She was sure something terrible had happened to him. She was facing towards the west, crying, when she saw the shape of a person coming up from the horizon. She couldn't believe her eyes, but she ran out to meet him happily. Then the young man told her about what happened to him, and he promised never to go down there again. He said, "I have learned my lesson. I will always listen to your counsel." They went back to their home happy that he was safe and able to see his home again. He was even happy to see X̱líipx̱liip, although she was sitting there all exposed!

Legend about Wormface

The chief's beautiful daughter thinks that she is better than everyone else. Her conceit almost gets her killed, but everything turns out all right after she learns that a good heart is more important than good looks.

THERE lived a chief in this part of the country, who had a beautiful daughter. She had long black hair and was a pleasure to look upon. One day the old women and also the girl's father told her that she was old enough to think about taking a husband. So all the eligible men began coming to the chief and asking for her hand. But this young lady was very conceited. She would not accept any of these young men. She would make fun of them, pointing out their defects. "Oh, that one looks funny, he has a large nose." The chief was very worried. He felt sad that she would not accept any of those who came to ask for her from their own part of the country.

One day, out of the woods came a stranger. This stranger was a very handsome man. He was dressed in beautiful clothes, his hair was long and beautifully braided, and he had very proper manners. They took him to the chief's teepee. They did that because a long time ago, it was the chief's responsibility to take care of strangers in their village.

When the chief's daughter saw this stranger, she was immediately attracted to him, and she began thinking that this was why she had been waiting. The stranger was also attracted to the girl. It was not long before the stranger was asking the chief for his daughter's hand in marriage. "I would like to take your daughter for my wife." The chief felt sad. This was his only daughter and she wanted to leave him to go to another part of the world to live with this stranger. Although she was spoiled and conceited, he still loved his daughter very much. Finally, he was forced to give his consent. "All right, if that's what she wants. I will give my consent for your marriage."

The chief gave a big feast. He invited all the creatures to announce that he was giving his daughter to this stranger from another part of the world. They celebrated and there was much rejoicing.

The stranger told the chief, "I must return to my own land. I come from way back east. I am going to take my wife with me to my land where I live." Then the chief became sad, but he realized that it was the duty of the wife to go with the husband. So the conceited daughter told her father, "I am leaving you, father. I am going with my husband."

They traveled three days. On the fourth day, just as it was breaking daylight, she awoke with a strange feeling. She turned to look at her husband, whom she thought was so good looking. To her dismay, she saw worms crawling out of his eyes, mouth, nose, and all over his head and face. He looked terrible! The girl was shocked beyond description. She could not take her eyes off this man whom she once thought was so handsome. When he woke up and found her staring at him, he said, "Why are you frightened? This is the real me. This is the way I really look. I turn myself into a handsome person when I hear there is a conceited girl someplace. I go there and take her for my wife. So why are you crying? You wanted a good-looking man, and that's the way I looked when you took me for your husband." Then he told her about his mother who lived in a big lake in the east. "She is a people eater. She eats only conceited girls, just like you." Then he laughed at her and said, "You are so skinny. My mother will not want to eat anyone so skinny. I must feed you and fatten you up before I take you to her. You stay here and wait for me while I hunt for food. Don't go anyplace because you will get lost."

Then he left her at the camp. She fell face down on the bed and began to cry. She was so sorry that she got herself into this situation. She kept thinking, "Oh, how I wish I was back home with my father, among my own people. I made a big mistake." Then she began to cry again.

Somewhere she heard a distant sound, as if somebody was trying to call her. The sound was faint and weak. She sat up and looked all around, but she could not see anything or anybody. She got scared and thought perhaps Wormface was coming back. She sat very still and was staring off into space when she happened to look down to the ground. She saw an

Conceited bride staring at Wormface

army of ants running around near her feet. But she ignored them. Then she heard this sound again, somebody calling to her. Then she realized it was the ants calling her. She got down on her knees, closer to the ground, and asked the ants what they wanted of her. They told her, "You don't think your husband is very good looking, do you? He looks terrible. We want you to give us your promise that you will no longer be conceited. Don't think that because you are the chief's daughter that you are better than other people. If you will promise this, we will help you."

The girl cried, "I promise I will never be like that again. I will never think I am better than other people." So the ants told her to fetch her bundle. They instructed her to make a pair of moccasins with a special heel. On that heel she was to sew a small piece of buckskin protruding from the back of the heel (just as the Indians make their moccasins today).

The conceited girl followed instructions just as the ants told her. She kept her project a secret from her husband. When he would return she would hide the moccasins in her bundle. But he kept feeding her to fatten her up for his mother. She ate everything he gave her so that she could work on her moccasins.

When they were nearing the place where his mother lived in the lake, the girl told her husband, "I want to rest. I am getting tired." He gave his consent. "You only have a few more days and my mother will eat you, so go ahead and rest."

While they were resting, she put on her moccasins. He saw them on her feet and he laughed at her. "What funny looking moccasins." Then he told her, "Let us hurry on. My mother must be very hungry."

When they arrived at the edge of the lake where his mother lived, the girl looked at the huge dark lake. It looked very scary. Wormface called out to his mother. "Oh mother, I brought you another conceited girl for your dinner." The water in the lake boiled and churned, and this huge monster came out of the water. She was a terrible looking creature, with large red eyes, flaring nostrils, and very sharp teeth.

Wormface took the girl and made her stand at the edge of the lake. The girl was very frightened, but she made herself brave and kept thinking of her promise to the ants. She thought, "I am keeping my confidence that the Creator will hear my plea, that I will never be conceited again, and he will save me with the help of the ants." Then she looked down on the ground and saw the ants climbing around her heels, riding on the little strip of buckskin behind her heels. They were riding on that little piece of buckskin.

The monster opened her mouth, calling to her son, "Throw that conceited girl into my mouth." Wormface grabbed her and tried to throw her into his mother's mouth, but he could not budge her. The ants were holding her down at the feet on the heel, and they were weighing her down by riding on that little piece of buckskin.

This happened five times. He tried to pick her up but he could not move her. After the fifth time, the monster told her son, "She is stronger than I am. Let her go. She is getting help from someplace. We should not harm her. Let her go free."

The girl was grateful. She returned to her home. But she was a changed girl. She had different thoughts. She was no longer a conceited girl. She changed her heart into a good heart.

When she arrived at her own land, she told her people about what happened. She told them that she nearly died. She said that she was taught a lesson. "It is a great sin to think bad things about people. Don't think you are better than other people."

The conceited girl married somebody from her own village and learned to live like other people. Her father was very happy. The Creator was happy too. So they had great feasting in their village, inviting all the creatures to come and hear what happened to this girl and how she was changed from a conceited girl to a new person.

The man she married was not good looking, but he had a heart of gold. He was considerate and kind to his wife and to all the people. He knew how to provide for her. He made her very happy and they lived happily until she had her own family. She passed on the lesson she had learned to her own children. They also passed this lesson to their own children.

Legend about Little Owl

A little curiosity is fine, but this young Owl woman was too curious for her own good. Because she invaded other people's privacy, we have skin disease in the world today.

ONCE there was a large camp in the mountains where everybody was busy working to preserve food for the winter. There were women working, scraping hair off the deer hides, cutting and drying meat, and grinding roots, while the men were hunting and fishing.

There was also a little girl living in this village who was always poking around and invading people's privacy. She was curious about everything and would ask questions all the time. Her mother was quite patient with her and she tried to answer her daughter's questions but at times she asked her to go out and play while she did her work.

Off living by himself was an old hermit who stayed inside his teepee most of the time, hovering over his fire. He had five smooth stones always warming by the fire which he used to scratch himself all over his body.

One day the curious little girl happened to see the old man sitting by his fire scratching himself. She became so curious she sat by the doorway staring at him and not saying a word. She would do this almost every day, but he kept on sitting there and scratching himself, ignoring her and not saying a word. She sat and watched him for five days, then he gave her one stone and she scratched herself all over her body. It felt good. Then she took the rest of the stones and scratched herself with them and it made her feel even better.

One day her mother noticed a change in her daughter and she asked her about it. She told her mother, "Oh, I'm going to have a baby!" Her mother became very angry, and when the rest of the villagers found this out, they were angry with her too. Her mother told her that it was the law that she must now move out of her mother's home and go live with the old man. The entire village packed up and moved away. She was cast out by the whole village, left all by herself with the old man.

They lived together for quite some time until one day he asked her to fix a sweatbath. She went down to the creek, gathered wood and some herbs for the water, and warmed the rocks until they were red hot for his sweathouse. When it was ready she called him. He told her that while he was sweating he would make certain sounds, but she was not to look inside the sweathouse no matter what! He told her she must obey him, and she promised she would do as he said.

The young woman went to the lodge to wait for her husband to finish his sweatbath. Then she heard this curious sound coming from that direction, "Whoooooooeeee!" but she remembered that she had promised not to look inside and she leaned back and relaxed. She heard this sound five times, until she became so curious she could not stand it and she ran down there and looked inside the sweathouse to see what was happening. Inside she saw a good-looking young man instead of the wrinkled old man. The old man had watery matter-covered eyes, and here was a clear-eyed young boy. His skin was smooth except for a few spots where there was a rash-like appearance, like small sores. He scolded her when she looked inside, "You should not have looked inside and looked at my body until I came out. Now you have broken the law and from this day forward the people will have skin disease. If you had obeyed me, there would never be skin disease!"

In the meantime the people who moved away and left them all alone were having a hard time finding game. They were starving. That's why some Magpies were flying around seeking food when they happened to land on top of this teepee and looked inside exclaiming, "Oh, look! These people have a good living. There is plenty of food!" With that, they flew down to the ground and began eating the scraps.

The young man went outside and saw the Magpies eating scraps, so he invited them inside to eat. They ate until they were satisfied, and then they began to look around. They saw the girl who was left behind with the old man, now living with this handsome young man. They wondered what happened to the old man. Then they told the couple about the village people who were starving to death because they could not find any game or food.

They learned that the young man was indeed the old man. They asked for forgiveness and asked the young woman if it was all right if they brought her parents to her because they were ill. She said it was all right and the next day the Magpies flew away to get her parents. They brought the entire village, everybody asked for forgiveness, and they settled down to living again.

It turned out that this young woman, who was a curious little girl, was the small Hoot Owl. She wears huge white earrings and has large curious eyes. She is petite and demure at all times. But if she had not been so curious we would never have skin disease today. Which goes to show that it does not pay to get too curious about some things we don't understand.

The Lakáaya

(Mice)

The Lakáaya (Legendary Mice) sisters were so intent on stealing other people's food that they lost their little sister who was dear to them. Because of their greediness, mice to this day are only able to take away tiny amounts of food at a time.

THIS is a legend about a place called Tamapáani (at the mouth of Rock Creek, two miles east on Highway 14). Lots of people lived in this village called Tamapáani. They were a happy people. They never experienced any kind of hardship, and they never had famine. Their land provided all kinds of roots for food which were dug, dried, and stored. They would string the roots, camas, buttons, and x̱awsh (breadroot) on long strings made from hemp. They were hung out until they dried. Then they were stored for use as needed. Each villager had an abundance of food stored for the winter.

Across the river there was another village at Lake Umatilla, and over the hill from this place lived a family of five Lakáaya (Mice) sisters. They lived close to the river near a small dam which was a catch-all for all sorts of debris—logs, twigs, and grass—which floated down the river during the high water season. The five sisters would take this material and weave a blanket camouflage to cover the logs made into a raft tied together with grass ropes. They took this raft and would float it across the river at night to Tamapáani and steal food from the villages. They would sneak into the teepees, quietly take down the dried strings of roots and tie them around their waists. They would take some and hang them around their necks like strings of beads. Then they ran down to their raft and sneaked back to their own home without being discovered.

When the people woke up the next morning and discovered their food missing, they began to suspect everybody, their best friends and their neighbors. People were going around mumbling, "I wonder who this person is who is not ashamed to eat food that is stolen! Every day I am missing food. He must have no shame to deprive people of food which was gathered with hard work. He must not have a conscience that he would watch the people starve!" They were beginning to suspect everyone. And all this time, it was the Lakáaya who were stealing the food.

Practically every night the Lakáaya sisters were carrying off food from this village. This is the only way these sisters existed. They never went out and worked to get their food. They always stole it!

One night they floated their raft across the river again to raid the village. This time the youngest sister became too greedy and she took more than she could carry. She had too much food tied around her waist. Around her neck was a huge string of camas which was heavy, which is heavier when wet. While they were floating back across the river the swift current tipped the raft to one side and the youngest Lakáaya fell off. She had so many strings of dried camas around her neck, they immediately pulled her down beneath the surface of the river. She had been riding in back of the raft and her sisters were so intent on sneaking back over to the other side that they did not miss her until the next day. In the morning the oldest sister was taking inventory of her loot, when she realized their little sister was missing. She asked her other sisters if they knew where she was, but they did not remember seeing her. It was at that time they agreed she must have drowned in the river. She had never separated from her sisters before. They put their food away and prepared to look for their little sister. They took their raft and floated out on the river crying, "Hii, hii, our little sister is missing!" They looked for little Lakáaya for days and days but they could not find her.

It was several days before the dried roots began to soak and expand in the water. As the roots expanded they became lighter and lighter and finally they floated up in the water bringing little Lakáaya with them, and she floated on top of the water. She floated down the river with the dried roots and became entangled in the small dam, across from the village they raided for food.

Mice Sisters stealing food

It happened that at this time Spilyáy was sauntering down the trail looking for something to do. He looked across the river and saw the home of the five Lakáaya sisters, and then he looked down to the shore by the dam and saw one of the sisters snared in the weeds all entangled in the small dam, dripping wet and wearing a necklace of wet camas roots. Immediately Spilyáy guessed what had happened. "Little Lakáaya must have finally met her punishment for stealing food! She became too greedy and stole more than she could carry and drowned in the river." He saw little Lakáaya's eyes staring blankly in death, as she dangled in the brush. He said to her, "Why do you look cross-eyed? You have been stealing from the people long enough. Hereafter you will not be so greedy. You will not steal all of the food, but only a small amount. The people will no longer starve because of you."

After he insulted little Lakáaya, he went down the river a little farther and he saw the four Lakáaya sisters weeping and beating the brush for their little sister. He went down to where the people lived and he informed them of his findings. The villagers realized then that it must have been the Lakáaya sisters who were stealing from them and they heard the sisters crying loudly across the river. They were sorry that they had blamed their neighbors for stealing their food.

They told Spilyáy to demonstrate his legendary powers by dealing with the Lakáaya sisters in his own way. Spilyáy found his way across the river to where the Lakáaya sisters were, and he hollered, "O-o-oh, w-i-s-e s-i-s-t-e-r-s! You Lakáaya sisters, what are you crying about? What kind of a song are you singing?" He knew what they were wailing about, but he made it sound as if he thought they were singing. The crying stopped. They held a quick conference and asked one another, "That Spilyáy wants to know what we are making noise about. What shall we tell him?" The oldest sister volunteered to answer Spilyáy. She hollered back, "Spilyáy, you are so curious about our actions, then you must be quiet while we tell you all about it. We don't want you to interrupt. Then you will hear what I have to say. Afterward my sisters will chime in with me, and then you will know what we are doing. We will not tell you before that what we are doing!"

Spilyáy answered, "All right, I am listening." He turned his head so his ears were pointed towards the Lakáaya sisters, to show his complete attention. The eldest sister began to sing a song. "We are s-i-n-g-i-n-g a l-o-v-e s-o-n-g a--a---ahn, b-e-c-a-u-s-e w-e a-r-e h-u-n-g-r-y, because we are the L-a-k-á-a-y-a s-i-s-t-e-r-s!" Then she finished by saying, "We will continue to plague you, you people across the river, although you are such magnificent beings. You will suffer from our pestilence!" They were crying about their little sister, but since all of those good people were standing on the shore of the river, they did not want to reveal the real reason for crying because then they would know who stole their food. So they had to fake by saying they were singing a love song, because when a love song is sung, there is some crying with it. Spilyáy was shocked! He said to himself, "What brazen women! I thought all this time they were mourning their little sister." He hollered across the river to the sisters, "S--T--O--O--O--P your love song. I wish to send some news!" The sisters stopped singing. Then Spilyáy told them that the day before when he was walking down the river he had found their little sister caught in the weeds all wrapped with strings of food hung around her neck and waist. Spilyáy said, "I thought it must have been one of your sisters. I insulted her and made a prediction for all the Lakáayas in the future. Now I have counted all of you. There are only four of you. There were five sisters, and one is missing. That is the reason I thought you were crying!"

The Lakáaya sisters were speechless. There was nothing they could say. They turned away, and with heads hanging in shame, they trotted off down the trail in single file away from the people, never again to steal so much food from people that it would cause starvation until the end of this earth!

K'aláasya

(Raccoon)

This legend reminds us how important it is to follow the rules of decent behavior, such as not being greedy with food, doing one's work diligently, and not molesting food.

A LONG time ago there lived little K'aláasya and his grandmother near a river. One day his grandmother asked K'aláasya to go down to their cache and bring her some wawachí (pickled acorns). His grandmother pickled the acorns with black coal dirt mixed with mud, buried deep inside a hole near the river where it can be preserved by the dampness. She gave him a ltáyltay (flat carrying bag), saying to him, "Bring some acorns back for our meal, and don't play on your way. Hurry back!" Little K'aláasya grabbed the bag and ran down towards the river.

While K'aláasya was skipping along, whistling and throwing stones as he loafed along as boys do, he had a sudden urge to defecate. He didn't bother to hide or anything, so he defecated right there in the middle of the trail. When he finished, he didn't cover it up, he just continued on down to the cache to get the pickled acorns.

After loafing for some time, he finally reached the cache. He stuck his head down inside the hole, which was so deep little K'aláasya was halfway inside the hole with only his backside and a twitching tail sticking out. He stuck both hands down inside the hole, scooping out the acorns into the bag until it was full. When he was finished, he covered up the hole and threw a few more rocks around and started back up the trail towards his grandmother's home.

The little boy disregarded his grandmother's instructions to hurry back and instead began to play a game watching the clouds in the sky. He ran back up the trail and as he was running past the place where he defecated, he stumbled over the small pile of waste and fell down, spilling all the pickled acorns on the ground.

Suddenly, he remembered what his grandmother told him. "My grandmother will be angry when she sees the soiled acorns. I'll eat them and go after some more." So he began to eat all the acorns which were scattered all around him. They were delicious, and it didn't take long for K'aláasya to finish them. At first he selected only those acorns which were split. He ate them so fast because they were the best. Then he ate the rest all up.

After he ate all the acorns, he went back again. He was daydreaming again, swinging the bag around and around his head, whistling around, jumping, and skipping as he went. When he reached the cache, he began picking out the split acorns again, scooping them into the bag. Again he started back up the trail, singing and skipping along. At the place where he fell down before, he stumbled again and fell down and spilled all the acorns. He already knew how good the acorns tasted, so he began to eat them all up again.

After he ate all the acorns he went back again to the cache. K'aláasya went deeper into the hole because the acorns were fewer, and he filled the bag again. He started back to his home, skipping and running as he went; then he stumbled on the pile of waste again and fell down, scattering his acorns farther away, the ltáyltay landing nearly out of sight. And for the third time he ate all the acorns.

He was getting pretty discouraged. He went back again to fill the bag, this time reaching farther down inside the hole because the hole was nearly empty by now. He started back up the trail a little more cautious, until he became absorbed in his daydreaming again and began to run. He came to the same place and fell down throwing his bag far away from him. He was very disgusted. He grabbed the bag and threw it even farther, thinking, "I guess I'll never get away from this place. I might as well go back and eat all the acorns instead of falling down and eating here." He went back to the hole and decided to eat the acorns instead of carrying them to his grandmother as he was instructed. (There he was, wiggling tail sticking up in the air, as he gobbled up the acorns at the bottom of the hole.)

Raccoon at the acorn cache

While this was going on down by the river, K'aláasya's grandmother began to worry about her grandson. Something must have happened to him. He shouldn't take this long to bring back a few acorns. She would walk down the trail and then walk back hoping he would soon show up. She did this five times. She was busily preparing tax̱ús (hemp) for weaving and she didn't want to neglect her work. She would lay it down and pick it up again, nearly leaving, then she would pick it up and sit down again. This went on for some time. Then she decided to go look for her grandson. She took with her the fire twanít'aas (stoking stick) to use for a cane and perhaps for future use (like a spanking).

Grandmother walked down the trail and nearly tripped on the pile of waste left by K'aláasya. She tracked her grandson down to the river's edge and found, to her amazement, something sticking up wiggling. It was the tail of her grandson twitching as he was gobbling up the acorns.

She grabbed K'aláasya's tail and pulled him out. He was still gobbling the acorns ecstatically, eyes closed. Grandmother took the poker stick and hit him across the nose, all the way across his body down to his tail. (When you hit something starting from one end to another it is called wák'alask-.) She was so angry she didn't realize how hard she hit her grandson. At last she realized he was no longer twitching and screaming. He was dead.

Grandmother felt so bad she began to cry. "Pináwakwyakuunaash káła káła. Pináwakwyakuunaash, káła káła!" ("I was carried away, grandson, grandson!") Then she grabbed him by his tail and threw him in the river. That was when he became K'aláasya. (That is how raccoon got those stripes on his nose, his black eyes, and large stripes on his back and tail.)

He floated down the river until he became entangled in a log extending across the river. There was another creature walking along the riverbank and he saw this boy hanging on the log. He wondered what he was doing there. He went down and pulled him out, laid him on top of the log, and was preparing to eat him when he suddenly lost his appetite. He decided not to eat him, walked away, and left him there.

K'aláasya lay there until some blackbirds came to drink and they found him. One began pecking away at his head, awakening him. He looked up and saw another huge monster getting ready to eat him. This thing walked towards him, licking his chops, anticipating a good meal. Suddenly the monster fell off the log and into the river. K'aláasya jumped on top of him and pushed his head under the water, keeping it under until it drowned.

The boy pulled the monster out of the river and laid him on the bank. He needed a flint knife to cut it up, to pack home to his grandmother.

When he reached home he heard his grandmother crying "Pináwakwyakuunaash káła káła, pináwakwyakuunaash, káła káła." He went up to her and asked, "Why are you crying?" She was so glad to see him, she grabbed him and patted him on the head, which is the Indian way to express affection and love. He told his grandmother, "I came home to get a knife. I killed a monster. We can cut him up and put it away for food. I need a sack and a knife."

She scrambled around getting a flint knife and sack. They went down to the river where he cut up the monster. He asked his grandmother, "What do you want to pack, grandmother? Do you want to pack the two shoulders?" To which she answered, laughing, "Hmmm, it might shoulder, shoulder, shoulder, shoulder me, your grandfather!" Then he asked her, "How about packing the legs? Or the ribs?" She would answer, "It might rib, rib, rib me, my grandfather!" Every part he named, she would answer it in this manner.

Finally, there were only the neck, the entrails, and the male parts left. K'aláasya asked her if she wanted to pack any of those. Right away she pointed at the male parts and said, "I want to pack that!" The old woman opened up her skirt and he dropped it inside for her to pack.

The boy packed part of the meat and carried it away. The old woman was slower, so she was way back on the trail. As she was passing their sweathouse she took her pack inside this sweathouse.

K'aláasya came back to get the rest of the pack, until he had most of it taken home. He wondered where his grandmother went with her pack. Then he began to look for her.

In the meantime, the old woman had carried this pack inside the sweathouse and began to play with it. She was giggling around, "Hee, hee, hee, hee," and there was a male voice laughing, "Ha, ha, ha, ha." The boy passed the sweathouse four times and heard all of this activity. He became curious and decided to investigate. "What are you doing? You should not do that! Don't do that," the voices were saying. He recognized the voice of his grandmother but not the male voice.

The boy grabbed the door flap and threw it back and looked inside. He saw his grandmother tossing the male parts around. He was angry and he ran back to the hut, picked up some pitch from their wood pile, lit it, and ran back to the sweathouse. He set fire to the sweathouse, all around the outside, while the old lady was still giggling around. The sweathouse burned up, and soon there was a loud sound like an explosion, "POW!" Something blew up and went flying into the water. It was the grandmother's female parts.

Nearby in the river was the fish called a Sucker. He was scavenging around for food, nearly starving to death. He saw this thing floating down the river and he dove at it, swallowing the whole thing. When you see the Sucker's mouth shaped like an "O," that is how he got that mouth. The Raccoon was ashamed of his grandmother for molesting food, so he killed her. The raccoon is a clean animal. He always washes his food before he eats it. If you are ever in the woods and you happen to see a raccoon, you will notice he is washing his food in the stream.

There is a rule to be learned from this story. Never molest good food by doing what that old woman did. Also, always listen to your grandmother when she asks you to do something. Never play around when you are supposed to be on an errand. Last, don't eat food without sharing it. Like the raccoon ate all of the acorns that were rightfully his grandmother's too. They did not have enough to last through the winter because K'aláasya ate them all.

Legend about the Thunder and Rain

When a young boy is carried away by an eagle and has strange experiences, he feels afraid and wants to cry. But by trying to be brave and using his wits, he does well in the end. This legend also teaches us that we should not insult the thunder and the rain because they have feelings too.

WHEN you listen to a legend, my children, take it into your heart and remember the lessons you learn from it. Keep your ears open to everything you might learn. Don't ignore the ways of your Indian people. Listen with your heart and remember.

Once there was a little boy, about five years old, who lived with his older brother. They lived by themselves, and the older brother had a bow and arrow with eagle feathers on the tips of the arrows. Every day, the older brother would go out into the forest looking for food while the little boy would stay home and guard their camp.

To keep his arrows shooting straight the older boy used to trap eagles to replace those feathers on his arrows. He built a trap like a cellar with a cage on one end which was held up by a large stick. He tied a cottontail rabbit with a string and attached it to the stick. When the eagle grabbed for the rabbit, he would upset the stick and it would come down on top of his head and knock him out. The boy would grab the eagle, pull out as many feathers as he needed, then he would release the eagle.

One day the little boy asked his brother for some eagle feathers for his play arrows. He wanted to go out and hunt for some squirrels. But his brother said, "No, you go find your own feathers," and he rudely walked away. The little boy's feelings were hurt and he cried, "Why does my brother refuse to give me some feathers? I must have some feathers or I'll never shoot anything!" Then he cried and cried, louder and louder.

In another part of the country, f-a-r a-w-a-y, a huge bird heard this little boy crying. He was sorry for him, and he decided to come over and find out why the poor little boy was crying so hard.

The little boy wandered from their home, and he went up the mountain where his older brother built this trap to capture eagles for feathers. He looked at it and decided he would build one just like it. When the little boy finished his cage for the trap, he was sitting inside it when this huge bird descended on him. He thought, "Oooh, that is the biggest bird I have ever seen! He is beautiful. What magnificent arrows I can make with his feathers."

The bird came down and sat on top of the cage with his claws over on top of the cage and the little boy. He reached up and felt those claws; they were strong. He examined the claws and found they were very yellow. While he was doing this, the claws closed around the little boy and pulled him out of the cage. The bird put the little boy on his back and flew way up into the sky and out towards the ocean.

The bird was flying west. Although the boy cried and cried, it made no difference. The giant bird tried to soothe him, "Don't cry—everything will be all right, you are safe with me." Soon they were flying over an island way out in the middle of the ocean. The bird flew down there and landed. He took the little boy off his back, "You can get off now," and he put him on the ground. The boy looked around and saw this tiny little island surrounded with water. He cried and cried some more, "How am I ever going to get off this island!"

"Don't cry, little boy. Everything will be fine. Soon you will experience an important incident in your life. Your grandfathers will soon come and talk to you. They will take you wherever you want to go. First there will be a small one, then they will get larger. When the giant grandfather comes, don't be afraid of him. Whatever he tells you to do, do it. I am leaving you now. Remember, you will be a great man someday!" Then the giant bird flew away, leaving the little boy on that island all by himself.

That evening the boy was wondering what to do. He finally decided it was no use crying anymore, since there was nobody around to hear him anyway. Soon the water began to rise up around his ankles, then it rose up to his knees. The fish swam up and began to frolic around (apparently to

Young boy seeking power with help from the giant bird

keep the boy's mind off the water). Gradually the water began to go down again. Then he saw this huge light coming towards him. It was coming from the east, and it threw sparks up into the sky like fireworks. It came right up to him. "Why are you crying, little boy? You must not cry. Don't ever be afraid of anything. You will be like me when you grow up!" With that, the creature turned around and swam back into the water and disappeared.

The next day the same thing happened. It was the same time of day, and the water came up around his ankles, to his knees, and then a little higher, and stopped. He stood very still like the first time. Then he saw this fiery looking creature coming towards him, shooting sparks into the air like fireworks. It was larger than the one the day before. He remembered what the giant bird told him, so he was not afraid. It came right up to him like the first one, and said, "Don't worry about anything. You will be a strong boy when you grow up. You will be like me. Look at me. I can travel in the water as far as the end of this earth." Then it turned and disappeared from sight.

The next day the same thing happened again. This time a larger creature came to visit him. The water climbed clear up to his waist, but he was not afraid because he remembered what the bird told him. The creature was shinier than ever, and his sparks flew higher into the sky. He swam up to the boy and told him, "I came to see you. Don't ever worry about anything. You will be like me. See how fast I can travel over the water." He, too, disappeared into the ocean. The little boy's eyes were still blind from the fiery lights and sparkling fire coming out of the water creature. "I can't see anything," he thought, but then he remembered that they told him he could see clear to the end of the earth.

The next day the same thing happened and the next. On the fifth day the water came clear up to his chin. He stood fast because he was no longer afraid. The little fishes came right up to him, peered into his eyes, and they tickled his ears. Then he saw this giant creature coming towards him. It was like a giant stoker shooting sparks into the air. The water parted in front of it like a huge steamboat as it plowed through the water towards him. It came right up to the little boy, "I have found you . . . my grandson." The boy was thinking, "The lights are flying so, supposing he blinds me with those sparks, then I won't be able to see anything." But the creature told him not to think that way. The water began to go down until it was completely gone, and he was again standing on dry ground.

The creature swam close to the boy, and he told him, "Climb on my back." The boy was undecided what to do, "How am I going to get on through all those sparks flying around?" The creature read his mind and told him not to doubt. Then the boy tried to get on, but it was four or five feet away and he hesitated . . . afraid he might fall in the water. He did this five times. Then it told him, "Jump!" The boy made one last effort and he jumped. He floated right on top of this creature with no effort at all. (This was a supernatural creature and it caused him to float.) "Hang on tightly," and it turned around and they dashed away, the little boy's braids flying in the wind, "Shux!" He was hanging on tightly as they cut the water.

The boy looked around and he saw the sparks flying all around, behind, and to the front. He must have been a long way out in the middle of the ocean . . . because it seemed like miles and miles before they slowed down and came to a landing on the beach. He looked around and found they were on land. When he tried to jump off, the beach looked a long way off. "I can't jump that far. I might fall in the water!" But, again, the creature read his mind and told him to jump. He tried four times and gave up, but on the fifth time he jumped, and he landed lightly on the beach.

For the last time the creature spoke to him, "Little boy, you are going to be like me when you grow up. No matter what happens, never be frightened of anything again. You are my grandson, remember that." With that the creature swam away and left the little boy standing on the beach. He watched it swimming away, sparks flying all around like fireworks.

He turned back to the beach and looked about him. He saw a long trail and an inclining meadow into the hills and mountains. Suddenly he was hungry. He decided to look for food, and he walked and walked towards the hills to look for berries, fish, or game. "What can I eat?" He was still carrying his little bow and arrow.

He walked until he saw a cottontail rabbit hopping down the trail. He pulled out his bow and arrow, aimed, and killed it. Before he met the ocean creatures he could not hit anything with his arrows. He remembered what his oldest Grandfather promised—he would never fail at anything. He tied the rabbit on a rawhide string and wrapped it around his waist.

He continued on his journey, and although the country was strange he was not afraid. He walked for a long time until he saw a teepee sitting in the center of a lush green meadow. Smoke was coming out of the top and made it look warm and comfortable inside.

He walked up to the teepee and found the door was facing east. He lifted the door flap and looked inside. There was one woman there. She was facing west with her back towards him. He called to her, "Ay, I just happened to find your teepee," but she would not answer him.

He saw some cedar roasting sticks tucked between the teepee and the poles. He walked over to them and took one down. He stuck his rabbit on it and anchored one sharp end into the ground to roast it over the fire. The fire was smoldering just enough to cook the rabbit. He did not eat raw rabbit.

Suddenly the woman turned towards him and she spoke some rapid words like bullets. She was so powerful the ground shook with vibrations. She spoke that way five times, and the rabbit on the roasting stick flew outside. The boy hid his face behind his hands and he bowed his head down close to the ground. All at once he thought, "Why am I afraid of her? They told me never to be afraid!" He turned to her and then he spoke some words and everything turned bright and sparkling like fireworks. The woman rolled all over the ground and she screamed at him, "Please have mercy upon me. You are indeed a powerful man. I wish to have you for my husband. I have five brothers. We will travel together and you will be our leader." He hesitated a moment, then he walked outside to get his roasted rabbit, brought it inside and sat down to eat.

Suddenly there was a sound, "Ḵux̱, ḵux̱, ḵux̱, ḵux̱, ḵux̱," like heavy footsteps. Five men came into view carrying packs on their backs. They came inside the teepee, went over to the north side and unloaded their packs. They looked the boy over carefully, and the oldest one sat down opposite him and spoke words so powerful it shook the earth. The boy put his face to the ground and he covered his ears with his arms. When the man was finished talking the next brother did the same. The boy put his head down again and covered his head with his arms. The third brother spoke making the ground vibrate like the sound of a drum, and the boy threw down his head and covered his ears. Each time they spoke the rabbit was thrown outside. The boy would get up and go after it, and his food was getting all dusty. The fourth brother spoke stronger words and the boy covered his ears between his knees and he put his head close to the ground. Now the youngest brother was observing all of this and he could see that this was not making any impression on this stranger. He decided not to test his power on him.

Five brothers testing the boy

Soon it was the boy's turn to speak. His voice was so powerful it made the five brothers roll all over the ground, blinding them with the sparkling light and deafening them with the clapping sound like the roar of the ocean. They became so frightened they begged him to stop, "Stop, stop! We are beaten. You are more powerful than we are. You will be our leader in everything! We have been killing all of the people around here, but now you will tell us what to do, and we will listen to you. When the people came to our house we would throw them outside and kill them."

The boy looked outside and then he saw all the bones lying around outside. He did not pay any attention to this before. "So that is what this family has been doing all this time!" That was the reason they were throwing his rabbit outside hoping they could throw the boy outside with it, but he was too strong for them.

He thought it over and then he finally decided to marry the sister and become their leader. The brothers said, "When you are displeased about something you will speak first and the earth will burn. Then we will follow after you." The brothers are the storm. The loud clapping sound you hear and the sparkling lightning coming down to earth is the boy. The brothers are the low rumbling thunder sound, and the pounding rain that follows is their sister, the wife of the boy. The boy has the power to set things on fire. He will speak, strike, and split a tree in two with his sparkling red-hot thunder eggs. Sometimes when there is trouble someplace, like drought, he will speak, strike, and the rain will come down. Other times he might become angry about something and he will rumble louder than ever, strike harder, making loud clapping sounds. When they strike the rain will pour down in large drops and drown everything. That's how they travel all over the world together. They are looking after this world. The boy changed the family from killers into good workers. Spilyáy decreed they will always travel this way and will no longer kill people as they did before. When there is a drought they work together to make things right, to make things grow. It is like medicine applied to the dry earth, like the people who irrigate the land. That is how this family works together.

A long time ago when an Indian became ill, the thunder and rain were able to cure him. One should never say anything offensive about them because they are like people and they can hear you. They keep this earth dampened. They water the plants, animals, birds, and the people.

One day the boy told his wife it was time to go to Ímatalam to see his parents. The land is nice and flat there. When they reached Bickleton Ridge at Timberline, she refused to go any farther. There were some lakes there which were brought there by this bride. (They were bringing a new baby boy to show his parents.) She had a reason for not going all the way down to where his parents lived, for she was a person that brought dampness and chill wherever she went. She created lakes and dew. She did not want to expose them to this, so she wanted to stay away from their village. That's why those lakes stayed there for a long time afterward. A few may still remain.

When he arrived at his old village, everybody was surprised and overjoyed to see him. Especially the parents. Everyone was admiring his little son. During this time, while they celebrated his return, the boy was noticing his parents had cut their hair in mourning, as is the custom when someone in your family has died. They had actually thought he was dead. He was sorry and he apologized for it.

Everybody was aware that there was a great change in the boy. He seemed different, more serious. They had great respect for him because of it. They knew something serious had taken place in his life to change it.

When Spilyáy saw the boy he too recognized the change in him. Immediately he ran through the village, because he was the village crier, announcing his return, "Thunderbird is back! Thunderbird is back!" Spilyáy gave him a name.

After he heard all about what happened to Thunderbird, Spilyáy decreed, "You are now the custodian of this earth. You will take care of it with your power. There are People coming soon—you can almost hear their footsteps. They will benefit from your gifts and powers."

Everything scattered to make room for the People who were coming. Thunderbird went back to his wife, Rain. He carried his son on his back. Just as they were leaving, one insolent creature complained, "Ah, that bride! She is causing me to catch a cold." He was complaining about the cold, damp mist that hung over the hills close to their camp. It covered the entire Bickleton Ridge. Somebody hushed him up, "Don't dare to say anything insulting to those people, not even in jest. They will hit you with lightning!"

About ten years ago, one woman was picking huckleberries. When it began to rain, she complained about it, saying bad things about the thunder and rain. She was angry because she could not go out and pick berries in the rain. All of a sudden there was this crackling sound, lightning shot across the sky, and soon there was a deep rumbling sound, and the lightning struck her camp. She was cooking in an open fire inside the teepee. Her children were standing around the campfire watching her. When this lightning came inside the teepee it threw her on top of the fire and all of her children on top of her. She was killed instantly. Her children were burned, and some of them never recovered.

That's why it's not wise to make insulting remarks or complain about thunder and rain. They can hear you, and they will punish you. This whole world is under the care of Thunder and Rain and their five brothers. If it were not for the medicine they put on the earth, nothing would grow. We would live in a desert.

The Chipmunk and Witch

Chipmunk learns that his grandmother had given him good advice. Never go too far away from home while you are playing. Listening to your Elders can prevent a lot of trouble or even save your life.

THERE lived an old lady and her grandson named Chipmunk. She used to tell him, "Don't go too far away when you are playing. There is an evil person around here. She might find you and eat you." The little boy used to play around close to home, climbing into small tunnels and climbing trees, just anything to keep himself entertained—jumping and running. Grandmother stayed inside the house doing her chores, weaving hemp bags or processing the hemp for weaving. The old lady would tell him to pick up wood for the fire to keep their house warm. The boy ran around picking up sticks of wood close to the house. Soon all the wood was gone, and he had to wander farther away from the house in order to find wood. He would run around looking for bark, chips, anything to build a fire. He brought this home, adding it to the fire for his grandmother, while she sat there working, winding the hemp, and tying it into small bundles for the time when they would need it.

After a while there was no more wood left to pick up and he had to wander farther away. He was walking around picking up wood when he found some pine cone skins and he found some nuts inside. He sat down to eat the nuts, forgetting to be careful. Álíx̱shtani, a witch woman, happened along and saw him sitting there eating nuts. She said to herself, "Oh, that's a cute little boy." Soon she approached him, "Here is some more," and threw some nuts at him. The little boy became suspicious. He thought, "Oh, this must be the witch that my grandmother warned me about." She picked up a nut, and she threw it at him saying, "There is another one for you to eat." The boy started to look around for a way to escape this witch woman because she was beginning to get more aggressive and she would try to get close to grab him. The boy avoided her grasp and he ran away. She tried to grab him five times. Then he climbed up a tree and sat down on a limb.

Álíx̱shtani waited for the boy so she could catch him and eat him. She kept thinking about how tender he must be to eat. Álíx̱shtani kept on waiting and waiting.

After a while grandmother missed Chipmunk. She looked around and he was nowhere in sight. She waited and waited for several days. Then she became alarmed. She thought, "Oh, 'the bad person' must have found my grandson." She cried sadly, "Oh, she must have eaten my grandson!"

The boy stayed perched on the limb above the witch woman. He would not come down, but the witch woman would not give up either. She kept sitting there waiting to grab him. Soon grass began to grow underneath the witch woman, and it became entangled between her legs. The longer she sat, the tighter the grass held her down on the ground.

When the boy noticed that the witch woman was not moving around anymore he grabbed a pine cone and threw it. She tried to jump up, thinking it was the boy coming down, and the grass pulled her down. The witch hollered with pain, "Áana naa naa, that hurts. That boy is causing me a lot of pain. Everything hurts, even my bottom hurts. That boy is playing tricks on me." She sat back down again and the grass pulled her down tighter than ever.

The boy began to think about his grandmother, who was probably worrying about him because he was gone so long. Then he made a plan. "I am going to throw a tree limb a long way and make her chase it." So he broke off a limb and threw it with all his strength as far away as he could. The witch woman jumped up, but the grass entangled her and pulled her down. She was so sure it was the boy that she gave one more big tug and the grass tore all her hair out. She lunged after the thump, thump of the sound made by the limb, thinking it was the boy getting away. She caught up with the limb and grabbed it, and finding it was only the limb she cried out, "Áana, that irritating boy is causing me all kinds of pain. The grass has torn me all up, oh how I wish I could gobble up all of his feet, legs, and everything. He must be very sweet tasting."

Witch woman coaxing Chipmunk down from the tree

While the witch woman was chasing the stick, the boy quickly climbed down the tree and ran in the other direction towards his grandmother's house. The witch woman was right behind him. Just as he was running into the house, the witch woman made a grab for him, but he ducked into the door and she could only claw him on his back, scratching him. She was angrier than before. "Oh, that Chipmunk, I could already taste him!" Since that time Chipmunk has those scratch marks on his back.

Chipmunk ran inside and told his grandmother that the witch woman was chasing him. He showed her his scratches. His grandmother took some deer salve and put it on the scratch. Then she told him, "She will not leave us. She is going to stay there." The witch woman sat down, blocking the doorway of their den. So the grandmother told her grandson that they would have to find another way out of their home. They dug, and dug, and dug, making another door. They tunneled far away from their home and got out.

After they were out of sight of the witch woman, she told her grandson that they were to dig a deep hole and fill it with lots of wood. They dug this hole, just as directed. In the meantime, old lady witch woman was still sitting at the doorway of their home. Again the grass began to grow, entangling her as before.

Chipmunk and his grandmother dug and dug until the hole was finished, and they lit a fire in the pit. When they finished their work the grandmother told her grandson that they were to go home. She was going to lead the witch out through the door of their house where the witch was blocking it. The vines and grass were growing all around the witch woman, entangling her more than ever. When the old woman went out the door, the witch woman grabbed her and tried to smash her. The old lady told witch woman, "What are you doing to me? I am a sick old lady and you are hurting me." The witch woman said, "Oh, is that you, old sister?" and she answered, "Yes, what are you doing to me?" The witch woman let her go.

Now grandmother was tattooed all over her body with beautiful designs. The witch woman began to lick her hand where it had come into contact with grandmother's body. Then the witch told the old lady, "Oh, you have a beautiful body. Those designs on your body are so pretty. You look so different and attractive. How did you get those designs on your body?" Witch woman asked her five times. Then the old woman told her,

Witch woman scratching Chipmunk's back

"Well, I never tell anybody how I got these designs on my body, but I will tell you since you want to know so badly. This is my personal secret. I warmed rocks on the fire until they were red hot. Then I lay down on top of them and covered myself with dirt and burned these designs into my skin with steam. When the burns healed I had these pretty designs all over my body." The witch woman said, "Oh sister, do you think that you could do that for me? Help me to get those beautiful designs on my body." Grandmother told her, "It's hard work. I'm not very strong anymore, and it takes a lot of energy to do this." They were going to leave, but the witch woman could not get up because the grass had grown into her hair and all over her body so that she was tied down. The old woman helped her get untangled and managed to get her up. She had to pull her up, roots and all. Grandmother scolded the witch woman. "You are wasting your time sitting here. You could have been out someplace picking up lots of nice tender children and eating them instead of sitting here in my doorway." Witch told the old lady, "Oh, I wanted that little boy so bad. I could just imagine how tender he is, and I could just taste him. That's why I kept sitting here, waiting for him to come out." The old woman said, "Oh, he's too small to eat anyway. Besides he's not here anymore. He went someplace else." The witch woman answered, "Oh, all right, but when you find out where he is, be sure and tell me."

They went away together. The old lady took her to the place where she and Chipmunk had dug this hole and built a fire. Grandmother pretended that she just discovered it, and she pretended to dig a hole. She said, "I used to use this hole a long time ago, and now you can use it. The coals are cold now, but you can try it out. It might make some kind of design on your skin. Go ahead and try it." The witch woman said, "Well, I'll give it a try. It might do something for me." They began to gather some ferns and they laid it on the witch's skin to make the designs. The old lady told her to lie down on top of the fire.

Suddenly Chipmunk came running out just as the witch lay down on the fire. He already had a forked stick ready, which he grabbed, and put the forked end part around her neck to hold her down on top of the fire. Chipmunk and his grandmother took two more forked sticks and held the witch's feet down. Then the old woman began to cover her with red hot dirt and rocks. The old witch tried in vain to holler, but they covered her mouth with dirt. She tried to tell them she was burning and that she wanted to sit up. The old lady told her, "No, you're not ready yet. You have to stay on the fire a long time. You want to get up too soon. It won't do you any good and you won't get a pretty design." They held her down tighter with the forked sticks, then quickly covered her over with the coals and hot dirt. The old witch woman struggled to get loose, but the rocks piled on top of her held her down. She stayed there and baked. She stayed there and died.

Later, two of her sisters came down there looking for tender little boys and girls. They smelled something cooking. They said, "Hmmmmmmm! Something smells delicious. There must be people around, and they are cooking something to eat." They wandered around looking for the place where something was baking. They looked and there was no one around, so they removed the rocks and uncovered the baked witch. They were very happy, and they said, "Oh my, we are going to eat our fill. This smells delicious. I wonder why the people baked this food and left it." They ate and ate. They were so hungry. They ate various parts of the food cautiously. "It seems like Álíx̱shtani had markings like this. It certainly looks familiar," they said. They found an arm that was broken and crooked. Soon they began to take more and more of her out of the pit. They finally recognized her. "Oh, something terrible must have happened to her," the sisters exclaimed. They examined her and found out why their sister died. There was a very bad smell there. "Oh, this is how she died—she was overcome by a foul smell. That's probably why she covered herself up so that the smell would be kept out." They cried and cried, "Oh, our sister died a terrible death. She was overcome by this foul smell." They covered her up and left her. Then they began to smell too. Everything in the woods could smell it. All the animals and birds could not tolerate them and they chased them out of the woods.

That's how Chipmunk got those stripes on his back, and that's how he killed the old witch. This is the reason the children are warned to stay close to home at all times for fear Old Witch might catch them.

Legend of the Crane

A Honker Goose maiden lets her curiosity get the better of her and associates with Crane, who has many strange customs. Her sad experiences teach us that it is better to stay with your own kind. We also see how a young man lets himself be talked into doing something unwise and gets in trouble.

ONCE there were five Honker Geese sisters, and they had five brothers. The sisters would fly clear across the ocean to dig roots and pick fruit. They would dig all day long in their secret digging place.

One day the Honker brothers were flying around in formation and they looked down to where their sisters were digging and they saw a strange looking creature standing in the water across from them. It was Crane. They commented on this, "I wonder what that man is doing wading in the water across from our sisters?" He was a very tall man. They worried about this. The next day they flew over the same place again and they saw this man still wading knee deep near their sisters. This went on for five days.

On the fifth day, the oldest girl finally noticed this tall man wading in the water. She became very curious about his activities. He would put his bill down into the water and swallow and swallow and swallow something, apparently eating. At close observation, she noticed he would swallow several times, storing it in his throat, and at a certain time he would swallow it all down at once. The girl became so absorbed in his activities that she was neglecting her digging. Her sisters scolded her for staring at the man. "Stop looking at that man. He is showing off. That is why he stands across from us! Don't pay any attention to him." It was about this time that Crane began to use mental powers on the young girls. He made them think he was good looking. He put yellow paint around the edges of his eyes to make himself look attractive. He was really a tall, skinny man. He had been using his mental power on them for a long time.

One day the oldest virgin girl flew up into the air, and the sisters wondered what she was doing. She flew across the river and landed where the man was wading around. She decided to ask the man about his habits. She was curious about why he kept swallowing and swallowing and never got full or enough to eat. She approached the man and asked him, "Why do you eat and eat and never get full? Do you have a bag where you keep this food?" The Crane laughed, "Ho, ho, ho, ho. What are *you* doing?" She answered, "Gathering food for future use. We prepare it, grind it down into meal, and dry it for preservation. When there is no food in the winter, this is our food." Then he told her, "That is not the way to prepare food. You have to swallow it and swallow it. Then keep it all in your stomach and you'll be full all winter." She did not believe him. Then he proceeded to prove it to her. He put his head down into the water and he swallowed five different kinds of food and put it all in his throat, and then put his head down into the water again and put more in his throat. He did this five times until his throat was all swollen up, and then he swallowed it all down at once. The girl thought this must be the right way to store food. She decided to tell her sisters to try this method of food preservation, and she flew across the river to tell them. Her sisters asked, "What were you doing over there? Why did you go to that man?" Then she told them what he told her. She said, "You are wasting your time digging, baking in the ground, grinding, and drying your food. You should swallow it and keep it in your stomach for the winter." But the sisters did not believe it. They told their sister to watch out; the man was up to some trickery. But the girl insisted she had witnessed how he preserved his food, and she described it to her sisters. She named all the things he swallowed and how he did it. She told her sisters she was going to use this same method. Her sisters only laughed at her, and they left her.

The girl began to dig and swallow, over and over again all day. Towards evening she began to feel sick. She did this for three days and on the fourth day she became very ill. The sisters found her in very critical condition and took her home. Things were happening as the Crane had planned it. He then proceeded to make himself into a medicine man.

Across the river he would sing his medicine song, keeping time with his knees. He would come out of the river and sit down on a log singing and knocking his knees together making a loud sound in time with his singing. This sound would echo and re-echo all around, making a beautiful sound across the river. The young girls heard this and they commented on what a beautiful song this man had. “He certainly must have a powerful medicine.” Actually he was singing so that the oldest sister would hear him and she did. She was thinking, “Oh, what a beautiful song.” The oldest sister then became very ill and she told her sisters to ask that man across the river to come and work on her with his medicine. She asked them five times, but they would not agree. They thought she was feverish and incoherent because her stomach was all swollen twice its size and she had constipation. She was nearly bursting from eating too much raw food, which was fermenting inside her.

One sister finally could not stand it any longer, and she decided to go after the medicine man. The other sisters did not comment, but they were still suspicious. Then one Honker said, “This man must have strong medicine because he has a powerful song. He might even be putting a spell on us. If we pay him lots of things, he might cure our sister or take off the spell.” This is as the Crane had planned! When the girl came to ask him to help the oldest sister, she said, “You must be a big medicine man. Our sister is near death. We want you to come and help her. We don’t want her to die. We will pay you well. We have lots of dried food stored away, or you can have whatever you want that we might possess.” Crane looked down at his feet and said, “Ho, ho, ho, perhaps it would be better if you asked somebody else.” This bantering went on for five days. Finally he said, “I guess I could come, but I don’t think I can help her. I already know that she is going to die!” He predicted this without even looking at her to show that he really had a powerful guardian spirit which made him into a medicine man. He prepared to go, trying to look reluctant.

Crane wished himself into a tall good-looking man painted with yellow paint around the edges of his eyes. When he arrived at their home, the young girl was already delirious and seriously ill. He told the sisters they had to leave the house, because he had to have absolute privacy while he worked. He told them that they must get some big sticks and beat them together to keep time with his song. The sticks all had to be the same size, and they must hold them all in a straight line while they kept time. They had to follow the same rhythm he pounded out with his knees. One sister did not like the sound of this and she hesitated, but the other sisters, seeing their older sister in serious condition, did not argue. So they convinced their doubting sister to consent and leave the house. They did not go too far because they wanted to be around if anything should happen to their sister.

Before they left the house, Crane told them, "You don't have to give me the food you promised. I want to be sure to cure this young woman before I am paid. If and when I cure her, then I might ask for something, but not your food." They thought he was truly a good man because he did not want pay before he cured their sister. They left the house.

Crane began to sing his song walking around the house, knocking his knees together in time with the music. The girls outside began to hit their sticks together and the sound was certainly convincing. He instructed them before they began that when he cracked his knees rapidly, they were to do the same because this meant that he was going after the evil thing that was making their sister sick. (Sometimes the medicine man goes after an illness with his mouth, sucking it out with his mouth, or sometimes he does it with his hands as if he was scooping it out. That is when this sound, which sounds like a pounding hailstorm on the roof, is made in rapid staccato.) Instead of doing this, he became so emotional that the rhythmic knocking of his knees was all mixed up, and the girls on the outside heard this and they thought he was going after the evil illness and they began to beat the sticks all mixed up. This went on for a long, long time and they thought this must surely be a serious illness because it is taking so long to take it out of her body.

At long last the knocking stopped, and the girl regained consciousness. She found herself all alone with that man from the river and wondered what happened. The sisters came inside to visit, and when she tried to tell her sisters what happened to her, Crane would immediately interrupt her by saying, "Don't pay any attention to her, she is still delirious. She was critically ill. She was nearly bursting open. It was necessary to pierce her so that the bad air came out to relieve the pressure. It will take her a long time to recover. I will go home now, but you let me know if she gets worse." He cautioned the sisters not to pay any attention to what their sister said, "She will be delirious for quite some time and will talk strangely saying things you might not understand." Then he went home.

The girl recovered rapidly. The brothers came home from a long trip and they noticed their sister was tired and she looked big around the middle. The brothers had been away for a long time and they were not home when the previous incident happened. The oldest brother became concerned about his sister. In fact, he was quite sure he knew what happened to her. She was pregnant.

The oldest brother held a conference with his brothers and told them, "We must get rid of that man. Let's tell him there are a lot of fish across the ocean and offer to take him there." They flew over in formation to where Crane was still fishing, standing on one foot. They came down and visited with him telling him what they planned. They were concerned because the youngest sister was running over to see Crane whenever she had the chance. They wanted to avoid further scandal in the family.

The Honker Geese brothers were very convincing when they told him, "We feel sorry for you. Here you stand all day long catching these little fish, while across the ocean there are a lot of fish twice as large as these. If you want, we will take you there." Old Crane said, "I'm not supposed to leave this country. I'm not making food for myself. I have a family too; that is why I am saving all this food. I should not leave!" They asked him five more times and finally he agreed.

The next day the Honkers prepared for a long journey. When they circled over Crane's home, where he was waiting, they were undecided who was to pack the Crane because he could not fly as far as them. They began to argue about it. They told the oldest one that since he was the one who planned this, he should pack him. This settled the dispute and he knelt down to let Crane on his back.

When they neared their destination, the Honkers wished this place full of big fish. It was a river flowing into the ocean, and the fish were swimming into the river from the ocean. They put Crane off there. He was so overcome by the sight of all those different kinds of fish that he had no time to worry about where he was. He fished all day and in the evening he wanted to go home.

The Honkers fell into formation and the oldest one put Crane on his back. Crane was very heavy because he had so many fish sticking out from his big long bill. When they reached the middle of the ocean, the carrier became very tired, and he asked the next brother to help him, saying that it was his turn to pack Crane. The brother flew beneath his brother to catch Crane and together they carried him home. Crane asked them to stop by and pick him up again the next day and they agreed. The two who previously carried him were all scratched up by Crane's talons when he held onto their backs, so they were very reluctant to carry him again. One of the others volunteered to carry him and they took him across and he fished all day again. It was harder to get volunteers to carry him this time, because they did not want to get scratched. Finally, the last two volunteered to carry him back. Crane was nervous about heights and he would hold fast, digging his claws into the back of his carriers. They brought him back again and afterward suffered from the scratches. "The next time we go, let's leave him," one said. The oldest brother told them that this time they would get rid of him.

The fourth time they took him, he was ready again, singing as he stood in the water. "This time I would like to go with you, my brothers-in-law! My brothers-in-law!" He kept singing this song all the way. The youngest one would listen to him and wonder about it. He came to the conclusion that he really must be their brother-in-law. He could not figure out how this was so because there was no wedding trade!

In the meantime, the oldest sister was getting bigger and bigger around the stomach. The other sisters thought she was getting fat because the food she ate was raw and it was growing inside her stomach.

The next day the oldest brother told his brothers he would carry Crane, but none of the others would volunteer to help. The Crane was so full of fish this time that he was dead weight, and his effort to stay on the back of the carrier made it very uncomfortable for the Honker, so he dropped him into the ocean. This is how it was planned.

When they arrived at their sisters' home, they circled the place in formation and the oldest sister missed Crane. She was sure they must have killed him and she cried. She grabbed her bow and arrow and shot her brothers down. She was angry because she was to have a child from this Crane, and now her baby would be without a father. The youngest brother intercepted her arrow under his wing and flew away with it. She killed four of her brothers.

The youngest brother flew back to where he had lived with his brothers. He still carried the arrow with him. The sisters scolded the one who shot her brothers. Then she told them she was to have a child fathered by Crane. When the baby was born he looked exactly like Crane, except he was more deeply colored. The mother was grey color and the father was white.

The sisters did not like their sister after she had the baby. It was a disgrace that their virgin sister had a baby by Crane. They were so ashamed, they abandoned her. This girl took her baby and began to travel all by herself. Nobody wanted to associate with her. They thought it was a disgrace to have a child with no father. Everybody avoided her and the child.

Soon the little baby grew into manhood (babies grew up faster in legendary days). One day everyone heard old man Crow was going to have a medicine dance. (Medicine dances are where the medicine men or women renew their powers to heal or whatever their guardian spirits designate.) The Honker mother told her son to attend this medicine dance because his father once was a big medicine man. The young man was anxious to see this medicine dance. He was carefully instructed by his mother as she prepared his elaborate clothing for the occasion. He had to dress according to his father's status of medicine man. The boy's mother had worked for a long time on his costume for the occasion, and she made a wish that he become very handsome and tall with yellow paint around his eyes. "You are to attend this celebration, and perhaps a young girl might want you for her husband. You will contribute at the medicine dance by keeping time to the singing with your knees, knocking them together in rhythm." She explained that the "knee-knocking" sound was characteristic of the Crane.

X̱ux̱ux̱yáaya (Old Man Crow) and his brother X̱atx̱áatya (Mallard Duck) and K'astilayáaya (Crawfish) were sponsoring this medicine dance to make the weather warmer because it was too cold and people were suffering.

The Crane boy went to the medicine dance. He heard some beautiful songs sung by some women. Old Man Crow was there all decorated in elaborate costume, beaded and feathered. Across from him sat a beautiful woman, his awít (dead brother's widow). She was dressed up and painted around the head and on her face with red Indian paint. She had long black braids and was by far the most beautiful woman there. Crow was singing and adding the words, "My brother's widow," in most of his songs. The boy immediately felt at home and he began to rap his legs together in rhythm with the song, "Yaw! yaw! yaw!" This made the medicine men very happy. They admired him for making this sound which accented their singing.

Spilyáy approached young Crane and suggested they "walk" Crow's awít down the aisle, which is a tradition practiced by medicine men and women at their medicine dances today. Crow was carrying a bag of bone meal while he sang his song, showing that this had something to do with his guardian spirit and his medicine as if to say, "This is what my guardian spirit told me to do when I sing for my power!" With this, Crow was challenging everybody that his power was greater than anybody else's. Spilyáy became envious of Crow, and to spite him he leaned over and whispered to Crane boy, "Let's take his awít and walk her down the aisle. He has lost his heart to her." Then they twisted some hemp and decorated it with beads and made it into a beautiful rope. Five creatures danced down the aisle following each other, right up to the woman. They pulled her out, tied the hemp rope around her neck and pulled her to the other end of the singing lodge and made her sit beside Crane. This upset the Crow so much he fainted, falling over. "Uh, uh, uh," like he was in pain. Everybody was excited. They wondered what happened to Crow. Then somebody said, "Oh, they made his awít walk the aisle. He is upset because he had lost his heart to her."

Crow turned to his brother Crawfish, "Quick, prepare to get her back. Let's declare war upon them." He told his brother Duck too, and then they prepared for war, taking off their dress clothes and putting on breech cloths and breast shields. The brothers all got together and charged down to the other end of the lodge, swarming around, fighting over the woman and tugging at her. They nearly choked the woman. Someone shot Crawfish in the head, and somebody shot Duck in the hip, and some of the helpers were wounded. An informer ran down and told Crow what was happening. "Your brother has been shot in the head. There is excrement coming out of the top of his head." "Ho ho, ho, whoever heard of excrement coming out of the top of anybody's head," said Crow. "Poor thing must have been keeping that in his head all this time!" They could not figure out if he was amused or hysterical. They told him X̠atx̠áatya was shot in the hip and could barely walk. "Ah, what is the matter with my brothers?! They have lost my awít," Crow said.

The Crow's sister-in-law was getting tired. They were pulling her back and forth until she could barely stand. But Crow would not give up. He called more of his friends and relatives together and told them to go after his sister-in-law. He did not want to lose her. He claimed he did not trust them, especially Crane whom he spitefully called Myáak̠in (child born out of wedlock). "I don't find anything attractive about him!" He made all kinds of remarks against the Crane boy. Then he asked them to charge again.

Crane beat them all up again. Spilyáy enjoyed watching Crow suffer. He was glad Crow was losing because he was bragging so much about his medicine. Spilyáy would joke, making fun of Crawfish, "Whoever heard of excrement coming out of the top of one's head! I thought he was supposed to be ferocious, always pinching people." (There was a time when Spilyáy wanted to be the interpreter for Crow when he was singing, and Crawfish had pinched him and sent him away. "Don't come close. You are spreading your fleas around here." Spilyáy had tried to tell him that he was an experienced interpreter, but Crawfish refused to listen. That is why he was angry at Crawfish.)

Again the Crow's people charged. They grabbed the hemp rope around the widow's neck and pulled her. This widow was actually Frog woman, very beautiful, all painted up with Indian paint. This Frog woman was all covered up with beautiful robes which Crane gave her. All this time he had been keeping them inside his stomach like his father. She had a robe made of leaves and grass which he decorated with shells and colored rocks from the bottom of lakes and rivers. Finally Frog woman decided to leave. She was afraid they would kill her or injure her. She braced herself and sprang way out into space, flying away carrying the robes with her into the water. Since that time, Frog has been living in the water and she is wearing robes with colors of the rainbow. She also has all the plants in the water that make her robes.

This is what the Indians follow at their medicine dances today. When there is an attractive unmarried woman in the congregation, some men will get together, donate something to the woman, decorate her with beads, robes, and walk her down the aisle singing a song. If some men want her back, they will go take her back. However, these days, it is those who decorate her the best that get her. They don't fight any more like when Crawfish got shot in the head and Duck was shot in the hind leg (that's why ducks waddle). They called this practice "the war." In the end they all lost out. The Frog woman jumped in the water, leaving all of them. Spilyáy started this when he talked Crane into stealing the Crow's awít.

When you find a frog in the mountains, usually at a freshwater spring, break off a sprig of grass and throw it at her and tell her, "You stay here and wait. He will come soon." You are making a gift to her, and it makes her very proud when you do this. She expects everybody to give her nice things. If you do not do this, she will follow you to your camp at night and she will sit on your head and pee on you!

Lesson of Palyuułá

(Bone Game Player)

Palyuułá was a gambler and all he ever wanted was more money. But he learns that actually food is more valuable than money.

THERE was a man living a long time ago whose name was Palyuułá (bone game player). He had a wife and two children, a boy and girl. This man gambled all the time, a game called Palyúut (bone game). Sometimes it is called the stick-game. He did not provide for his family like other men, and as a result his children were ragged, his teepee was old and full of holes, and his wife was poorly dressed. There was no food to cook and they were hungry all the time.

One day Palyuułá, out of desperation, told his wife he was going to visit the chief of the village and bargain with him for food. He said, "I will trade with the chief for food, and I will give him what I value most, money! I will trade him money for salmon and we will eat it together." Then he walked over towards the chief's lodge and went inside. They visited for awhile, talking about everyday things until he finally came to the main reason for his visit. He told the chief, "I came to see you because of hunger, and this is what I brought to trade for some salmon." The chief looked at the piece of coin and pondered for a long time. He thought to himself, "I will teach you a lesson today, Palyuułá!" He took the gold coin and laid it on top of a piece of dry salmon. Then he took out his hunting knife and, using the coin for a pattern, cut out a piece of dried salmon the same size as the gold coin. He picked up this piece of salmon and gave it to Palyuułá without a word. Palyuułá looked at the piece of salmon in the palm of his hand with disbelief, then he stood up and walked out.

As he was walking back to his teepee he was thinking, "He could have at least given me a little more salmon than this for all that money." But there was nothing he could have said to the chief. He looked at the small piece of salmon and wondered what he was going to do with it. That night he took it out and let the children smell the salmon, since it was so small dividing it was impossible. Smelling that salmon made them more hungry!

The next day the chief called all the villagers in for a council. He told the people, "We must move away and leave Palyuułá. We will move downriver. We must teach him a lesson. He never goes hunting or fishing for his family. We must leave them to their fate. Whether they survive or not is their problem." They all packed up and left Palyuułá and his family behind.

Palyuułá and his family were positively starving because there was nobody around to provide them with scraps or handouts as their neighbors had done when they felt sorry for the children and his wife. On that day, he was lying down with his back against the teepee wondering how he was going to feed his children, when he happened to glance up towards a rocky ledge and thought he saw something, "Swish." He kept his eyes on that spot for another few minutes and saw the same "swishing" movement again, and then he focused his eyes better and saw a small deer. He crept up the side of the ledge and then peeked over and saw a large herd of deer grazing all over the meadow. He became excited and called to his wife, "Quick, help me. We must plan how to kill all those deer, so that we may eat!"

The entire family got together and began to gather branches and grass to build a trap for the deer. They built a fence leading towards a cliff. They narrowed the fence at the end down into an opening over the high cliff. When they finished this fence, they sneaked behind the herds of deer and maneuvered them towards this opening. Some ran away in the other direction, but some went along the fence down towards the cliff edge and jumped over the side to their death. The family ran down there and began to skin and cut up the deer as the children prepared the fire for cooking the meat. They had so much food! They did this five times, had enough food for the winter and they had plenty of deerskins for their clothing, moccasins, and even enough for a brand-new teepee.

In the meantime, the chief was worrying about Palyuułá and his family, wondering if he did the right thing by leaving them to their own fate. He wondered if they were still alive. One day he could not contain himself any longer and he asked his wife to prepare a bundle of dried salmon to take on a journey. He told her, "I am going to visit Palyuułá and his family." Then he turned towards the direction where their old village was located when they left Palyuułá behind. As he neared the place, he saw a brand-new teepee standing in the place of the old one, and he heard people laughing happily inside. He quietly approached the teepee and cautiously peeked inside. He was ashamed when he saw Palyuułá sitting down inside this new teepee. He was sorry for leaving his friend behind like he did. Palyuułá was very happy to see the chief and he greeted him joyfully, asking him to sit down in the best place inside the teepee, offering his best hospitality. The chief could hardly believe his eyes when he looked around and saw the new teepee, the new clothing on the family and all the food. Everybody looked healthy and happy, no longer hungry and desperate.

While they were visiting and eating, the chief could not control his curiosity any longer and he told Palyuułá, "I want to confess. When we moved away and left you, I was responsible for that. It was to teach you a lesson!" But Palyuułá answered, "Do not apologize. We understand. You have truly taught me a lesson!" The chief asked, I am curious, how did you get all this wealth? You have all this meat and new clothing, even a new teepee. How did you do it?" Then Palyuułá told him all about the huge herds of deer and how they caught them and preserved the meat. He assured the chief there was still a lot of deer left for everybody. Then he told the chief about how they were starving and he saw this small movement on the ledge and then he saw the deer. He told how they all worked together to build the fence and prepared the hides and meat.

After a while the host asked his wife to prepare a large bundle of dried meat for the chief to take back home. They shook hands and the chief asked him if it was all right for them to move back and live together again. They vowed to work together in keeping the villagers fed and clothed. Palyuułá said, "You will provide the salmon, and I will provide the deer meat. We will trade this with each other and live happily together."

There is a lesson in this story that money is not as valuable as food. Some people today do not value food like they did in the olden days. Money is valued more than preserved foods. We Indian people have our own food which was created for us and we do not place monetary value upon it. To some of us this food could never be purchased with money. We will never sell it because it is reserved for us.

Story about Chakyáy

The chief knew that Chakyáy was a thief, but he baited him with valuable things just to see if he could catch him. In the end the chief lost everything, including his life, showing that you shouldn't get carried away with proving your own cleverness. The story also shows that if you are too rich and greedy that Chakyáy can take over your soul and your wealth.

THERE was a small boy living all by himself named Chakyáy. Living in a small village nearby was a rich man. This man had all kinds of workers and he had everything he needed to make a comfortable home. He had a wife and a daughter, and he had all kinds of animals on his land. That is why everybody thought of him as a chief.

The boy was an absolute thief. He could steal anything from anybody. He would even go to the chief's home and steal just about anything he wanted. This aggravated the chief and he thought, "If this boy is such a crafty thief, then I wonder if he could steal my prize horses?" He baited him with his most prized horses, but he told his helpers to take extra precautions and to have somebody on watch all the time. Each group was to take turns watching day and night, and he provided tame horses for those sleeping at night. They had to sleep with their horses close by in case of an emergency.

Chakyáy observed what the chief was doing and he said to himself, "I am an immortal thief. I can outwit anybody. This is my gift! My guardian gives me invisibility, and I can hypnotize anybody to do as I please! That is I, Chakyáy." Then he hypnotized all the helpers into deep sleep, examined them all to make sure they were sound asleep, found some logs with branches and laid them on the logs with their hands holding the small branches. He did this to all the helpers while they were snoring out loud. Then he led all the gentle horses away. The next morning the chief woke up early and he went down to check on his helpers, and found them all sound asleep. They were holding branches from the logs. He woke them up and reprimanded them soundly, "Why did you sleep on the job? He has stolen my tame horses. I have none left." The thief had taken all his gentle horses, and the chief was very bitter, and he walked home defeated. When he reached his home some strangers came to visit him and he told them his problem. Then he exclaimed, "If this thief is so crafty, I wonder if he could steal my closest possession, my wife. I don't think he can!"

The strangers left the chief's home and they met the thief and told him what the chief had said. "You have taken everything from the chief?" He answered, "Yes, I have stolen from the chief," and then he showed them where he stored all of the things he had stolen from the chief. "As long as I live, I will oppose this rich man. Everything you see here is stolen from the chief." They told him what the chief had said, that the thief had stolen everything he prized from him, but he does not think he can steal his wife, nor the things he has left.

After the strangers left, Chakyáy sat down and pondered what he just heard. Then it turned evening and a full moon came into view. He could see everything like it was daylight. Then he remembered the chief had many baby pigs. He knew it would be no problem to catch one. He went to the chief's home and he grabbed one small piglet and carried it under his arm. He went to the house and looked inside to find out which way the chief faced when he slept. The chief was sleeping with his gun tucked inside his arms, ready for use, because he planned to kill Chakyáy if he tried to come inside his house. The chief told his wife, "Chakyáy is peeking around at us from the outside; he is here again. This time he will die. If he really is an immortal thief, the next time he peeks inside I will kill him!" Right at that moment Chakyáy put the piglet in the window and the chief shot it. The piglet squealed and the chief thought he had shot Chakyáy. Then Chakyáy grabbed the piglet and ran zigzagging back and forth leaving a trail of blood, finally throwing the piglet away into the brush down the canyon. He ran back to the chief's house while the chief was tracking the bloody trail left by the bleeding piglet. There was no Chakyáy to be found. The chief was confident he had wounded the thieving boy and was thinking that if he found his body he would burn it.

Chakyáy escaping

got off his horse to investigate. Chakyáy called out loud, "Ohhh, I've changed my mind, I've changed my mind!" The man became curious and asked, "What are you, and what are you talking about?" Then Chakyáy told him, "Don't you know? I am the man that the chief's daughter is supposed to marry, and I refused. This is why I am all tied up. But I have changed my mind. I will reconsider and marry the chief's daughter!" Then he told the man because he refused to marry the chief's daughter, they were going to drown him in the river. The man exclaimed, "Oh, I've been trying to court the chief's daughter for a long time. I will untie you and you can tie me up inside the sack! Then when they come back I will agree to marry the chief's daughter!" He untied Chakyáy and exchanged places with him. Chakyáy tied him all up and quickly jumped on the man's horse and galloped away. The man was left on the ground all tied up in a sack.

Later the men came back, all fed and ready to work. They found the sack rolling around on the ground. The man inside told them, "Oh, you have returned? Untie me. I've changed my mind. After thinking about it for a long time, I have decided to marry the chief's daughter!" One of the men told him, "Oh, you don't deceive us any longer. We know you are Chakyáy, no matter how you try to fool us. You can no longer outwit us!" Then they picked him up and threw him in the canoe and took him out to the middle of the river and drowned him. The man was gone forever. But Chakyáy was still alive, galloping away on a horse.

A few days later he decided to return to that place. He turned back and he drove all of the animals he had stolen back with him. While he was traveling, he sensed the chief was coming down the road. "Uhh! He's coming! I wonder why?" thought Chakyáy. The chief came up to him on the trail and asked him, "You truly are Chakyáy, aren't you?" He answered, "Yes, I am Chakyáy." Then the chief told him that he thought he had been drowned, but Chakyáy told him, "No, you did not kill me. This water is only on the surface and underneath is a rich land. When I fell in, I landed in the middle of this rich country and the people untied me. They gave me all of these animals, and I drove them up to the surface of the earth. If you had taken me farther out I would have been able to reach the more wealthy land, where the people are more handsome. But your men did not take me out far enough and I was only able to reach an ordinary land." The chief immediately became restless and wanted to leave right away. He told Chakyáy, "I'm going home and I'll instruct my workers to take me way out and drop me into the river. I want to see this land you are talking about." He did this, and he told them about the place where Chakyáy was given all of those beautiful animals. He said he wanted some of that wealth too. His workers did this thing. They took him out into the river and threw him in. He went under, and to this day, was never seen again. This is how Chakyáy tricked the chief and took possession of everything he owned, and he became a wealthy man.

Sháapshish

Sháapshish looks for his guardian spirit even though he is not successful the first few times. Finally his efforts are rewarded and the guardian Mouse woman gives him the spiritual strength and guidance to accomplish great things.

Sháapshish was a small boy and he lived with his grandmother. They were very poor; so poor, in fact, that the people in the village did not want to associate with them. The village people would not make their camp nearby because they wanted to keep their children away from Sháapshish. Whenever they moved to another place, they had to camp away from the rest of the people. His grandmother would tell him, "Don't go near the camp, and don't play with other children. Don't make them angry with us."

The boy would hunt for food for his grandmother, trap rabbits, and shoot small birds with his bow and arrow. One day his grandmother became ill and she died suddenly. He was all alone, and nobody wanted him. The people would move to another place and he would just follow along, leading his grandmother's kawxkáwx (palomino) horse. He sought his own food and whatever he could find he would throw into the fire and eat it. He was truly an orphan.

One day the chief of the village began to worry about this boy and thought he should take care of him. Sháapshish was ragged and thin and the chief felt sorry for him. The chief sent a messenger to the boy inviting him to his teepee to eat, but the boy would not come. He told the messenger, "I am all right," although he was nearly starving to death. The chief would not give up and kept after the boy to come live in his camp, but the boy refused.

Finally one day in the winter time when it was cold, his grandmother's horse died from hunger and old age. In the springtime his own horse died, which left him without transportation. But he kept on living alone in his makeshift camp. The chief saw an opportunity to persuade the boy and he offered to give him a horse if he would come live with him. Even this would not persuade the boy. Sháapshish did not want to obligate himself to anybody and burden them with his presence because he had been taught that he was an outcast.

The boy would often go out into the wilderness and camp overnight looking for his guardian spirit, but he could not find one. All the creatures kept very still and they would not make any overtures to the boy. Although the boy went to places where no human had ever been, he did not see or hear anything. When the people in the village would have their medicine dance, he often wondered how they received their songs and power. When he went out to the wilderness to seek this power he was unable to find it. He even went out in the dark night looking for his guardian spirit but nothing happened.

Finally the chief caught him in a weak moment and he consented to live with him. He was very careful not to offend the chief. He would not eat too much, nor would he use the blankets, because he was always afraid of the chief's wife who might get angry with him. Nobody noticed him much, and as a result, they moved away one day and left him while he was out hunting. When he returned to the camp, he found only the empty campsite. He walked around the abandoned camp and heard a female voice weeping. He thought someone must have been left behind and he went over to where he heard this weeping. He found a Mouse woman sitting on the ground, and when she saw him she said, "Oh, I'm so glad to see you. I'm crying because the chief must have taken all my children. My children are where the chief keeps his medicine pouch, and they are still too little to take care of themselves." Then she named all her children. "I want you to go after them for me, and I will reward you."

He followed the villagers that night towards where the woman told him they would be camping, and he caught up with them at daybreak. He went directly to the chief's teepee just as the mother-in-law was stirring up the fire for cooking. He went inside right to the place where the chief kept his medicine pouch, pulled out the parfleche, and was opening it when the mother-in-law attacked him with the poker stick (a stick used to stir up the fire). The chief woke up and told her, "Leave him alone. Don't hurt him. Let him do whatever he wants!"

The boy opened the parfleche, took out the medicine bundle and opened it and began counting the babies inside, putting them in his soft belt pouch as he named each one. She had told him not to hurt her babies and he was very gentle with them.

He put the chief's property away again and he hurried back with the babies to where the woman was waiting. The chief observed all this, and he knew that something very important was happening to the boy that would probably affect his entire life.

That evening he reached the place and found Mouse woman still weeping. He brought the babies to her and told her, "I brought the babies," and he named them all. "They are all safe and healthy." He laid them down in front of her.

Mouse woman told him, "I know you have exhausted yourself trying to find your guardian spirit. Your soul is crying out for this strength and spiritual guidance. I am going to tell you a secret. All of the creatures don't want you, even the people don't want you. All the creatures have warned each other not to take pity on you because you are a mean boy. But I will reward you for this big favor you have done for me. You must clean yourself up. Pick the leaves in the autumn, fix a mud bath, and rub yourself with the leaves all over your body. Boil some leaves and drink the juice. Your body will discard all its impurities, and afterwards everything will accept you." Sháapshish followed her instructions.

The boy ran home, but everyone had moved away again. The Mouse woman had already told him where they would be. She also told him that his life was going to change; he would be accepted by everything and everybody. Soon he would be superhuman in all his accomplishments.

The village was moving to a place where the women would dig camas and the men were forming a war party to go to another village to steal back some horses which the enemy had stolen from them. The people were preparing by singing songs and asking for help from their guardian spirit.

Sháapshish's younger sister was living with another family, since they had been raised separately. He approached her and told her he wanted to go with this war party. He told her he did not want anybody else near him.

So she said she would stay near him. He gave her all his worn-out moccasins to mend. She begged some scraps from other people and began to mend his moccasins.

All of the accomplished warriors were preparing for the raid. They sang their songs all night. Sháapshish and his sister joined the crowd. She tied all of his old moccasins on the end of a pole and she carried it over her shoulder. The people observed them and were amused, wondering what they were doing with all of those warriors, where they had no business. Sháapshish told his sister to stay close to him, not to let anybody behind him. She stayed right with him. People were making fun of them. They thought they were only playing children's games.

The chief sent scouts out to find out where their enemy was camped. The women had nearly completed their work of digging camas and drying it. They were in the process of grinding it to store when the chief ordered the war party to get ready to leave. They were ready to take their horses back from the enemy.

The boy and his sister would not give up. They mingled and sang right along with the rest of them. The chief called the boy to his teepee and told him, "Are you determined to go along on this war party?" He answered, "Yes, I am ready!" The chief said, "All right, I have an experienced war horse. You may have him. If something should happen and you get lost, he can find his way back." The boy agreed to take the horse, and the women prepared his food to take along. They tied a bundle of sapk'tɨ́t (dried root biscuit), x̱yaaw nɨkwɨ́t (dried deer meat) and x̱yaaw núsux̱ (dried salmon).

The war party reluctantly agreed to let the boy come along. After a few hours of traveling the boy had a premonition. He went ahead spiritually and found the enemy camp. He saw the chief's favorite horse (which had been taken in a raid) and was sure this was the camp of the enemy. He went back and told his war party, but they would not believe him. They finally sent another scout with him to have a look at this enemy camp. The scout saw the camp and it was as the boy had described. The enemy were having a good time of games and gambling, unaware that they were being watched.

After the scout reported what he had seen, they prepared to raid the camp. During the night the boy went down into the camp. He found a watchman riding around the camp. He jumped behind him on the horse and cut his throat. He took off the clothes the watchman was wearing and put them on. He threw the watchman into a creek bed and went into camp on horseback, checking all the horses. Quietly, Sháapshish untied all the horses.

Before he did anything else, he remembered the chief telling him to bring him a war bonnet and some fancy beadwork for him and his wife and mother-in-law. So he peeked in a teepee and saw two women making tallow and throwing away the membranes. He stuck his hand inside and grabbed the membranes and ate them because he was very hungry. This gave him some strength.

Sháapshish wandered around camp afterward and looked around while everyone slept or celebrated. Eventually he came to where he saw the reflection of a war bonnet with a long train hanging inside the teepee. The man inside the teepee woke up and was preparing to go out. He said something in his own language to his wife and got up and went out. The boy saw the war bonnets and all the beadwork belonging to the woman. He remembered what his foster father had told him. He quietly walked inside and got into bed with the woman and put his arms around her. She giggled and told him to leave her alone, that she had already made love with him. He kept on fondling her until he put her to sleep. He heard the other woman leave her bed, and he quietly got up and took down the chief's war bonnet. He gathered the beadwork and everything the chief told him to bring back and carried it all outside to where the horse was waiting. He put all of his loot on the horse and tied it securely.

Sháapshish then went inside the other teepees without anyone seeing him. When he found something, he took it and left quietly. This was the trait Mouse gave him when he did her a favor by saving her children. When he was ready to leave, he led his horse ahead. His horse whinnied softly to the others and they followed.

When they were far enough away he got on the watchman's horse and galloped away fast. The people heard the noise and they followed him on the few horses they had left. The horse the chief had given him with the pack on his back galloped away, leading the others. Sháapshish was riding the horse of the watchman, the one he killed in the enemy camp.

His people were still asleep when he thundered into camp with the enemy not far behind him. He woke them up. The enemy went into combat with the war party while Sháapshish drove the horses towards home. On the fifth day the horse belonging to the chief galloped into their camp with the pack on his back. The other horses followed and the people ran to claim their own horses.

Sháapshish took the chief's favorite horse to him and gave him the war bonnet with the long train and the beadwork for his wife and mother-in-law. The chief was very grateful and he wanted to reward him by making him a subchief. The boy refused. He said, "I grew up poor and I will remain poor. I don't want any chieftainship bestowed on me. Someday I will be justly rewarded if I carry my obligations as I have been directed by my spiritual guide."

When the people heard that he could be made into a subchief, they objected saying, "Oh, he has no royal blood. He is just an urchin, a nobody! How could a person like that become a chief?" Sháapshish was hurt, so he went out and killed a nighthawk. He pulled its feathers and made a tassel for his hair. He had in the meantime taken a wife, and when she saw him decorating his hair, she asked, "Why are you fixing yourself up?" He said, "Oh, I'm going to visit some royal blood people." But his wife cautioned him not to do anything foolish. She thought his feelings were hurt because they called him those names. She told him they would someday find their reward for the bad things they had said to Sháapshish. "Someday they will find out the good things you have done for them," she said, and she begged him not to make any mistakes. He smiled at her and said, "All right."

He got on his white horse and galloped away, stripped down to his skin, wearing only a breech cloth and the feather tied in his hair. He went to the teepees of the men who were mocking him and galloped up and down the racks of drying roots, ruining their food. He went to their teepee and cut up their teepee while they were away from the camp. He did everything to make the men angry but they would not challenge him. Everyone was afraid of him.

Later in life, when the Indian wars developed, this man became famous for his feats in battle. He was able to withstand any kind of hardships while in battle, and he came out without a scratch or wound. He was able to sneak into the enemy's camp, strike, and leave without being detected. He had supernatural powers and he eventually became a leader in his tribe. The people in his lifetime remembered this man for the leadership and wisdom he provided for them, and they still talked about it in the early century.

This is how the Indian people get their spiritual guidance through some creature of nature. They are bestowed with supernatural powers and spiritual strength. It is to protect us when we are in dire need of some superhuman guidance.

Some people have the ability to withstand tribulations of war. They can run through a hail of bullets and not receive a scratch. They have the ability to see clearly at night, or to sneak up on the enemy without being noticed. That's the way this man Sháapshish became, when he began to practice his superhuman gifts. He could predict things, and they would come true. He could hear people talking about him many miles away, and he could see at night. I don't know if he received all of these gifts from Mouse, or if he found another creature to guide him, but this is the way he was.

Legend about Blue Jay

One should not make fun of ugly or deformed people as Blue Jay demonstrates in this tale. Someday these very same people may become powerful.

ONCE there was a real fat boy with a huge stomach. He was so roly-poly that he rolled around like a ball. People would push him away with their feet and he would roll away. They'd tell him, "You are always in the way. Stay out of the way." He would roll away from them. It seemed that he was always falling down and getting in the way. He was an ugly boy. He had pimples all over his face and body.

People played tricks on him all the time, but the Chief told them to leave him alone. He said, "Don't play tricks on that boy. Leave him alone." Every time they played pranks on him, putting their feet in front of him, and making him fall down, they would find small items lying around where he had fallen down. They became curious, and they talked about it among themselves.

The Chief had a beautiful daughter. One day the daughter became of age and experienced her first menstruation. They built a cellar and put her in it. There is a law that when a girl has her first menstruation, she is not to touch food or plants that grow, and she is not to touch her body. She is to use a long stick to scratch herself, and she is not to touch anybody else. They isolated the girl away from other people and covered her eyes with cloth so that she could not look at people. She was served by older women while she was in isolation. The girl was put away in a cellar. She stayed there until her menstruation was over, and when it cleared up, she was able to return home.

After that the Chief announced that his daughter was able to accept proposals of marriage. He announced to all the creatures that they could come and ask for her hand in marriage. "There are a lot of you who are great warriors capable of taking care of my daughter. Whoever wants her hand in marriage is welcome. It is up to my daughter to choose the one she wants for her husband."

All the eligible creatures were clamoring to ask for her hand in marriage but she turned them all down. All this time, Fat Boy kept rolling around and laughing loudly, "Ha, ha, ha." People would trip him and make him roll around. He would laugh and laugh. He had a huge stomach and tiny legs and feet.

All the creatures were turned down by the girl. Fat Boy wanted to ask her, but he thought he could not ask for her hand because he was too closely related to her. He was thinking about the wealth that he kept stored in his body. That was why he had such a large stomach, because that was where he stored his wealth. He would think, "What am I going to do with all this wealth? I don't want to marry a stranger and give it all to her. I could ask the Chief's daughter to marry me and keep it all with us." But he thought about how ugly he was and how everybody made fun of him. He had a blue body, and his hair was tied in a knot on top of his head. He had skinny arms and skinny legs. The only thing big about him was his stomach. His name was Tɨmsk'aplúya—he was Blue Jay.

The girl would not marry any of those asking for her hand. The Chief was very worried. He was afraid if Blue Jay asked her to marry him, he would be so disgraced. He did not want Blue Jay for a son-in-law because they were too closely related. But Blue Jay kept thinking about his wealth, "There isn't anybody else more deserving of my wealth. I guess I will ask her to marry me."

Blue Jay had been raised by his grandmother and when she died she left all her wealth to him. She told him that he would be ridiculed later in life, and that all the women would not want him for a husband because of his appearance. "Secretly swallow your wealth and keep it in your stomach. When you marry, take it out and you will be wealthy," she said. He did as she told him to do. That was the reason he was so fat. That's why he caused so much curiosity when the people rolled him around and afterward, they found valuable articles lying around. Nobody ever found out his secret.

Blue Jay made up his mind that he would ask for her hand in marriage. Blue Jay knew that the Chief was worried that he was going to ask her. So he prepared by weighting himself down at his feet with heavy rocks, because the girl said that she was waiting for a tall heavy man. The girl heard his steps. She said to herself, “Here comes the man I am waiting for.” She heard him coming, “Thump, thump, thump.” That night Blue Jay married her. The next morning she looked at her new man. She recognized him, “Oh, it’s Blue Jay.” He lay there fat and round, with his skinny feet and hands, his hair tied up on top of his head. She knew that the damage had been done and it was too late to do anything about it.

The next day Spilyáy made an announcement that Blue Jay had become the son-in-law of the Chief. He called Blue Jay all kinds of names when he made his announcement to the people. The Chief woke his wife and told her to prepare to leave. His wife told him that he should not abandon his daughter because he had announced that anyone could come and ask for her hand. The Chief was so embarrassed, he did not want to claim his son-in-law. His daughter was too ashamed to come out in public; she hid away from the village people who were all laughing about her. Blue Jay told her, “I have embarrassed you. It was a hard decision to make to marry you. Do not worry, I am going to leave you for a little while. I am going to a place at Warm Springs to take sweatbaths. When I am ready I will return.” He knew that his wife was pregnant.

He went away to find this hot springs his grandmother had told him about. He bathed until all of the poison was steamed out of his system. His appearance changed gradually, and he became a handsome young man. He was no longer the fat roly-poly boy with pimples all over his face. He was a lean, handsome looking young man with a clear complexion.

In the meantime, the Chief and his people had moved away, abandoning Blue Jay’s wife. The girl’s mother pitied her daughter, and she left some food buried in the ashes at each fireplace. The girl found this food and survived, otherwise she might have starved to death.

When Blue Jay returned to his wife, he brought the wealth he kept hidden inside his stomach. It was necessary to enlarge his home to store his wealth. He went hunting and brought back all kinds of food and he stored it in his house. His son played with scraps of fat, using it for targets for his bow and arrow. Blue Jay was shooting all the game and depriving the Chief and his people of their share. The Chief’s people were starving.

During this period of famine, some magpies happened to pass by Blue Jay's home. They saw the little baby playing with pieces of fat. They thought they were dreaming, as they flew down to get a closer look. They found Blue Jay and they begged him for some food. Blue Jay was reluctant to help them because the magpies were the ringleaders when he was taunted about his appearance by the villagers. He gave them only scraps.

Blue Jay told his wife to prepare for guests, because he knew the magpies could not keep a secret, although he made them swear to secrecy. This came true one day when the magpies were quarreling violently over a scrap of meat. Their quarreling voices interrupted the Chief while he was singing and praying to the Great Spirit for help. He sent one of his messengers to find out why the magpies were making so much noise. He said, "Oh, what are they whispering about? Somebody go see what they are doing." The messenger went over and he saw the magpies eating the fat. Immediately he ran over to tell the Chief. They grabbed the magpies and broke their legs, trying to make them tell where they got the fat. But the magpies were sworn to secrecy and they would not tell. Finally when they twisted their necks, the magpies gave up and told the Chief where they got the fat. They told him that Blue Jay had lots of food.

Everybody packed up and moved back to their old village. They found everything as they were told by the magpies. When they arrived back at the village, Blue Jay met them. He wondered why they were moving back because he was using all of their space for preserving and storing food for the winter. Everyone noticed that Blue Jay looked different, not like he was when they made fun of him, rolling him around and calling him names. He told them he would help them by showing them where the deer was located, and they would shoot it for themselves. They were so weak and hungry that they could not go hunting. Blue Jay felt sorry for them and gave them food. The next morning he woke up early and told them that they should get up and go hunting. Everybody went hunting, all those good hunters—Cougar, Wolf, and Wildcat.

While they were hunting, it snowed and they began to freeze. They crawled inside their prey to keep warm. When Blue Jay returned home the villagers asked him where the rest of the hunters were. He told them that he had shot some deer and they were to skin the game and bring it home. He left them and came home with some game that he had killed. He went back and found them inside the deer. They were eating the deer from the inside. He pulled them out and made them take the game back to the camp. When the meat was brought back, the Chief distributed it among the people. He tried to give some to Blue Jay, but he refused it.

They had a council and decided they wanted to make Blue Jay a chief, but he said that he did not want to be a chief because he grew up poor and he had a hard time. He told them about how they mistreated him when he was ugly and fat, how they rolled him around and made him lose some of his wealth.

Blue Jay promised he would help them out sometimes when they went hunting. He would give them signals. But when they did not shoot anything, Blue Jay would make fun of them. Today when you go hunting, you can hear Blue Jay say, "Why, why, why, why!" When you make mistakes he will make fun of you, "Ha, ha, ha, ha!" Especially when you miss the deer, he will laugh and laugh.

Mountain Goat

When Spilyáy visits his in-laws, he does not watch his manners and insults everyone. Then he gives in to greediness and steals from his own relatives, almost getting himself killed as a result. This story stresses how important it is to behave properly when visiting your relatives.

A LONG time ago during the animal world days, there lived a girl at Camas Prairie. She was the daughter of Spilyáy who was the chief of Camas Prairie. She was a beautiful girl, and all of the young eligible bachelors wanted to marry her. There were so many, in fact, that it was hard for Spilyáy to pick the best one for a son-in-law. Finally he decided the best way to do this was to have a contest. He told the young men, "The one who can beat my daughter in a foot race can marry her." All the young men—Swift Deer, Grizzly Bear, Black Bear, Marten, all of them—gathered at Camas Prairie, getting ready to beat the girl in a foot race. Each one took his turn and she outran all of them.

Way up in the mountains above Icicle, there was a Mountain Goat living who was the eldest of three brothers. He told his two younger brothers to go down and beat Spilyáy's daughter. He was the older brother, so according to tradition, if he wanted the young woman for his wife, he could send his brothers to compete for her.

He prepared his brothers for the race. He gave one brother a medicine bag containing powder made of tips of his hooves and some whole hooves. To the other brother he gave a medicine bag with powder from the tips off his horns and horn tips. Then he told them, "When you get there, watch the girl. When she walks around before the race, put the powder in your mouth and follow her and spit in her tracks. Tell her father, Spilyáy, that you will both race with her. He will laugh at you, but don't pay any attention to him." The race was to go the entire length of Camas Prairie, which is about two miles long, and back to the starting point. This is a place where the Indians dig camas. Then he instructed the brothers how to use the hooves and the tips of horns in the medicine bags. They were to use the hooves to put on the girl so that she could climb up the Icicle Mountain because it's steep and slippery.

Down at the Camas Prairie camp it became real foggy. Everything was hazy and they could only see a few feet in front of them. They wondered why it became so foggy. Then all of a sudden the two mountain goats appeared in front of them. At the same time the fog lifted and everything was clear again.

As soon as Spilyáy saw them he laughed, "Ha, ha, ha, ha, we are now at the very last part of the earth. This is all there is left to race my daughter. Look at all the swift running young men my daughter outran. They are athletic and they have long legs, not short ones like these things standing in front of you." They disregarded the insults from Spilyáy and one of the goats answered, "Yes, we are here to race against your daughter. Our brother told us to come."

The girl was getting restless. She was pacing around. When the Mountain Goat brothers saw her doing this, they began to chew on the hoof and horn powder that their brother gave them in a medicine bag, and they followed her and spit in her tracks.

Everybody was making fun of the poor Mountain Goat brothers. They were poking fun at their short legs. Some were betting on the race. Finally everything was ready and they lined up to start. The brothers, standing on each side of the girl, got set and they started the race. The girl immediately took the lead, leaving the poor short-legged Mountain Goat brothers behind. Everybody began to laugh and laugh. The girl was out of sight and the brothers were still bouncing up and down trying to catch up with her.

When they were out of sight, everybody was holding their breath waiting for the girl to come around the turn first. Instead, they were surprised to see the Goat brothers taking the lead down the prairie. They said, "Where is the girl? What happened to her?" The goats came back and they said, "Well, we beat her." When the girl came into sight, she was barely walking. She said, "I don't know what happened. I was running real good

The one who can beat my daughter in a footrace can marry her and then all of a sudden my legs began to hurt." Spilyáy was very disappointed, but he made the rules and he had to observe them. He said, "You outran my daughter and I have to let her go with you." So the two little goats took the girl back to their brother.

They traveled for several days, and when they reached the Icicle Mountains the girl was unable to climb the mountain. They made her rest and they put the hoof tips on her feet so she wouldn't slip on the ice and rocks. They went on up to Icicle, in the Cascade Mountains where their brother lived.

One year passed, and Mountain Goat told his wife, "It's time for you to return to your father's home for a visit." He packed a sack full of dried goat meat for her to take with her. Blue Jay was living with them. He was the brother of Mountain Goat. Blue Jay said, "I'm going along." But his brother told him, "You don't behave. I'm not happy about your going along! You'll probably embarrass everyone while you are there." Blue Jay persisted, "Oh, I'll behave myself. I want to see that country, and I want to meet the chief, Spilyáy." Finally Mountain Goat consented to let him go.

When they reached Camas Prairie, Spilyáy was glad to see his daughter. He invited everybody to come inside his home, "Come inside, my Píwnash (in-laws), and have something to eat." Spilyáy's family rushed around getting the food ready. They had camas and bitterroots cooked and ready for the visitors. The little Mountain Goat brothers accompanied their sister-in-law and so did Blue Jay. They seated themselves around the table. Spilyáy's family set the food in front of them. Blue Jay wrinkled up his nose and said, "I don't eat that kind of food!" The Mountain Goats were so embarrassed. They said, "We knew you were going to embarrass us. That's why we did not want you along." They told him, "You could have tried to eat some of it, instead of being so impolite." Blue Jay brazenly complained, "But I don't eat that kind of food."

The old lady asked the Mountain Goat brothers, "What kind of food does this man eat?" One of the goats told her, "He eats moss." Then she went out and found some black moss for Blue Jay to eat. When Blue Jay tasted the moss he exclaimed, "This is what I like to eat. I don't like that camas and bitterroots they tried to feed me!"

The visitors stayed there a few days, and then they prepared to return to the rocky mountains. Spilyáy wanted to go along. His daughter told him,

What makes you think you can outrun my daughter?

is Spilyáy doing with his son-in-law's flint ax?" Spilyáy was surprised, "I thought I left this place." He sat up and found himself back where he started. He pretended to wake up as if nothing was wrong.

Mountain Goat was not happy that morning. He was thinking, "I invited this man and treated him like a guest. Now he is stealing my flint ax." That night after Spilyáy was asleep, Mountain Goat, Spilyáy's daughter, and the rest of the family left Spilyáy. They left him lying in the iceberg.

When Spilyáy woke up he felt crowded. Blue Jay had been sleeping with him while he was a guest in Mountain Goat's home, and he thought Blue Jay was crowding him. He nudged around, "All right Blue Jay, why don't you start laughing? You're always making fun of me!" When he was fully awake he looked around and found himself inside an iceberg. He lay there starving and shivering with cold.

One day there was a little bird playing in the ice. It was X̱átx̱at who lived with his grandmother. They lived there by themselves. Spilyáy would see this little boy and he would think, "Oh, how I wish my little friend X̱átx̱at would come and help me." This little boy would flip around in the snow and ice. And then he would listen. "I seem to hear something that sounds like Spilyáy." He scouted around, listening intently. Then he saw an iceberg with something in it. Spilyáy could see the boy and he tried to attract his attention by blowing on the ice to make a hole. Then the little boy finally saw him and exclaimed, "Oh, it's Spilyáy!"

The little boy ran home to tell his grandmother about Spilyáy's plight. He said, "Spilyáy is in trouble. He is trapped in the ice, and he wants me to help him." His grandmother said, "No! Do not help him. He is not a nice person. He tried to steal from his son-in-law. That's why they left him like that." But the little boy insisted, "Oh, I want to help him. He might die."

X̱átx̱at's grandmother finally gave in and let him help Spilyáy. The boy flew up into the sky and then he dove down and hit the ice. Some of it chipped apart, and then he went up again and again. He did this several times until he finally broke through and released Spilyáy. Poor Spilyáy was nearly dead.

X̱átx̱at went back to his grandmother's home to recover. His face and nose were all bruised up and swollen. His grandmother told him, "I told you not to help him. He won't appreciate it. Besides he was being punished for doing wrong. He was stealing from his own son-in-law."

That was how Spilyáy barely escaped death. He was saved by X̱átx̱at, who was bruised up and his nose was flattened in the process. That is the reason his nose is flat and he has black rings around his eyes which look like black eyes.

Legend about Black Spider

Spilyáy ends up humiliated in front of everyone because he did not control his desire to have his son's wife for himself. We also see how the black spider got the long hemp that he spins today.

THIS is a story about Spilyáy. He and his family were traveling around. His son had two wives—one was Duck and the other was Mud Hen. The Old Spilyáy was always dreaming about stealing Mud Hen from his son and making her his wife. He would scheme and try to think about how he was going to steal this pretty woman from his son. It finally became such an obsession that he forgot how much his son meant to him. Instead he began to see him as a rival.

One day he told his son, "Son, way over there is a big tall tree. At the top of this tree is an eagle's nest. We must catch this eagle. Let's go over there and catch it today." His son was interested because eagles are valuable and scarce. His son said, "All right, let's go." So his son got ready and put on his usual fancy buckskin clothes, because in those days the younger men wore fancy beaded buckskin clothes while the older men dressed more conservatively. Then they started out to find the tree.

As his son began climbing the tree, Spilyáy was at the bottom pushing the tree up like a telescope, making it go higher and higher. Finally the son began to tire and he looked down. He found himself up so high, he couldn't understand what was happening. But then he thought, "I'm this high, I might as well go the rest of the way." In the meantime, Spilyáy continued to push the tree higher until the top of the tree went right through the sky.

When the son found himself in the sky, he realized his father was trying to get rid of him. Then he walked around all over in the sky, but he couldn't find anybody there. He became curious. "There must be somebody living here. I'll look a little longer." Then he walked and walked until he saw a flicker of light. He trotted toward it and came upon Spider. Old Spider was very busy twisting his hemp, making a rope. He would wrap it around his leg, pull it, and spin some more and wrap it, but the rope wasn't getting any longer.

Spilyáy's son stood there and watched Spider work for a while, and then he hollered, "Hey, Grandpa!" Spider jumped with fright, dropping his ball of hemp, and he immediately turned fiery red, which is the way spiders get angry. Spider said, "What are you doing here?" Spilyáy's son said, "I'm just looking around." Spider replied, "I don't allow anybody up here." Then the son told him what his father had done to him. How he tricked him into climbing the tree and that was how he came to be there. After he explained all of this, Spider was a little more sympathetic and allowed him to come closer.

Spilyáy's son had been watching Spider spinning and trying to stretch this hemp and knew he wasn't getting anywhere. He thought he would help him out, so he took a little piece of it and went outside to urinate. He wet down the hemp and it immediately grew and grew. He picked it up and brought it inside to the spider, saying "Here, Grandfather, take this and spin it." This made Spider very happy, so he took it and began to spin a longer rope.

After a while Spilyáy's son asked old man Spider, "Grandfather, I am getting homesick. I don't know how I'm going to get down. Can you help me?" Spider said, "If you can go out and get some more long hemp, then I will help you." So the son went outside and he wet all over and the hemp sprang up like magic into tall plants. He picked it and brought it to Grandfather Spider. This made the old man so happy he began to spin more rope, twisting and twisting it around his legs. Finally he said, "I think we have enough rope here for you to reach the earth."

In the meantime, Spilyáy waited until he saw his son reach the sky, and he was sure he was rid of him, then he pulled the tree back down. Then he put on his son's clothes. He took his skin with both hands, pulled it tightly back and he fastened it tightly to make himself look young. When he was sure he looked like his son, he started back to camp.

When he got there, he began to howl. "Poor Dad, my poor Dad. He was killed. He was climbing the tree and he got lost. He was killed. Oh, my poor

Dad!" When he was sure they accepted him as the younger Spilyáy, he told them they had to abandon their home because this was the custom when a member of the family died. They got ready and they packed everything up, burning the rest of Old Spilyáy's things, and abandoning camp. He would cry loudly, "There are too many memories here about my Dad. I don't want to see anything that reminds me of him!" So the women packed everything up and they moved away.

While they were moving, Spilyáy was very attentive to Mud Hen, but he was cold towards Duck. He told Duck, "You stay back. I don't want you to come close. You follow way in the back. I'm feeling bad enough without having to look at you." Duck had a little son, so she put her little boy on her back and stayed behind. Spilyáy was way ahead, practically packing pretty Mud Hen in his arms. When they camped he would tell Duck, "Don't come close, stay away from us!" But Duck knew this was not her husband. This went on until the fourth day.

In the meantime Spider had spun enough hemp to let Spilyáy's son down to earth. The young man went to where he left his clothes and found they were gone. He looked around for his father but couldn't find him. Then he went to where they were camping and found it abandoned. He found some tracks and followed them. He found the camping places where they had camped while they traveled. This went on for four days, then he caught up with them. He came up behind his wife, Duck. His son was riding on his mother's back, and when he saw his father he smiled and said, "Táta!" (baby talk for daddy). His mother would tell him, "Hush! Don't say that. Your Tá, Tá is gone. Then he gurgled again, "Táta!" Finally his mother turned around and she saw her husband. She stopped and talked to him. She told him what was happening. The young man said, "Oh, I knew something was wrong. He wanted to get rid of me so he could steal my wife." Then he told her to unroll the blanket. She rolled him up inside this blanket and put it on her back. Then she put her baby on top of it. He told Duck, "Don't listen to him when he makes you stay away. Keep right on walking towards him, until you get ahead of him."

That evening when it was time to camp, Spilyáy began to holler at her again, "Stay back, don't come here." But Duck did not pay any attention to him. She kept on walking until she was ahead of him, and then she threw her bundle down on the ground. Old Man Spilyáy scolded her, "I told you to stay back." All of a sudden the son stood up. Old man Spilyáy was shocked.

He began to babble, "Here, Son, I've been taking care of your clothes and your family." Old Spilyáy began to fumble around trying to tear the clothes off and he tried to put them on his son. The fastening in the back of his head came off and his wrinkles fell back into place. Mud Hen was glad to see her young husband and she pushed Old Man Spilyáy away, looking scornfully at him. He lost out all around for being so deceitful.

That is how the Spider got his long hemp that he spins today. Remember it is not wise to deceive your relatives and try to steal somebody's wife, husband, or friend.

Legend of Prairie Chicken

This is a story about Coyote. He had strong powers and he was quite a character. The people do not look upon him as a god. He was looked upon as a great magician, the great seer, an astrologer; sometimes he was even looked upon as a prophet. This story is about one particular time when he committed a serious criminal act.

ONE day Coyote was walking along the trail and he came to a house that belonged to Prairie Chicken. In this home there were some baby Prairie Chickens staying home all by themselves. The mother and father were away for the day apparently looking for food to feed their little babies. When Coyote came to the house he saw these little babies and he gave them the usual greeting. "Ah, my little nephews and nieces, I'm glad to be here. Where is my good brother?" This is the greeting he gave to everyone, to make himself look like a good fellow. These little Prairie Chickens were not old enough to talk and they did not know how to answer him. All they knew how to say is, "K̲un k̲uun Sh..pu..pup!" Coyote was quite baffled and he asked, "What does that mean?" The oldest baby Prairie Chicken jumped up and ran up to him and said, "K̲un k̲uun Sh..pu.. pup!" This did not make any sense to Coyote. (It has no meaning to anybody for that matter.)

Coyote was losing his patience. He became very angry and he said, "I will ask you just one more time! If you don't answer me correctly, I am going to slaughter all of you for disobedience. Now, WHERE ARE YOUR FATHER AND MOTHER?" The little Prairie Chicken was frightened because he was able to understand. Bravely, he jumped up and ran up to Coyote, ruffled his feathers and said loudly, "K̲UN K̲UU---N SH...PU...PUP!"

Mother and father Prairie Chickens killing Coyote

Brother Red Fox reviving Coyote

Prairie Chicken flew up and struck him full in the face with all her might. This blinded Coyote, and he turned around and he thought he was running back up the trail. Instead he was running towards the edge of the cliff where he went over the edge, falling down to the bottom of the canyon where he fell on top of the rocks. That was the end of the bad Coyote who killed the innocent little baby Prairie Chickens. The father and mother went home satisfied, and they raised another family of baby Prairie Chickens.

Later on that year, Brother Fox, who was Coyote's brother, was walking down the trail and he looked over the edge of the cliff and he saw Coyote lying in the sun decaying. Brother Fox said, "Oh, oh, my brother must have done something very wrong to get punished like that. There he is lying in the sun decomposing like any ordinary thing. I believe I will bring him back to life." So Brother Fox stepped over him three times and brought him back to life. (In the Winátshapam legends, this is the way it was done.)

Coyote sat up and rubbed his eyes, stretched and yawned, saying, "Oh, my Brother Fox. I'm so glad you came along and woke me up, I thought it was such a nice day to rest, so I lay down to sleep for a while." Brother Fox laughed loudly and said, "Yes, you were resting all right. You were rotting in the sun. You must have done something awfully wrong. Tell me or else I will let you lie down and stay the way you were." Then Coyote remembered, and he told his brother that he killed some baby Prairie Chickens. He excused himself by blaming them for not talking properly to him.

Brother Fox was very disgusted with his brother. He told Coyote, "You will no longer be so conceited and expect everybody to please you. You must repent for what you did to those little babies." Coyote said, "All right, Brother Fox, from now on I will be a better person." Then Brother Fox let him live. Ever since that time Coyote never killed another Prairie Chicken.

CHAPTER III

Legends and Stories about Landmarks

Landmarks have deep meaning for the Yakama. They remind us of times past and teach many lessons. Many of the legends presented here refer to landmarks that were created by legendary figures such as Spilyáy. They are sometimes grim and sometimes humorous, but they are always easy to remember. In fact, legends connected with landmarks are often more easily remembered and more widely known than other legends. Perhaps the most important impact of legends about landmarks is to make the environment a more familiar and easily understood part of human existence.

Black Bear and Grizzly Bear

Because Black Bear and Grizzly Bear were so jealous and suspicious about their husband, they were turned to stone and can be seen at the place called Saddle Rock.

IN Wenatchee at a place called Saddle Rock, there are stones standing there. The white people call it Saddle Rock, but actually they are a black bear and a grizzly bear sitting up there quarreling over their husband. The small rocks scattered around them are their children.

One day Grizzly Bear was performing her wifely duties and decided to go out and dig camas. She was very suspicious of Black Bear and had to watch her all the time because she was very jealous of her. Black Bear was more efficient than the Grizzly, and she got more compliments from their husband because Grizzly was a grouchy wife, always suspicious and grumbling around, complaining about everything.

Black Bear was crafty too. She would outwit the Grizzly by taking off her digging pouch, throw the belt clear across the Columbia River, use it for a bridge, walk across the river to Rock Island while the Grizzly was trying to catch up with her and find Black Bear clear across the river. This would make Grizzly more angry, and she would throw a tantrum, tearing up trees and brush and making loud growling noises. Grizzly would have to go down the canyon and find a place to catch up with Black Bear, making her more angry.

Grizzly was so busy chasing Black Bear around all day that she would neglect her duties, and when evening came she had to hurry around to get enough camas to take home. In her haste she would dig up only half a camas, breaking it up, which is not good digging for a wife. When she

Black Bear and Grizzly Bear

would get home to feed her husband, he would not eat it because it was inferior food.

Black Bear would bring in real nice food, all clean, whole, and steaming hot. He would rather eat her food than Grizzly's, naturally. Grizzly would become very angry and say, "Oh, Black Bear must have more sex appeal than I have!"

They quarreled so much over their husband that Spilyáy punished them by turning them into stone where they sit today, quarreling over their husband.

The Stone Woman

This interesting legend traces the footsteps of a young woman bent on outwitting the Black Widow Spider brothers. Although she dies in the end, she creates many landmarks.

ÁWACHA NAY! Once upon a time there lived a young girl at White Bluffs. She used to take a bath in the Columbia River every morning. She was a beautiful girl. One day she went down to the river as a young man happened to be passing by. He was from the far west and he saw her. He followed her because she was such a pretty woman. He watched her as she bathed in the river. All of a sudden she saw a bunch of brambles floating around in the water near the bank. She became curious and swam over to this mass of weeds which she thought was just a bunch of grass. She grabbed on to it and it carried her out into the middle of the river. The water was so swift she became frightened and could not let go. Suddenly she heard a voice talking to her, "Hold on tightly, don't let go. I am taking you home with me! Do not be afraid." The young man took the maiden far away to the west, over rivers, lakes, and creeks towards his home.

One day he was out hunting for food and she ran away. When he returned to the camp and found her gone, he followed her. He did not want to force her to stay with him if she had to run away from him. He told her she could go home. He said, "You may go home, but you will have a child. This child will take care of you; it has supernatural powers," and he let her go.

The young woman traveled for several days until she came as far as X̱átash, where she stayed until she had the baby. The child was a boy. She stayed there for five days and the baby quickly matured. When they were preparing to leave X̱átash the baby told his mother, "We are going to arrive at a place where the monster Tíshpun (Black Widow Spider) lives.

There are five brothers and they kill anything that passes by their home; they will not let us pass." With this knowledge she was busy thinking about ways she could outwit the monster Tíshpun brothers. Finally she thought of a way. She would pretend she was their long-lost sister.

The young woman walked up the trail towards the Tíshpun's home and she bowed her head in sorrow shedding tears as she walked. As she neared their home she began to wail loudly, "Oh, oh, this is where my father and my mother and my brothers used to live!" The monsters heard her and they asked one another, "Could it be that she is our sister?" The youngest one was suspicious. He did not believe she was their sister, and he tried in vain to convince them that this was a trick, but when they saw her they refused to listen. As she came closer she cried louder and louder, and they felt so sorry for her. They called to her to come inside the house. They gave her food which could only be eaten by a Black Widow Spider. It was food collected when they killed the creatures passing their home. It was meat and bones of these creatures. She pretended to be very hungry and bent way over as if she were eating, when she actually was shoving the food into a large bag she had hidden tied to her belt around her waist.

The spiders watched her, twirling their long whiskers. They said, "If she eats this food then she surely must be our sister." Afterward, when they saw her eat all the food they were convinced she was truly their sister.

That night after they prepared for bed, she told them about her travels in the west. She told them many stories because she wanted to keep them awake so they would sleep soundly. The Black Widow Spiders had long black bushy beards that hung clear down to their knees. While they slept, she tied their beards together and set them on fire. However, she must have tied the youngest spider's beard too loose and he ran away. But the other brothers burned up. From that day on it was decreed that the Black Widow Spiders would no longer prey upon people and kill them and eat them.

The young woman ran and ran until she came to a place called Cháwi-sha (place of the dead) where she camped for the night. In the meantime, the youngest brother spider went back to where his home used to be and he found all his brothers had perished in the fire. He became very angry and he followed the young woman to avenge his brothers. He found her camp and sneaked up on her while she slept, and he stabbed her with his stinger. She woke up and grabbed the knife out of her chest, broke it in two, and threw one part to the east and the other to the west. She began

Black Widow Spider stabbing Stone Woman

to bleed from the wound and she became very weak. She turned to the baby and said, “You must go back home to your father. I am going to die!” She undid the sk’in (cradleboard) and turned the baby loose. She took the sk’in and set it up against the hill where it is today at Cháwisha. There is blood on the edge of the stream coming down the canyon stream at Cháwisha, which resembles soda water, where the young woman bled after she pulled out the knife in her chest. There is one crumbled piece of the knife in the eastern part of the canyon and also a part of the knife on the other side.

She started back towards her home, but she was so weak she could walk only a short distance at a time and the first place she rested was K̲w’ayk̲w’áylɨm (K’úsi Creek), then she staggered onto a place called Támchatani (Soda Creek). Then she went on to a place where there is another spring where her blood spilled out, and on up the canyon where there is another Soda Spring. She rested near the Sheep Ranch where there is another spring, and on up to Páwankyuut, and on down to Tł’úmni, and to the last stop X̲átay, where she fell down and bled. She nearly reached the top of the hill when she could go no farther and she collapsed. She tried to stand up but she would fall over backwards. She could not get up. That is where she lies today, on her back, arms and legs outstretched.

The young woman died there on top of the little hill near the Goldendale Highway where she lies today. In Yakama language the place is called Shapák̲anaykaash, which means lying down on your back.

The Giant Owl

Below Wenatchee, towards Malaga, there are two rocks with holes bored in them. These were once owls who wanted to destroy people.

ONCE there were three sisters. They lived way up on top of the hill above Winátsha. One day they came down and peeked over the hill down into the valley. They saw a lot of people camped near the Columbia River. The people were busy doing their chores, not knowing there was danger nearby.

One sister said to the other, "Let us go down there. There are a lot of people in that camp. We can kill and eat them." That was when the owls were bad people. They would eat everything.

They came down the hill towards what is now called Wenatchee. Before they reached the village, however, X̱át X̱at (Sparrow Hawk) would not allow them to kill and eat the people. He flew up in the sky as high as he could go and he came down on them like a bullet. He struck one, then the other, boring holes through their bodies. He killed one, and she fell down into the canyon. The other two he attacked again and again, making holes all over both of them.

Spilyáy happened to be there at that time, and he saw what took place. At the foot of the hill where Sparrow Hawk was attacking the owls he decreed, "The Owl sisters will no longer kill people. They will remain here for always." And he turned them into stones. Then he said, "The owls, after the People come to this earth, will be harmless little creatures." That's where the owl stones are today, on the road between Malaga and Wenatchee on the southeast side of the Columbia River. They are bored full of holes, but they still stand there just as Spilyáy predicted.

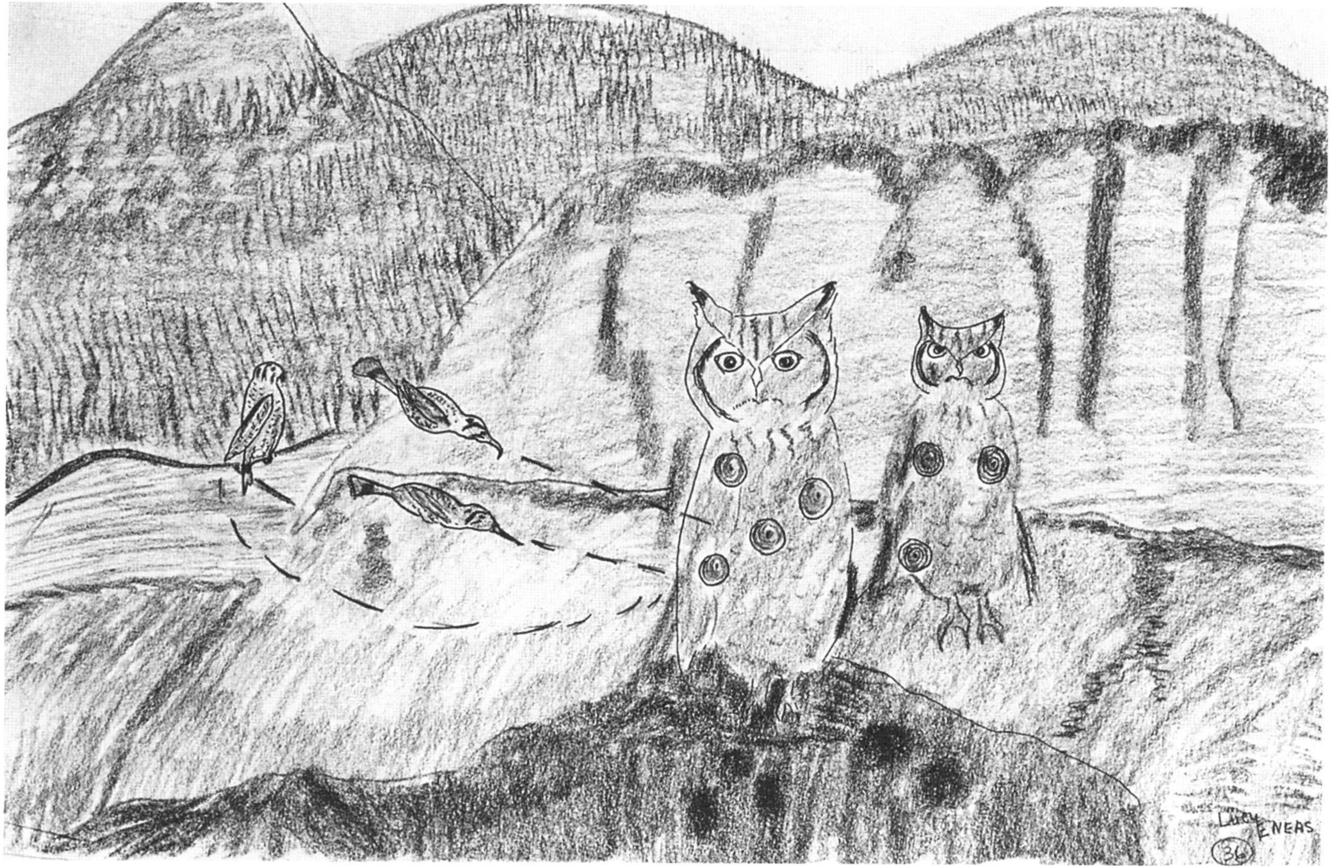

Giant Owls attacked by Sparrow Hawk.

In addition to the Giant Owl rocks, there are other stones scattered around Wenatchee worth mentioning. My mother took me down to Wenatchee and she showed me the huge stones that look like folded Indian blankets. These stones are lying all around the south residential area. They are blankets that were turned to stone after the Princess at Lake Chelan turned Spilyáy down and refused to marry him. Spilyáy's relatives were preparing for the Indian wedding, but when he was turned down the blankets were turned to stone.

Myáwax̱

(Chief Mountain)

Two sisters ignored their grandmother's rules about how to behave at bedtime and got into a very unhappy situation as a result. This legend explains that there are many kinds of food, fruits, nuts, and roots on the mountain because maidens brought these things as gifts to a handsome young man.

This legend is about a place called Myáwax̱, who was the child of a heavenly being. A long time ago when the mythical beings existed on this earth they were people just like we are today. When the Creator changed this world, destroying all the bad people who did not follow his teachings, he separated the people. He made the good ones into good omens. Some went to heaven and became stars, planets, or moons.

Everything is created by our Creator and everyone is required to follow certain rules on this earth. Some mythical beings were very bad and they were destroyed by the law they broke. We are all watched every day on this earth by the Creator. We cannot hide anything we do, good or bad, that he does not know about. If you do something bad and you know it's bad, but you hide it and think nobody will find out, the Creator knows. He's watching you. Each one of us is responsible for everything we do in our daily living regardless of the color of our skin. We owe this life we have to the Creator who created us and gave us life.

We are like a plant, and just like when we plant a potato, we expect it to grow and produce more potatoes. That's how our Creator planted us here on this earth, all different kinds of plants, all different colors. It is up to us to follow the rules he set for us to follow—to become good or bad.

If you are bad then you have only yourself to blame for it and you will have to pay for it. If you are good then you will be rewarded for it with His own kind of reward, which I'm sure will make you happy. That's the way it was before we were put on this earth. There were people here then too. They broke the law by disobeying the rules and the Creator destroyed them. When he destroyed the bad ones they became ugly crawling creatures. Those people who took care of their life, observing all the good ways, were made into good things. That's the way it was. The stars were good people and they were put up in heaven.

Down below at a place called Cowiche, near a place called Nax̱chíish, lived five virgin girls with their grandfather and grandmother. Their grandmother always cautioned them, "Do not sleep on your backs out in the open and do not look up into the sky, and don't talk about the stars at night. Always sleep on your side."

One day the five sisters prepared to go up in the hills to dig roots in the early spring where there was still snow on the ground in some places. They were very anxious to get out and dig roots. They told their grandmother they would stay overnight and dig roots all day the next day. She told them to be very careful while they camped, and they promised they would behave. They went up in the hills and made camp and prepared to sleep early because they had to start digging early in the morning. Their grandmother told them not to talk way into the night.

The oldest sister and the next one to her questioned the reason their grandmother was always telling them not to look at the stars and not to talk to them. One sister told them to sleep, but they kept on giggling and talking. They broke the law and lay down on their back looking up at the stars and talking about the stars. One small star was glimmering off and on, and the girl told her sister, "Oh, look at that star. It's winking at me!" Her sister tried to get her to sleep but she persisted and finally she looked up in the sky and she saw the star winking down at them. Then the girl said, "Oh, I wish that one was my husband! He looks so small and young." Her younger sister told her, "That one, the largest one shining brightly, is the one I would want for my husband!" Her older sister teased, "He would get near and blind you with his light. Then it would hurt your eyes! Mine is small and dim. He would not hurt my eyes!" They kept joking. They tried to get the other sisters involved in the game but they refused. The older sister was named Yáslams, the other one was X̱átash. They all had names. Finally they fell asleep, tiring of the game.

The stars they were talking about came down and took them up to their home while they were asleep. Yáslams woke up and looked around at the strange surroundings and found herself in bed with an old, old man. She pushed him away and looked for her sisters but they were nowhere in sight. Then she saw her younger sister sleeping beside a handsome, young man. The old man looked at her and said, "Why are you pushing me away? You said you wished I would be your husband! You have had your wish. You are my wife!" (The star had been on earth and he had an earthly wife. Because he was a good man he was put up in heaven and he was an old man when he died. He will stay that age forever.) He told Yáslams that he would never grow any older, but she would age and someday she would be older than he. Yáslams did not want this old man for a husband and she yearned to go home. She felt strange in this vast land, and she tried to persuade him by telling him that her grandmother was old and needed her. He told her it was impossible for her to get back home. That was how she ended up there in the heavens.

The sisters still had their kápɨn (root diggers). The stars brought them along when they carried the sisters to the heavens. Yáslams told her sister she was not happy with her old husband. But the younger sister was quite happy with her husband and she was content to stay there. But Yáslams would not give up. She kept persuading her sister as they were looking for roots while their husbands were out hunting. It was very difficult to find any kind of roots because the ground was dry as ashes and there was no vegetation. Then they found a bunch of vines, the first green growing thing, thriving in a small meadow-like place. One sister, thinking it might be edible, stuck her kápɨn down beside it and dug it out. When she pulled out the plant from the ground it suddenly exposed this huge hole with air blowing through it. They peeked down into the hole and looked down on the earth. It was beautiful! They recognized the place and finally realized they were up in the sky! One sister said, "Quick, let us make ropes with these vines!" They wove the vines into a long rope and lowered it down to earth. When they were sure it was long enough the younger sister climbed down first, and then when she reached the ground, the older sister started down. In the meantime, the men felt the strange air circulating around and realized something had happened. Immediately they knew what it was. They hurried to the hole and looked down and saw the oldest sister halfway down the rope. The old man became angry, "Why is she running away when she is the one who chose me? She broke the law, and she is insulting me by rejecting me." He cut the rope and Yáslams fell down the vines and was killed. The youngest one survived and went home telling her grandmother what had happened and that her sister was dead.

There was one strange thing they could not understand. The youngest girl was glowing so brightly they could not look directly at her. She was now pregnant and she was glowing inside. This was the origin of Myáwax̱, the son of a heavenly creature, the North Star.

One day the grandmother told them they were moving up in the mountains to dig camas. They stayed farther up into the mountains from Nax̱chíish with the four granddaughters. They stayed there for quite some time . . . from early spring to fall (I guess the mythical beings had children sooner than the present human beings). She had her baby there at Myáwax̱ located across from Wenas, a high rising sharp rock mountain.

The baby grew up quickly because he was a heavenly creature. The sisters kept the child hidden because all of the other creatures were jealous and wanted to kill him. They did not want a foreign person coming into their land to become their chief. Even Spilyáy was jealous, claiming he was of royal blood and should be the next in line for the chieftainship. He said, "That baby has no father and he is not fit to be a chief." Spilyáy even tried to hire some of his relatives to kill this child. The mother named this baby Myáwax̱ and it made the creatures very angry. Why should a stranger be called Myáwax̱ in their part of the country?

Myáwax̱ grew into young manhood in spite of all this fighting. (That's the way it is today. People get jealous and say bad things about other people who are different.) The young man was outstanding in everything. He was strong and could defeat anybody in combat. Even Grizzly Bear could not kill the young man who was glowing like fire. Instead he high-tailed it for the mountains as fast as he could go. Then Timber Wolf went after him, and he too took one look at this strange glowing being and turned tail and went back to the forest. This happened with all of the rest of the killers from the forest. They could not kill him. In a huge lake on the other side of Myáwax̱, there was a giant monster who tried to swallow him, but until your body is clean. Then you take your gift to him and exchange with him. You can be lucky in anything you want but you have to lead a clean life and have a clean body, have good thoughts! The stones around the Myáwax̱ are shiny and sparkly. It shines when the sun hits it. But you must be clean before you take anything, or when you ask for help before it will work.

Raccoon's Grandmother

This story explains how Raccoon's grandmother came to be sitting up on a hill by the Columbia River.

ONCE there was a raccoon and his grandmother living down at Wíshx̱am, down by a rock called Ḵwilkúla at a place called X̱aslúwaykt (Star Crossing Place) where there were lots of berry-bearing trees growing.

Raccoon was playing around with his grandmother's hat, pounding it with a rock. (The Wíshx̱ams wore grass hats shaped like a flat cone.) His grandmother called to him, "Grandson, pick some berries for me." Raccoon went out and picked the berries and he also picked the thorns from the trees with them. (This particular tree has long sharp thorns and the berries are as big as huckleberries.) He brought the berries to his grandmother and he told her to open her mouth wide. Then he threw them into her mouth. She began to sputter and choke, grabbing her throat, trying desperately to push the thorns back up from her throat. She called to little Raccoon, "Quickly, go get some water from the river. I am going to fly away like a crow! Hurry up!"

Little Raccoon grabbed his grandmother's hat, which he had been pounding with a rock, and ran down to the river, scooped up a hatful of water and ran back with it. But before he reached his grandmother the water dripped out through the holes he pounded in the hat. He ran back five times, but in the meantime his grandmother was choking. Then she changed into a crow and flew away.

To this day Raccoon's grandmother is sitting up on the hill where she landed when she flew away with thirst. She sits over on the Oregon side the youngest one made it home to deliver the message. He rushed up to his father saying, "K̲aamúukii!" Spilyáy said, "Yeh, that's what I thought all along!"

Spilyáy and his children went out into the plains to gather the hemp to process and weave the net. They were all picking the plant and diligently processing the hemp, spinning it into string, while Spilyáy was weaving it into a dip net saying, "This is the way the People who are coming will prepare to catch salmon. They are coming closer. I can hear their heavy footsteps. They will be catching salmon here at this place."

When Spilyáy finished his net he decided to consult his wise sisters. He walked away into the sagebrush and defecated them out onto the ground, "Tell me!" One sister said, "No." "Tell me, or the rain will come down and wash you into the ground," Spilyáy demanded. Then he stuck his nose in the air and said, "Tux̲, tux̲, tux̲, tux̲, tux̲!" (This is the legendary way to summon rain.) His sister was afraid of the rain and she frantically replied, "Catch one salmon. Bake it by the fire and feed it to your children. They are to take this salmon and chase one another around, throwing pieces of it at each other. This will be the tradition here at this fishing place." (By throwing the salmon in this manner one could acquire "good luck" for the fishing season.)

Spilyáy took his net and dipped it into the water there at Palouse Falls and he brought up one beautiful salmon. He told his children, "Build a fire," then he roasted this salmon on a stick by the fire. When it was cooked he called to his children, "Come here, we are ready to eat. This is the first salmon. Throw it at each other!" They did this, setting the precedent for the People who were coming.

Afterward Spilyáy decreed, "This land will be called the Repeater. When the people holler into the mountains it will repeat back to them. They will be called Echo Mountains." Then he decreed all of his children would remain there as landmarks to exhibit Spilyáy's powers. They were turned into stone images, still there today. There are five stone images for people to see. If you happen to be in that area sometime, you will see them near the falls.

After he did this he traveled on to another part of the land.

The Widow Rock

This story tells how the Great Spirit punishes a disrespectful widow by turning her into a rock. This rock can still be seen at Wíshx̱am.

WHEN a woman becomes a widow she is supposed to cover her eyes with a black cloth, so that she does not look upon anyone. She is to mourn her husband for a minimum of a year. She is not to participate in social affairs, must wear black clothes, and must keep her eyes partially covered at all times.

There was a woman who lost her husband. He died and left her a widow. Her in-laws cut her hair five times until it was clear up to her ears. This woman did not observe the traditions. Right away she began to look at people and going to social gatherings, like she did before she became a widow. She was especially attentive to the men.

The Great Spirit was very displeased with her actions and he turned her into stone. She is there today looking at everybody. There is a stone cliff at Wíshx̱am (Spearfish) with a face imprinted on it and it is called the Widow Rock. When you go up to it, her eyes are upon you, and no matter where you stand on either side of her, the eyes are upon you. Even when you walk away she is looking at you.

Some people thought she was taboo to young girls. They would caution them, "Never look upon the Widow Rock for you may become a widow someday." They said skeptics would become widows every time they marry. For good reason, the girls always stayed away from the rock, which is located at Wíshx̱am.

Widow Rock smiling at a fisherman

Wíshpush

On top of a hill near Goldendale Highway, you can see a rock called Shapáḵanaykaash, which is really Wíshpush after he was careless and lost his power. But Wíshpush's sister finally learned how to be strong and take care of herself instead of depending on everyone else.

At one time there was a big flood in this area, the river bottom being the Yakima Valley we now live in today. During this big flood, there lived a young man and his sister at Páx̱utakyuut (Union Gap). This young man's name was Wíshpush (Beaver). His younger sister was very dependent on her brother. She was not able to comb her own hair, so he had to take the oil from his tail and grease her hair with it to make it lie down smoothly. (Beaver tail oil is used as hair oil by the Indians.) As long as he was able to take care of her, she looked neat. But when he was away from home, she would neglect herself and become very shabby. Her hair would become all tangled and she looked frightful.

One day Wíshpush fell in love with a beautiful young woman named Weasel. He pursued her out into the middle of the river and they were carried away by the swift current. While they were desperately trying to stay afloat, at a place called Walawitís (Willow Creek), he heard a voice, "Quick, grab hold of the willows!" He did this, and he was able to save himself by swimming out of the swift current into a lagoon where he was able to rest, still holding onto the willow.

After he was stronger, he crawled out of the water and he came up the hill to a place called Shḵ'íyachash. He reached the peak of the hill and he sat down and looked towards Union Gap longingly, "I wonder if I will ever get back to my own land?"

Beaver receiving his power from Willow

Grizzly taking power away from Beaver and he turns into stone

He journeyed up the canyon to Goldendale Hill where he encountered a family of killer grizzlies. These were ground grizzlies who lived in a hole in the ground. This hole is still there today in the forest. They challenged him to battle. Wíshpush was given supernatural powers by this willow, which he still carried in his hand. He killed the grizzlies, except for the youngest one. Spilyáy was there and he predicted that, "Grizzlies would no longer kill all the people and eat them," like they had been doing.

After Wíshpush killed the grizzlies, he continued on over the mountains and down along the canyon by Satus Creek to Logy Creek. He was so tired from fighting the swift current in the river, and also from fighting the grizzly brothers, that he lay down on top of a hill and went to sleep, still holding the willow in his hand.

The creatures were observing the activities of Wíshpush and they were worried. They felt he was truly a powerful shaman and he must be curbed from using the powers of the willow. They held a conference and decided something must be done about Wíshpush. If he was allowed to continue using this power, he might kill all of the creatures and there wouldn't be anybody left on this earth.

They picked the youngest grizzly, the one that Wíshpush spared, to avenge his brothers and take the willow out of Beaver's hand while he slept. Young Grizzly agreed and he sneaked up on Wíshpush while he slept soundly. He quietly slipped the willow out of his grasp. Grizzly had hypnotic powers too, and he was able to hypnotize Wíshpush into a deep sleep. As soon as this willow was out of Wíshpush's grasp, he lost the power of protection and he died on the spot in his sleep. That is where he is today on top of the hill.

Wíshpush's sister waited and waited for her brother to return so he could comb her hair, but all in vain. Finally a bird came and told her that her brother had been killed by the creatures and that he would no longer be able to come back home. She cried and cried helplessly until something with supernatural powers took pity and changed her into a person so that she could take care of herself and not be so dependent on anybody. After that she was able to comb her own hair and take care of herself.

Steamboat Rock

There used to be all kinds of berries, roots, and fruit growing in the meadow on top of Steamboat Rock. Spilyáy planted them for the people just to win the love of a beautiful young woman.

A LONG time ago in the animal world days, Spilyáy was traveling along the Columbia River and he happened to meet the people living in that area. He found them to be very friendly and they treated him royally. He thought this would be a good place to find a wife, so he began looking around for a beautiful woman.

He found a girl that met his favor and he wanted to make a good impression on her parents and on the people there. He told them, "You have treated me well, and I want to return the favor. I would like to give you something that will benefit your people all the time." Spilyáy looked around and found their diet was lacking certain things and then he knew what he must do. Spilyáy had supernatural powers. He could wish things to happen anytime he wanted. He looked around some more and found a place rich with fertile soil. This place was the top of Steamboat Rock. He made a meadow on top of that rock. He planted service berries, chokecherries, huckleberries, black camas, Indian carrots, bitterroots, and onions. He told them, "Anytime you need food go there and take all you want. This is my gift to you for treating me so nice and making me welcome in your midst."

Spilyáy did all of this to win the favor of the young woman and her parents as well as the people in the village. He did this everywhere he went. He was always alert and looking for a beautiful girl. Sometimes he succeeded, and other times they refused him, at which time he made bad things happen to the people or to the girl. He would dry up the streams and make it into a desert. He could change the pretty girls into dried up old women or turn people into stone. Spilyáy had all of these powers, and he used them all the time.

It is not known what Spilyáy did so that the food on top of Steamboat Rock did not remain. People used to go there to dig roots and pick berries, but now it is dry and arid, so it seems that Spilyáy was not satisfied with his plan. There are huckleberry bushes on top of Steamboat Rock today, which is a miracle because huckleberry bushes grow only at high altitudes up in the mountains. Steamboat Rock is located in a desert area, on Banks Lake.

Twit'áaya

(Grizzly Bear)

Because Cottontail Rabbit was too afraid to say "No," he got himself into terrible trouble with Grizzly Bear. Twit'áaya can be seen at the base of Pátu (Mount Adams) today, her arms extended in rage.

ONCE, after Grizzly Bear's husband was killed by the monsters, she was traveling around because she had no home. She would go here and there but she was not content to stay very long at one place, so she kept on traveling. At another place there lived a boy, Aykwíisya (White Cottontail Rabbit), who was very mature for his age. He had everything at his home—food, plenty of wood, a cozy place to live. He was always busy accumulating all of these things for his own comfort.

One day Grizzly Bear met this boy while he was hunting. She saw all of the food he carried and she said, "You are an outstanding young man. Who is providing you with all those things?" She called to him five times. He would not answer her at first. He was so frightened of her that he was shaking all over. "Do you hear me? Where are your parents? I am poor. I don't have any place to live." He finally replied to Grizzly Bear, "I don't have any parents. I am all alone and there is nobody providing for me." Grizzly Bear immediately responded, "Since we are both alone, why don't we live together and keep each other company!" He tried to make believe he was just passing through and was resting. She was very persistent, insisting that he accompany her as long as he was traveling alone. He was afraid to say, "No," so he agreed to go with her. She told him they should find suitable quarters for both of them so they could live together all winter.

Grizzly going to boy’s cave

Grizzly inside cave, yawning

They looked for a cave until they found they were at the foot of Mount Adams. While they were looking around, she began to make horrible noises, "Ohhhh, Ohhhh, Ohhhh," as she went around on her haunches. He couldn't imagine what was happening to her and he waited for her, as she crawled around near a huge stump. He waited because he was afraid of her. She was well known for her bad temper and she was known to eat people. In a few days they finally reached the foot of Mount Adams.

The Grizzly Bear was thinking all the time, "My, what tender meat that boy must have. He must taste awfully sweet!"

They traveled on and on until the boy saw his cave where he made his home and he told her, "Sometimes I camp at this place. Maybe we can stay here for a while." By that time Grizzly Bear was very hungry, so she agreed to stay as long as he provided warm quarters for her. The cave was quite small; it was not big enough for anyone as huge as Grizzly Bear. They both began to dig around, enlarging the cave, but she could barely squeeze through the opening. They made their beds, one on each side of the cave across from one another, and they lay down on their backs beside the fire. The door was already closed for the winter and they were snug inside, with only a small opening for emergency exits. Grizzly made her bed across the opening of the cave so she would have complete control of all the entries and exits.

Grizzly Bear informed Aykwíisya, "I am very ill. Would you go find some herbs for me?" The boy went outside to find some herbs for her. Because all of the plants were dry and wilted and frostbitten, everything was dry and he brought only what he could find at that time of the year. She continued to groan around, evidentially in great pain. This frightened the boy because he was afraid she would become more ferocious with pain.

On the fifth day she began to yawn around in the evening, "Y . . a . . w . . n, all of a sudden I have this strong craving for cottontail rabbit!" The boy was immediately on the alert, and he thought about what she said. "I knew she was up to something when she insisted I live with her."

The cave was nearly completely dark inside, since there was no opening to let in the light. About that time of year, too, the Grizzly Bear is partially blind. The little boy began to dig a hole in the ground real fast, making a tunnel away from the entrance of the cave. He worked as quietly as possible while Grizzly slept.

Grizzly chasing Cottontail Rabbit

One day Grizzly Bear asked the boy to go find some food. She claimed she was terribly hungry. She let him outside. He brought some yellow moss from the trees, which was all he could find for food. He gave it to Grizzly and she complained that she was not used to eating such inferior food. Again she yawned, "Oh, how I wish for white cottontail rabbit." Aykwíisya became so afraid he wept. He knew that Grizzly Bear wanted to eat him. He was paralyzed with fear.

That night they prepared for bed again and the boy sneaked quietly to his tunnel and began to dig some more after Grizzly Bear fell asleep. He dug and dug all night until it was daylight, and Grizzly woke up again. He did not finish the tunnel. He had to postpone his work until Grizzly went back to sleep again.

The next day Grizzly asked him to go find some more food. She accused him of being a loafer, "You should be out there looking for my breakfast. You should not wait to be asked." The boy crawled outside and began to scramble around looking for food. He was afraid to make an attempt to run away because she could very easily catch him. Grizzly Bears are fast runners, especially when they are angry. He found some berries that bears like to eat. They are bright red and taste bitter, but the bears like them. He picked a lot of them and brought them to her. After she ate them she said, "That was good but I am still hungry for white cottontail rabbit." The boy was becoming irritated. He was getting tired of running errands for her, especially when he could not please her.

One night after they retired again and Grizzly was asleep, snoring in the doorway, Cottontail dug and dug his tunnel all night. The next morning she woke up and growled that the boy did not have her breakfast ready. When he went out to find food, there was nothing left but some pine cones. He picked them and carried them to the cave. He gave them to her but she complained, "I don't eat this kind of food. Do you want me to prick my hands with the pine thorns? Why do you give me such food? I crave for white cottontail rabbit!" That was the fourth time she said this.

That evening she went to bed early. As soon as she began to snore, Cottontail dove into his tunnel and began to dig again. He dug until he saw some daylight. He ran back to the cave as she was beginning to wake up. She was grumbling around for him to provide her with some food. He was terribly afraid, so afraid, in fact, that he was shaking all over and his teeth were chattering. He ran and ran down the trail to a blackberry bush. He

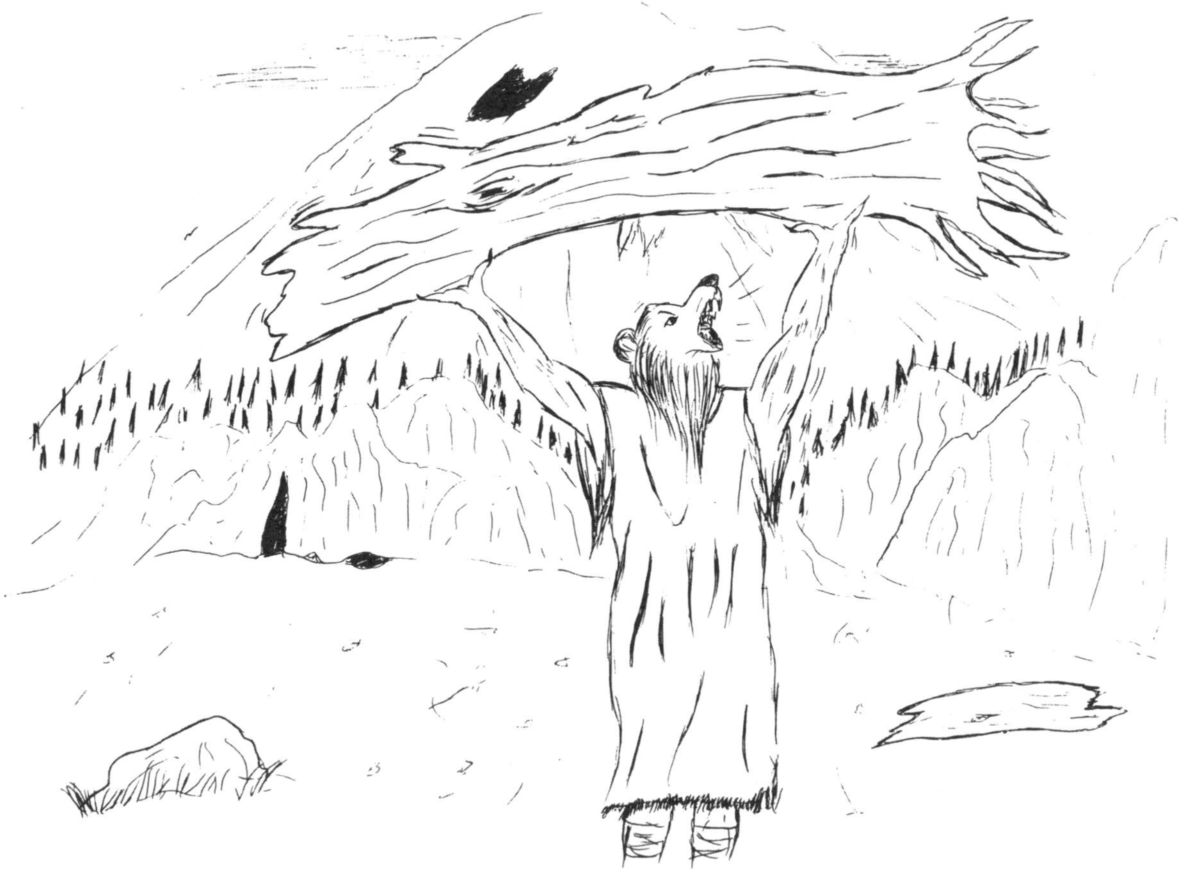

Grizzly furiously tearing up trees

picked the berries and brought them back to her and he informed her, "This is all there is left." She began to eat, still growling that she was dying from hunger for white cottontail rabbit.

He waited until she nearly finished when he stretched himself to full length and yawned, "Y . . a . . w . . n, Oh, how I wish I had some Grizzly Bear to eat!" She was furious! She roared at the boy, "WHAT DID YOU SAY? Just wait until I get my paws on you!" She crawled across the cave trying to grab him. She could not see and she had to feel around for him. The boy jumped away from her reach, crawled into his tunnel and scrambled down to the opening, and came darting out. Grizzly was grabbing at everything she could feel inside the cave, tearing everything up. The boy ran and ran over five mountains while Grizzly was still trying to crawl out of the cave. She was stuck in the small opening because every time the boy went out to look for food, he would drop a rock in the cave opening to make it smaller. Grizzly Bear was stuck in this small opening, roaring with rage. Her stomach was fat from eating too much and she could not get through the cave opening.

While the boy was running away over the five mountains, Grizzly came crashing out. She grabbed at everything—a tree, rocks, a log—anything she could feel she would grab and tear to pieces.

Since that day she has been sitting down at the bottom of Mount Adams, her arms extended in rage. Her mouth is wide open in anger like she's growling. That was the way Spilyáy decreed her to be. "The People who are coming will be telling stories about you. They will tell about how mean you are, always tearing things up. They will talk about you, about your bad temper!"

Conclusion

WHEN the Old People told legends in ancient times it was a serious ritual because this provided training for the little children as they progressed towards adulthood. Each clan or tribe had their own legends about the immediate surroundings or habitat. The storyteller would imitate the characters with singing, dancing, or mock battles. It was the same thing when they indicated the landmarks; they would point them out and give the proper name mentioned in the legend. The reasons for the landmarks are emphasized by the predictions made by Spilyáy.

A legend is an explanation for certain phenomena for being what they are in Indian education. Nobody knows when they first developed a spoken language; it is supposed they communicated by writing on stone and by sign language. Who knows when anything happened? The important thing that matters right now is that the children continue to study and learn their culture and retain their traditional values.

When we were created we were expected to do certain things for a good reason. Every child is expected to be proud of what he is but not to be better than anybody else. To think you are better than somebody is only fooling yourself, like Coyote in the legends. He was always bragging about himself, but he had to stop and ask his wise sisters for help when he got into trouble. That's why it is wise to listen to someone with more experience and knowledge. Nobody is so smart that he does not need help at one time or another.

There are some people who say the Indian legends are a myth. But who can say what a myth really is? Look at the stars in heaven; why do they resemble a dipper, an archer, a bear? Why do we have a certain mountain that has the face of a woman, or a big stone mountain that looks like a chief, or like an animal? Why does the Chipmunk have those stripes on his back? Where did Duck get that beautiful necklace he wears around his neck?

Was it not a reward for something he did in a legend before the People came? Do you suppose the Stone Woman really was punished for smiling at the men before her mourning period was up?

We have many landmarks in our Huckleberry Mountains which denote our Indian legends. There are the Ice Caves near Trout Lake and the lakes near Mount Adams. Each landmark has a lesson or it records a prediction made by Spilyáy. Some legends are very long and more detailed than others because the legend-teller takes the time to emphasize more of the details.

There was another reason for telling legends. If a family experienced a tragic incident—for instance, when the children became orphaned—the Old Legend-Teller would bundle up some bedding and he, or she, would go to this home and stay a few weeks. Each day there would be long sessions of legend-telling to entertain these children, to keep them occupied, to help them forget their grief and loneliness for their deceased parents. It was like how our present-day children watch television or attend the movies at the theatre. This was the way the Elders provided entertainment, learning instruction, and consolation.

The other reason for using this method was to preserve history. It was passed on by the Elders to the younger generation through repetition. They had no written language to preserve this important part of life. They could only use the oral method which made it a serious ritual.

There are certain types of legends for boys and appropriate legends for girls. They teach the serious facts of life which affect the child's entire life and his future mode of living. These lessons are handed down throughout the consecutive generations. The important details are not glossed over with unnecessary words. They state it as it was meant to be; they do not mellow it down with dainty words. To learn the "Indian way" is to listen and learn the legends as they are told by the Elders. They are meant for each individual to face the facts as they encounter them in everyday living. This method of training is jealously guarded by the clans, tribes, or families and usually is not told outside of their respective circles.

There are legends that have gone into written materials and are sold to the public in book publications. They are usually the humorous or entertaining legends, not the serious kind.

As time goes on, every race on the face of this earth will have forgotten its heritage. This is the reason we have people wandering aimlessly around the country seeking their identity. They have no knowledge of their heritage and culture. This is the reason the American Indians are concerned about the future. They want to teach their children to learn their ethnic background, to retain their culture, and to practice it along with the second culture.

VIRGINIA BEAVERT

Tribal Storytellers

The following biographies from the 1974 edition of Anakú Iwachá *provide the ages and background of the storytellers at the time of the original edition. Where possible, a few biographies have been briefly updated for the new edition.*

Annie Jim, age 84
Yakama (Alderdale)
Annie's Indian name is Popkiawahnee Hienstulle. She follows the old traditional ways and lives in a rustic home. She emphasizes the importance of holding on to the land and home promised to the Indians by the Federal Government when they ceded their land holdings. She refuses to move and abandon her homesite on the Columbia River although moving might provide her with a modern house. She retains the gentle ways typical of her traditional nature. She values her grandchildren and great-grandchildren. She thinks of them as "growing plants" requiring the nourishment of love to make them grow. She is concerned they don't understand their native language. She volunteered her legends to help them understand their people better—and to preserve them for future generations.

Mary Jim Chapman, age 64
Yakama (Palús-Walúula)
Mary is one of the original Palús people. She knows the history of the Palús and Walúula area as it was negotiated with the Federal Government. She is an active member of the Shaker Church, devoting all her activities towards helping her people. She was successful in raising her family, educating them to be self-sufficient and independent. Her husband, Jesse Chapman, died many years ago. Although her children have been assimilated

into the white society, they still retain their native language and are comfortable around their own people. She says, "Spilyáy was a seer. He planned our destiny in the animal world. The landmarks indicate this. Why would they be there otherwise?"

Sallie Wachalka George, age 80
Yakama
Sallie is an active member of the Shaker Church. She firmly believes the Indian children should know their native religions. They should study it and then choose their own church afterward. She has lived all her life believing the Indian ways. She respects everything that is traditional because God created us that way. "There is nothing anyone can do to change that." She risks criticism by recording the history of the Shaker Religion because she wants the children to know about it.

Otis Shilow, age 78
Yakama
For eight years Otis worked on the Yakama Tribal Council fighting for tribal rights. He worked on many committees, specifically on hunting and fishing and water rights. He can recite many incidents and names about this reservation. He is one of the last known traditional Announcers. This is the only way to explain it in English. He is called upon to announce at funerals, memorials, medicine dances, and other functions which are not social. This is where the person speaking does not speak directly to the people but is echoed by the Announcer. This is a very respected position because one must learn more than one dialect to efficiently perform this work.

George Foreman, age 81
Yakama (Wíshx̱am)
George Foreman is a historian and he was born and raised at Wíshx̱am, living there until he was forced to move when his village was inundated by the Dalles Dam. He recalls all of the fishing sites, the families who fished there, and where they came from. He, like Ida White, can recite legends about the landmarks around Spearfish and Wasco. He speaks the language fluently. He is retired and living with relatives but has no permanent home.

Emma Bellinger, age 84
Yakama (Wíshx̱am)
Emma lived most of her life in White Swan, Washington. She was educated at Fort Simcoe Indian School, one of the early Government schools. She is able to recollect historical events about Fort Simcoe. She successfully raised and educated her children after her husband died, then she moved to Toppenish where she lives at the present time. Emma is a member of the Bahá'í Church and the local chapter of the Society for the Blind. She is active in the Community helping the blind although she too is blind. While working with Dr. Silverstein as a resource person in conducting a study on the Wíshx̱am language and history, she laughingly comments, "I had to brush up on my Indian language recalling words I nearly forgot."

Pauline Wahsise, age 47
Yakama (Columbia-Umatilla)
A lifetime resident of Satus, near Granger, Washington, Pauline graduated from Granger High School. Since that time she has been active in the community working in education. She works for the Granger School District, Tribal Community Action, and the Satus Longhouse in educating children in Indian culture. She teaches beadwork, tanning deer hides, moccasin making, and Indian language. Her legends are flavored with the Umatilla dialect. She knows many legends but they are portioned with forgotten bits and pieces, names of places and so on. Experience has convinced her of the importance of preserving Native legends and historical events recorded by the elderly.

Harris Beavert, age 81
Yakama (Cayuse, Táp'ashnak̲'it/Timberline)
Harris is also known by the people as Henry Beavert; his Indian name is Wataslâyma. He is the minister of the Satus Shaker Church, active in that capacity for many years. He served on the Yakama Tribal Council for eight years. He was active initiating with other members of the Council the scholarship program for Indian students. He lived his childhood at a village on Bickleton Ridge called Táp'ashnak̲'it, which means "the edge of the timber." The people who lived there were very traditional. They survived on wild food, lived in teepees, observed their Native religion,

and spoke their own dialect. They did not believe in white man's education in the earlier days. They were gentle people. That's why Henry is always on call for spiritual guidance, especially to children.

Henry George, age 65
Yakama (Rock Creek)
Henry resides near Roosevelt, Washington, along the Columbia River. His older brother was Gus George, the religious leader of the Rock Creeks. After his brother died, he did not wish to take over that position, and he relinquished it to another. Henry is knowledgeable in history, and he loves to tell Spilyáy stories but he felt they might be too spicy. He says, "Through Spilyáy many lessons can be learned, both good and bad. I hope the children will learn and retain the good parts."

James Alexander, age 82
Yakama (Winátshapam-Klikitat)
Born and raised in Ellensburg, Washington, he was elected to the Yakama Tribal Council in 1944. He served in the Council for twenty years until he was replaced in 1967. Mr. Alexander was active in the following committees: Fish and Wildlife, Timber Industry, Economic Development, and the Tribal Executive Committee. The General Council, consisting of Tribal Government, elected him to a committee to do research on the north boundary claim. He speaks several dialects in the Yakama language. He knows many legends but wants to keep them within his own family. He is presently residing at Cooks, Washington, a small fishing village on the Columbia River. He is still actively involved in disputes, fighting for Indian fishing rights. He is a principal member of the Treaty Indians of the Columbia, Inc.

Mary Tomieth Schuster, age 97
Yakama (Páwankyuut-Pshwánapam)
Her Indian name is T'swas'palu. She is an ardent believer of the traditional ways. She wants to live the old way. Exercising and keeping your body physically fit is the right way to live. She exercises by taking a walk every morning before breakfast, which is the secret for her longevity. She is training her grandchildren in traditional ways, and they respect her for it. To periodically rejuvenate her spirit she sings her medicine songs,

and her grandchildren dance and sing for her. "Like praying, one does not require a big audience to get results. I sing in my humble home all by myself."

Louise Billy Howtopat, age 53
Yakama (Rock Creek)
Louise resides in a small village near Goldendale. They named this village Billyville because most of the families, relocated by the U.S. Corps of Army Engineers when they built the McNary Dam, were named Billy. There is another village near there named Georgeville, also of relocated people from Rock Creek but mixed with other families. Louise is very active in her Seven Drums Longhouse Church. She leads when the First Foods Feast is held, teaching the younger people the right way to observe this important ceremony. Her contributions to this book relate to areas close to Rock Creek, the Columbia River, or the root digging meadows of her people. Her reason for recording is to teach the Indian children to respect their Indian ways and to refresh the memory of the older generation. "We become so involved with other activities and we forget our legends and stories."

Anita Sampson Lewis, age 40
Yakama (Táp'ashnaḵ'it)
The youngest informant, Anita is tutored by her grandmother Aas'maatqw. When her grandmother was too ill to record, Anita offered her contribution. She is attending Haskell Institute, an Indian College, at Lawrence, Kansas. She is majoring in Business Law and Business Administration. Her views as a younger person emphasize the importance of preserving our traditions for the children. "When it can't be taught at home, it should be available through the schools."

Hazel Smiscon Miller, age 55
Yakama (Wánapam)
Ḥazel is a Yakama Tribal Indian Culture Specialist. She is involved with the local schools in providing cultural information to students and teachers. She works for the Native American Programs. She lectures in secondary schools demonstrating beadwork, traditional child raising, foods,

preservation of foods, legends. She is available through her employer and is a valuable resource.

Wilson Charley, age 72
Yakama (Wíshx̱am)
Wilson is a former Tribal Councilman. He was active in various committees working for the tribe, concentrating on hunting and fishing rights. His knowledge of the traditional ways comes from Chief Joe Charley, his father, who was a recognized humorous legend-teller. Wilson resides at Wapato, Washington. He is helping his nephews and nieces in education. His reason for recording and contributing to this book, "There is so much misunderstanding about our Indian culture. This misunderstanding creates prejudice towards our children attending school. Sometimes it makes the children ashamed they are Indian. Perhaps when they learn about their own traditions and culture, they will be proud they are Indian."

Lizzie David, age 103
Yakama (Cowlitz-Táytnapam)
Lizzie was born in Cowlitz County. As a small child she was taken to Oakville, Washington, to attend school. There she met her husband, and they lived there most of the time until his death. Then she moved back to Randle, Washington, where she lived with her dear relative, Mary Kiona. Together they were the most talented cedar basket weavers in this territory. Lizzie contributes this knowledge for this book. She is presently residing in a nursing home at Goldendale, Washington.

Mary Dick John, age 61
Yakama
Mary lives in White Swan, Washington. She operates a thriving berry farm. Her husband Hadley is a trapper. Together they are busy throughout the year. She takes time, however, to attend the White Swan Longhouse, which is the Seven Drums Religion Church. She is one of the leaders when the root diggers and hunters or fishermen take their vows and go out to gather food for the First Communion Feast of the spring roots and fish and the berries and game feast in late summer. She confirms the importance of educating our children to respect their own traditional ways.

Ellen Saluskin, age 76
Yakama (Silá-Tx̱ápnish)
Ellen has been a resident of Toppenish, Washington, all of her life. Her Indian name is Hoptónix Sawyalíl Wantúx̱. Ellen's knowledge of culture and Indian history is passed on from her Elders. Her father was Oscar Wantúx̱, a Yakama and graduate of Carlisle College, Pennsylvania. Her grandfather was Yakama George Sawyalíl, a historical figure on this reservation. Her grandmother, X̱ax̱ísh, raised Ellen and later raised Virginia, and Ellen and Virginia learned many legends from her. She unfortunately did not acquire an education because she had tuberculosis until she was too old to enroll in school. She realizes that every child is not born with traditional knowledge. She wants to live to see the day when we can, again, make the child accountable for his misbehavior. "The modern way has obviously failed, and we are following Spilyáy's predictions."

Celia Ann Dick, age 65
Colville (Winátshapam-Pshwánapam)
A direct descendant of the Winátshapams, her father was the Chief of that tribe. Her grandmother was from Náanum (Ellensburg). This tribe was called Pshwánapam, and she recollects legends and landmarks conveyed to her by her grandmother. She thinks that if the landmarks are taken away, the stories will disappear. "I could not recall the stories if it were not for the landmarks." Celia is presently involved in cultural education with secondary schools. She lectures and demonstrates the native culture and crafts. She expresses the importance of teaching Indian culture to our children because she feels they will lose their identity. "People should know who they are." Celia resides in Nespelem on the Colville Reservation.

Isabel Arcasa, age 84
Colville (Columbia)
She was born and raised on the Colville Reservation. She was a cook at the Corps of Conservation Camps for many years, and then she worked in various restaurants as a cook. She is very active in church activities. Before the hospitals were built on the Colville Reservation, Isabel assisted the Government Nurse for the U.S. Indian Service. She was a midwife, and she delivered twenty-eight babies into this world. She raised five

motherless children. She is still raising one eight-and-one-half-year-old, who is her grandchild. At her age, she is still preparing to go root digging in the mountains.

Lillie (Lela) Yoke Whitefoot, age 65
Yakama Tribe
Lillie has lived in White Swan all of her life. She is active in the community and has cared for many grandchildren and foster children. She is interested in their welfare. She taught the children to be grateful for every day, to be thankful for the gifts of the Creator. She was such an effective teacher for the children—even the little tiny children would carefully listen to her. Some of our Tribe's future leaders were among these children who were taught in this way, including Patricia Whitefoot, who has served as the President of the National Indian Education Association.

Moses George, age 66–67
Colville Tribe
Mr. George is a descendant from one of original bands of the Wenatchapam tribe. He is a retired land surveyor. He was employed as an engineer-surveyor for thirty-five years, and he also taught surveying for several years. He attended school at Saint Mary's, is a graduate of Chemawa Indian School and also of Haskell Institute of Lawrence, Kansas. He served on the Colville Housing Authority for approximately three years, is a veteran of World War II, and served in the Corps of Engineers for two years. He resided in Wenatchee, Washington, for twenty years with his wife and family. He returned to the Colville Reservation in 1970 where he is presently residing. He is active in promoting cultural and historical programs on the Colville Reservation and is a well-known lecturer.

Louie Wapato
Winátshapam-Chlálpam
Is the oldest living resident in Chelan. He was born there, and he is still residing on Indian land. He attended local schools in Chelan, and he graduated from Carlisle Indian College in Pennsylvania. He is still active in politics involving Indian rights and laws. He is a historian. Mr. Wapato lived at Lake Chelan for the rest of his life. He used to have racehorses and would race thoroughbred racehorses at Ellensburg. He told the legend about why

there is no salmon in Lake Chelan. He was generally hesitant to share legends with people who wanted to record them but decided to participate in the *Anakú Iwachá* project because Virginia was such a renowned racehorse jockey and often outrode Mr. Wapato's jockeys at the aforementioned horse races.

Tribal Illustrators

Biographies for illustrators have been added for the new edition. Calvin Charley was not listed in the 1974 edition as an illustrator but is now included. Two artists, Shayleen EagleSpeaker and Michelle Saluskin, are new illustrators for the new edition.

Calvin Charley
Calvin was from Wapato, Washington. He was quite young when he did his artwork of Crane. Virginia recalls that he was a dreamer and poet. He was also a World War II veteran.

Shayleen EagleSpeaker
Shayleen (Wasco, Warm Springs, Yakama) is a tribal member of the Confederated Tribes of Warm Springs. Shayleen attended the Northwest Indian Language Institute Summer Institute and has studied Ichishkíin at the University of Oregon with Virginia. She has also studied Chinuk Wawa at Lane Community College. She is now working with her Kiksht (Wasco) language as a linguistics doctoral student at the University of Oregon.

Lucy Eneas
In preparing the new edition of *Anakú Iwachá*, Virginia shared that Lucy had, at the time of the original project, a severe case of arthritis in her hands, with her hands all curled up. After making the illustrations for the book, her hands became healed, and she became a very celebrated artist having her own shows. Reflecting on Lucy's experience, we see the power of our traditional stories to help heal us.

Johnny Jim Jr.
Johnny illustrated the battle of North Wind and South Wind. He graduated from Toppenish High School. Virginia shared that Johnny's artistic talent was natural, without formal training. He was also a famous runner at Toppenish.

Bobby Maldonado
Bobby's mother was Winátshapam. She was fluent in her language and in Ichishkíin. He and his brothers were all artists, Virginia remembers. They lived in Toppenish.

Nathan Olney Jr.
Nathan was a trained artist. He volunteered his talent and was a great resource for the original project. Nathan was a Yakama Tribal member, and Virginia remembers his kindness and generosity to participate in the project.

Julie Saluskin
Julie was thirteen years old when she volunteered to draw the flower girls. She attended Toppenish schools all her life, and she graduated Toppenish High School. As we were preparing the new edition in 2019, we enjoyed reflecting on her being a Lady Boss Jr.! Julie retired from working at the Yakama Nation but continues to go back and help train accountants.

Michelle Saluskin
Michelle Alice M. Saluskin grew up on the Salish and Kootenai Reservation in western Montana. She is married to Brian Saluskin (Yakama). After graduating in 2009 with a BFA focus in painting, she is now a stay-at-home mom of four children as well as a part-time artist.

James Telekish Jr.
James was from Satus, Washington. He had a background in art and did a lot of work around the Yakama Reservation in art. He preferred not to elaborate too much about himself, but his artwork in *Anakú Iwachá* is very outstanding. He worked with Indian education programs.

Legends in Ichishkíin and English

Introduction

Readers hold a finished, edited book in their hands and only see the final product. However, years of work have gone into this new edition. We want to share a glimpse of this work with readers, so they might understand the process used. The four legends included here in Ichishkíin and English are beautiful examples of how the work is done. As we sat with Virginia Beavert in her home in Toppenish on a cold day in December 2018, we were aware that being part of this project is a special gift, to sit with Elders and learn things that only they know. Only Virginia knows what it was like to record the storytellers for the original edition of *Anakú Iwachá* over forty-five years ago. Now we, along with our students, are fortunate to continue this work in a small way.

In the following conversation between Virginia and Joana, edited for ease of reading by Michelle, Virginia prepares to retell a story in Ichishkíin. The conversation transcript also provides an introduction to the first legend. Her telling shows how the stories of our people are intertwined with one another. Virginia notes the many explanations contained in this version of the legend: how it is that we use shells to decorate our dresses, how Turtle got his shell, how Beacon Rock came to be. Each of these stories could also be told as its own legend.

VIRGINIA: There are different races of people. Here we are the red people. Those are the people that Creator put here, on this earth. And Creator placed them in their own territories, clear around, and he put us here, the red people. We speak different languages. He placed us here close to each other, but we're one people. Our language is slightly different, but we understand each other. And that's why we are here as people, but this legend is going to be from way back. It was told to children to be aware of their self, their culture.

And this is the legend I am going to tell: There was an old couple living over there, in the ocean. They were maternal Elders who raised these three girls. They were Abalone, there was a Dentalium, there was Cowry (also called Monetaria) Shells, the three girls. So the Elders prepared them for their journey; they were all ready to get married, you know, because this announcement came out that Coyote's son is mature enough now to get married. He's been trained to his responsibilities about looking after a family, and now he's ready. An announcement was sent all over the country to send their girls to come court him. He learns a lesson here.

And in the next episode of the story I am going to talk about the crane who was called the ferry man *nakwaykłá* and he used to spread his leg clear across from that island [the Hawaiian Islands] and the girls are going to walk across his leg over here to our place from the ocean, from that big island. Then they are going to come and court this young man. So that is what this legend is about. Now I have to think about what they call a crane . . . [*she laughs*] . . . You know too much English is causing me to forget. Hmm . . .

JOANA: So nakwaykłá that is just what he is in this legend?

VIRGINIA: Yeah.

JOANA: Sandhill crane.

VIRGINIA: K̲w'áshk̲w'ash—

JOANA: k̲w'áshk̲w'ash—

VIRGINIA: k̲w'áshk̲w'ash—

JOANA: k̲w'áshk̲w'ash—

VIRGINIA: is the crane . . . [*she laughs*] . . . now you can remind me if I forget again . . . and dentalium, mark that—

JOANA: áx̲sh'ax̲sh—

VIRGINIA: áx̲sh'ax̲sh.

K̲w'ashk̲w'ashmí Watít, ku Túyaw Alashikmí Psa Átx̲anana (Watít Atachiishpamá Ttmayimamíki)

(Related to "Amushyáy and Wɨx̲inshyáy")

Awkú, K̲w'ashk̲w'ashyáy ipáwawaykika pɨnmínk wɨx̲á, iwachá waníki nakwaykɬá K̲w'ashk̲w'ashyáy. Waayk ipáwiwaykika íkuuni nch'ípa, anakwnák iwachá nch'iii tiichám páchupa atáchiishpa (nch'ípa ɨmawípa).

Crane extended out his foot. Crane was called the ferryman. He extended his foot clear across (the ocean) to a big place, where there was a large piece of land in the middle of the ocean (a big island).

Ku íkwɨn awkú patkw'áwaykma ttmayíma íichɨn tiichámyaw. Ku kwnak awkú pat áwɨna, "Íkuuni pam wínata, íkwnak kw'ɨnk iwá ɨwínsh." Awkú pawínama ttmayíma.

And from that land the maidens walked across (on Crane's leg), clear over here. And they told the maidens, "You go that way, that's where that man is." And the maidens came.

Wat'uymá Wɨx̲inshyáy, iwachá mayktɨmnáyi, anakú iwachá wat'uymá. Ku pachupamá iwachá Amushyáy.

The eldest Wɨx̲inshyáy (Abalone) was the kindest because she was the most mature. And the middle one was Amushyáy (Cowry/Monetaria Shell).

K̲w'ashk̲w'ashyáy ipáwawaykika pɨnmínk wɨx̱á. Crane pole-boated his leg across.

Ku tɨ́knik'a láymut Ax̱shax̱shyáy, pɨ́nch'a iwachá láymut, pɨ́nch'a táaminwa anakúsh túnx̱ ipx̱wí-nx̱ana, pinápx̱wini, anakúsh chaw iwachá káakɨm íx̱wi sápsikw'ani, "Chaw nam íkush wáta, chaw nam íkush kúta," anakú iwachá láymut, ku pat anakúsh álaaknx̱ana anakú pɨnch'á iłḵ'íwix̱ana ámchnik anakú pasápsikw'ashana káłayin ku tílayin napwiinanák nápu.

In contrast to those two, the youngest, Ax̱shax̱shyáy (Dentalium), that littlest one had always thought and behaved differently. She was not fully taught, "Don't be that way, don't do that." This was because she was the littlest one and they forgot about her when she was outside playing in her own little world at the time their maternal grandparents were teaching the other two.

Ku pɨnch'á awkú iḵḵánaywisha túkin, chaw imɨts'íx̱washa, kunkínk iwachá mayktúnx̱.

That youngest one was occupied with her own things and did not listen, and in that way she was the most different (of the three sisters).

Ku awkú mɨ́taawma pawínama, aw pawyánawya íkwɨn sáats'at pawínama.

And then the three sisters came; they traveled all the day clear into nighttime.

Wɨx̱inshyáyin awkú pá'ɨna, "Íchna na mɨnán wáwt'ɨkwta kú na maysx̱ awkú áwinanuuta."

Then Abalone said, "We will camp here and tomorrow we will go to him."

Láymutawkúikkáasana,pinápx̱wi-shana "Shix̱ natash wa ḵ'ínupa ku tash 'ii' ikúta niimanák." "Chaw, íkuuk na wínata laak na túman túnx̱ma pat áwashuuta ku na awkú chaw niimanák isáp'awita."

The youngest one was in a hurry, she was thinking, "We are beautiful and he will say yes to us." She said, "No, let's go now, today, because some others might go to him and he'll select them and not us."

"Chaw," pá'ɨna pátiin. "Anakú iwáta aan ḵayx̱ ku na iḵ'ínuta awkú ḵayx̱."

"No," the older sister told her. "When the sun is up shining then he'll be able to see us clearly."

“Chaw, áwna wínata íkuuk.” Awkú wáa’aw ikúya. Pátiin awkú pá’ɨna “Kuu mish.” Awkú pawínanuuna sts’átpa.

“No, let’s go right now.” Then she won her argument. Her older sister told her, “All right.” So they went to him that night.

Pat awkú áwitax̱shya, “Aw natash wyánawi, aw nam wínamta ku nam ḵ’ínuta, ámchnik natash wa!”

Then they woke him up. “We’ve arrived now, come see us, we are outside!”

Ku tɨ́knik’a awkú pɨnk Ax̱shax̱shyáy pɨ́nx̱ush iwináynakuuna láymut anakwnák ipnúshana kw’ɨnk ɨwínsh, awkú ɨwínsh iwachá isht Spilyaymí.

Dentalium ran in first, that youngest one ran in to that man who was sleeping. That man was Spilyáy’s son.

Huuy pápawaynana ku pá’ɨna, “Íkuuni wínak, chaw pá’ihananuykɨm, pnúshaash!”

He tried in vain to push her away. He was telling her, “Go away, don’t bother me, I am sleeping!”

Ánach’ax̱i pá’itax̱shiya. Huuy ánch’ax̱i pápawaynana, “Wíyat wínak, shaláwishaash kush pnuwát’asha!”

Again she woke him, and again he tried to push her away, “Go away, I am tired and I want to sleep!”

Ánach’ax̱i iwáynanuuna mɨ́taatiyaw ku kuuk pápaptɫ’ka tpɨ́shpa. X̱túwiki ápaptɫ’ka íkush.

After the third time she approached him he slapped her. He slapped her face hard.

“Aah!” Awkú ináx̱tiya, iwinátma pináwipiksha tpɨ́shpa anakwnák pápaptɫ’ka, “Páyuush ikú, páyuush ikú!” inánax̱tisha.

“Oh!” Then she came running out, crying and holding her face where he hit her. “He hurt me, he hurt me!” she cried.

Awkú Amushyáy isx̱íx̱na ku iwináynakuuna "Mish nam ámi ínpsitsnan?" Ku ánach'ax̱i pɨnách'ak'a pápaptł'ka tpɨ́shpa ku iwinátma.

Then Monetaria Shell was angry and ran in to him, "What have you done to my sister?" And he slapped her face too, and she came running out.

Awkú isx̱íx̱na Wɨx̱inshyáy ku iwináynakuuna pɨ́nch'ak'a, ku pinách'ax̱i awkú pápat'k̠a tpɨ́shpa. "Íhananuykshapam, huuy nash wíihaashhaasha, aw nash shaláwik'aysha."

Then Abalone got angry and *she* ran over to him and that one again slapped her face. "You are all bothering me, I can't rest, and I am getting so tired."

Awkú iwinátma Wɨx̱inshyáy pináwipiksha tpɨ́shpa anakwnák pápapłka páyu. Awkú panáx̱tiya, pawyánax̱tiya awkú patkw'anátika awkú, pawyánax̱tika:

Then Abalone came running out, holding her face where he hit her. Then they cried, they went along crying a sad, sad song:

Ahaayiya, hahaayiya, ahaayiya, hahaayiya, pawyánax̱tisha. *Aahaaa, a'haaa'aa'haaa, a'haaa'aa'haaa*, pawyánax̱tisha. *Ahaaay . . .*

Ahaayiya, hahaayiya, ahaayiya, hahaayiya, they went along singing. *Aahaaa, a'haaa'aa'haaa*, they went along singing. *Ahaaay . . .*

Awkú papx̱wína, "Hmm, páchix̱ash iwá iwɨ́nsh, chɨlwítx̱ash áwa tɨmná, áw na paysh kw'ałá chaw awamanyú!" Kuuk awkú shix̱ papx̱wínkika! *Ahaayiya, hahaayiya, ahaayiya, hahaayiya, a'haaay'aa'haaa . . . Ahaayiya, hahaayiya, ahaayiya, hahaayiya, a'haaay'aa'haaa . . .*

Then they thought, "Hmm, he must be a bad man, with a bad heart, we are happy to not be married to him!" Then they began to feel happy and sang a happy song!

Kw'ałáni awkú kw'áx̱i patúx̱-ɨnkika, awkú pawyánawya kwnak ilá'ayksha Ḵw'ashḵw'ashyáy.

Happy again, they decided to return home and they arrived at the place where Crane sat leisurely.

"Aw natash kw'áx̱i túx̱sha. Itíwish natash ɨwínshnɨm, páyu tash ikwíini tpɨsh, ku tash aw kw'áx̱i túx̱sha."

"Now we are going home again. That man beat us up, he hurt our faces, and we are going home."

"Aaaaaw," awkú ipáwiwaykika wɨx̱á waayk atáchiishnan íiiikwɨn ɨmawíyaw. Awkú patkw'áwaykika.

"Aaaaaw," then he pole-boated his leg, stretching it clear across the ocean there to the island. And then they (the older two) walked across.

Awkú papx̱winúuna awkú Ḵw'ashḵw'ashyáyin, "Páyux̱ash iwá pinápx̱wini íchi pt'íniks láymut." Awkú ának iwáayka, itkw'anátishayka ának Ax̱shax̱shyáy, awkú míimi pawyánawika pátiin.

Then Crane thought, "Apparently this youngest girl is very conceited." Then Dentalium was walking across last, way after her two older sisters had already arrived home.

Awkú Ḵw'ashḵw'ashyáy ishapáwiisklika pɨnmínk wɨx̱á ku ix̱átamaniina awkú Ax̱sh-ax̱shyáy atáchiishyaw. Wíiiiiii-yatyaw awkú kwnak awkú iḵá'ɨsha ɨmíti atáchiishpa. Kw'áx̱i awkú Ḵw'ashḵw'ashyáy icháwii-waaykma kw'áx̱i pɨnmínk wɨx̱á.

Then Crane twisted his leg around, and Dentalium fell into the ocean. Faaaaar down below in the ocean she fell and lay in a heap. And then Crane pulled his leg back again from the island.

Tɬ'anx̱ íchi Spilyaymí isht iyíkna walptáyktyaw pt'ilímaman, "Aah, paysh nash aw wyákwshtiksh! Paysh íkwak pawachá kwmak pt'ilímaash kumanák awiwáx̱ishana. Áykshanaash shii'iix̱ pawá k̲'ínupa."

Aaaah, kw'áx̱i awkú ik̲áchaykma, iwinátma, Aah! Áaawna íchi ɬp'uɬ tɬ'áax̱wpa mɨnán áwiit'ishksha íkuuni.

"Aaah! Aw nash chaw shix̱ kúya, aw nash átwapatisha!" Kw'áx̱i awkú itwápatima pt'ilímaman.

Ku iwináchikma kwnak K̲w'ashk̲w'ashyáy ilá'ayksha. Ik̲'uk̲'úwisha, ik̲'uk̲'úwisha ik̲'uk̲'úwisha.

Ku páshapnya K̲w'ashk̲w'ashyáynan, "Mɨnán íkw'ak pawá kwmak ayáyat pt'ilíma? Páyuush wyákwshtiksh kush átk̲'ix̱sha kw'áx̱iish áwanpimta, aw nash ánaktux̱ta."

Ku sha'áaat, K̲w'ashk̲w'ashyáy ilá'ayksha awkú pákatɬ'inashana K̲w'ashk̲w'ashyáyin. Icháwinatx̱amak'a pɨnmínk kátɬ'yaas ku ikátɬ'inashax̱ana awkú, ánach'ax̱i wyákw'aɬayashana, ánach'ax̱i, ánach'ax̱i.

Meanwhile Coyote's son heard the maidens singing. "Oh! Maybe I have made a mistake! Maybe those were the maidens I was waiting for. I heard they are good looking."

He jumped up and ran out in horror and saw their tears splattered everywhere.

"I've done wrong! I'm going to catch them!" And then he chased after the maidens.

And he arrived where Crane was sitting. Crane was coughing, coughing, coughing.

And he asked Crane, "Where are those beautiful women? I have wronged them and I want to call them back to me and take them home with me."

Unconcerned, Crane sat leisurely, then he spit on the young man. He kept coughing up his thick stringy spit and spitting it out onto Spilyáy's son, smearing it on him, again and again.

Ku awkú payúwya kw'ɨnk áswan. Awkú payúwishana, awkú pákatł'inashana pakatł'inashana awkú, íx̱wi awkú iwáx̱ishana kwnak.

Then that boy became sick. He was sick and still being spit upon, spit upon, even so he waited there.

Awkú aswanmí pshɨt, Spilyáy, iyíkna X̱wɨ́łx̱wɨłnan. Pínch'a iwá patamunłá X̱wɨ́łx̱wɨł. Patalwaskłá pat áwanikx̱a X̱wɨ́łx̱wɨłnan, mɨlíish íkush ikúx̱a, "X̱wɨ́łx̱wɨł, x̱wɨ́łx̱wɨł!" Sínwit táaminwa, itámunx̱a tíinmaman.

Then the boy's father, Spilyáy, heard X̱wɨ́łx̱wɨł. X̱wɨ́łx̱wɨł (Meadowlark) is a news reporter and also a gossiper. He's always slipping his tongue back and forth in his mouth, "X̱wɨ́łx̱wɨł, x̱wɨ́łx̱wɨł!" This is his way of speaking, and he is always telling people the news.

Ku pátamuna, "Aw mash payúwisha ku tł'yáwisha isht. Áwɨnpata!" Íshtapa ináktux̱ana.

And he reported to the elder Spilyáy, "Your son is sick and dying. Go get him!" He brought his son home.

Ku Tamanwiłáyin pá'ɨna ináawnan, "Aw nam wa pinapx̱winúuni, iksíks ɨwínsh, ku nam aw íchna lá'aykta táaminwa. Shapa'isíkw'at íkush nam wa, ímch'a nam wa pinapx̱winúuni. Chaw nam átmaakna ttmayímaman. Chaw nam ák̠'inanya tɨmná.

And Creator said to Spilyáy's son, "You are a childish, arrogant man and you will now sit there always. You'll be thus made into an example for others. You are conceited. You did not respect the young women. You did not see their kindness (their soft hearts).

Íkw'ak mash wa k̠w'iit ku pinapx̱winúunt. Ku nam páyu páyu ákuya ttmayímaman.

This shows your arrogance and conceit. You wronged those maidens deeply.

Íkw'ak iwá isíkw'at: Tł'áax̱w-maman shin átmaakta. Áwiḵ'inanitaam tɨmná. Chaw nam awkú pinapx̱winúuta, 'Shix̱ nash wa ɨwínsh kush átḵ'ix̱shaash shɨ́x̱tx̱aw áyat, ásap'awita.' Chaw.

This is the lesson you will show: Respect everybody. Take some time to see their heart. Don't think only of yourself, 'I am a fine man, and I want only the best woman. I will seek her out.' No.

Aw nam átk'ina, átk'inanita tɨmná, átk'inanita wáwnakw-shaash. Tł'ápx̱i chaw shix̱ ḵ'inúpa áyat áwa shix̱ tɨmná ku nam shix̱ inaknúwita. Íkush nam wáta isíkw'at tł'aax̱w awinsh-mamíyaw kúshx̱i ayatmamíyaw. Átmaaktaam wáḵ'ishwit laxsmí, chaw nam áwałata."

Take your time to look at their heart, look at the whole person. Although she may not be the good-looking woman you think you want, she has a true heart and will take care of you. Thus, you will show this lesson for all men and women. Respect a person's spirit, do not reject them."

Íkush awkú páshapa'ayka kwnak ɨwínshnan. Ku íchi íkuuk ilá'ayksha, ḵw'laapsh, íkush iwá ḵw'laapsh. Chaw iwá ḵ'ínupa shix̱. Chaw nam áwinanuuta ku chaw nam áwayayata. Ilá'ayksha nch'i wanapáynk, iwaníksha Isíkw'at Pshwa.

Thus, Creator made the son sit there. And to today he is sitting there, bare; he is bare stone without life. He is not good looking. You will not go to it (the rock) and admire it. He sits by the Columbia River and is called Beacon Rock.

"Awkłáaw nam kwnak tíinma patk'íta, 'Aw íkwaalx̱iish íchna panátitax̱nay!' Ku nam pawípanatita, awkú awkłáaw. That is all.

Creator said, "The people will see you there and say, 'Oh, I can climb up that far!' And they will climb up on you.
That is all.

Chaw nam túyaw awkú ánach'ax̱i wa shix̱ áwtik'a nam aw tx̱ána, awkłáaw isíkw'at."

You will not be good for anything after that; you will instead only be a lesson there."

Tɨ́knik'a íkwna, tɬ'áax̱wshin ipx̱wípx̱wina Ax̱shax̱shyaynmíki. Mish awkú yanwáy íkwna táaminwa itx̱ánata?

Meanwhile, everyone worried about Dentalium. Will that pitiful one remain there always?

Wyánch'ima ápx̱wipx̱wina, "Átḵ'ix̱shaatash kw'áx̱i wáḵ'ish itx̱ánata niimí myánash." Patámuna awkú tɬ'áax̱wnan shiin, "Aw pam shix̱ ánatɨmta kw'áx̱i kwɨ́nik anakwnák iwíishtkshax̱ash kwnak ɨmíti."

The Elders worried, "We want our child to live." The message went out to everyone, "Bring her out from where she is tangled down below!"

Íkw'ak, tɬ'aaaaax̱w túman, kákyama, pawínana atáchiishkan anakwnák Ḵw'ashḵw'ashyáy ilá'aykshana.

That's when all of the creatures gathered at the ocean where Crane was sitting.

Ku pá'ɨna Ḵw'ashḵw'ashyáyin, "Pt'íniks iwá, ayáyat ḵ'ínupa, ix̱átamani, ku pam wáḵ'ish áwanitax̱nay, anakw'ɨ́nk inátɨmta atáchiishknik, ku awkú áyat átx̱anata."

And Crane said, "There's a good-looking girl, she has fallen, and whoever of you saves her and brings her from the ocean, she will become his wife."

"Uuy, ii," awkú tɬ'áax̱wma panuú. "Ash ink, ash ink!" Náx̱shk'a! Náx̱shk'a!

"Ooh, aah, let me, let me!" They all said this, one after the other!

Tɬ'aax̱w íchi kákyama anakwmák pawá tiichámpa ku túx̱ɨnpa, chíishpa, íkw'makx̱i awkú, pahúuyna.

All the creatures, those of the water, the sky, and the land, they tried and failed.

Náx̱shk'a ilamáylakx̱ana, "Ii, uuy!" Kw'áx̱i ix̱átamaatx̱ana. Náx̱shk'a ilamáylakx̱ana, kw'áx̱i ix̱átamaatx̱ana.

One by one they tried. "Aah, ooh!" One would dive, then immediately pop back up again. Another would dive and immediately pop back up.

Wíyatyaw iwináynaka tmáy kwnak áwku ilá'ɨshana. Cháwiyat awkú itł'yáwishana.

The girl fell way down deep, and that's where she lay. She was near death.

Ku áwku, náx̱shk'a iwachá láymut, náx̱shknik ttáwax̱tknik, Spilyaymí isht.

Then the next one to have a turn was another youngest son of Spilyáy (from a different family than the one who scorned the sisters).

Pɨ́nch'ax̱i áwku iwachá pinapx̱winúunix̱i,

This one was also vain.

"Aaah, ink nash wa x̱túx̱aw, ink nash ánatɨmta."

"Aah, I am the strongest one, I will bring her out."

Áwku pɨ́nch'ax̱i ilamáylaka, kw'áx̱i ix̱átamaatɨma.

So that one also dove in, but then he too popped back out.

Tł'aax̱w awkú haasht anakúsh k'aywá. Chawmáal palamáylaka.

Everyone must have run out of air down there. They couldn't dive for long.

Ku x̱wayamá, "X̱túx̱aw nash wa ink," pɨ́nch'a áwku ilamáylaka kw'áx̱i ix̱átamaatɨma.

And Golden Eagle said, "I'm the strongest." He too dove down and right away popped back out again.

Tł'aax̱wma áwku pahúuyna.

They all failed.

Ku pɨ́nch'a ikwíitama, xwɨ́saat, áwtya pɨ́nch'a kwnak itkw'aníntkw'aninx̱ana, cháwtun, mish imíshana?

Then this old man (Turtle) came walking along. He was not involved in what had been going on; he just happened to come by.

Pat áwɨna, “Ímksasimk’aam aw wa. Mish nam chaw wáḵ’ish áwanisha, ánatshamsh tmáynan. Ayáyat iwá ḵ’ínupa. Ku mash áwku áyat tx̱ánata.”

They told him, “You are the only one left. Why don’t you try to save her, to bring out the maiden? She is beautiful, and she will become your wife.”

“Uuuh, x̱wɨ́saat nash wa, túyay nash áwku ink shix̱ ḵ’ínupa áyat wáta? X̱wɨ́saat nash wa, íkwɬpam húuyna. Mish nash áwku ink ámita, x̱wɨ́saat nash wa.

“Why should I have a beautiful wife? So many of you have already failed. What could I do, I’m an old man.

Anatúmantya pat átḵ’ix̱ta ku túuman pɨ́nch’ax̱i itḵ’íx̱ta ku aw paysh pɨ́nktya ishúkwaaya mish iwá. Ku paysh itx̱táymata tɨmná ku tɬ’ápx̱i chaw shix̱ ḵ’ínupa ɨwínsh ku áwa shix̱ tɨmná ku páwɨnpta, pananaknúwita kwiiník. Cháwk’a awkú itḵ’íx̱shata shíx̱tx̱aw ɨwínsh. Ku anashíyin pátḵ’ix̱ta ku pánaktux̱ta.”

Rather, whoever might want her and whoever she might want, she will accept this person. And perhaps she alone knows why she fell in and she will change her heart, only she will determine how she is going to emerge. She will perhaps accept a man who is not good looking but has a good heart. He will take her and take care of her. She will choose the best man, the one who will desire her and take her home.”

“Iyúushtamatash. Tun nam awkú átḵ’ix̱sha?” Alashíknan pat áwɨna.

“We will compensate you. What do you want?” they told Turtle.

“Aaw, táaminwaash ínch’a k’asáwisha. Huuy nash piná’ilats’muynx̱a. Chaw nash wa tun útpaas. Átḵ’ix̱shaash útpaas.”

“Oh, I am always cold. I can’t keep warm. I don’t have a warm robe. I want a blanket.”

Aw pat áwna, “Kuu mish, aw matash nísha útpaas, paysh nam ánatɨmta tmáynan.”

“All right, we will give you a robe if you bring out the maiden.”

Ku awkú pɨ́nch’a iwá ikush-pamánk, íchi atachiishpamá Alashík. Awkú itkw’anátika ɨmíti tiichámpa, x̱álukt chíishpa. Itkw’anátika, iiii, iyáx̱na! Íchi ilá’ɨsha tmay.

And since this one, Turtle, was a creature of the ocean, he walked to the bottom of the ocean. He walked in under there and, yes, he found her! Here the maiden is, lying down.

Awkú iwɨ́npa ku ik’álaka. Awkú kw’áx̱i itkw’anátima awkú atá-chiishknik, k’álaki tmay.

He took her and put her on his back. And he walked out of the water, with the maiden on his back.

Tł’aaax̱w kákyama patamá-chayka anakú inátɨma tmáynan. Awkú pat áwitax̱shya tmáynan ku pat ánya awkú iyúush x̱wɨ́saatnan ku pat áshapa’utpa kw’ɨnk útpaas.

All the creatures cheered when he brought the maiden out. And then they woke the maiden and they paid the old man; they put a blanket around him.

Ayáyat útpaas, iitii, ts’muuy iḵáwa x̱wɨ́saat. Áḵ’inutaam awkú íkuuk, ayáyat áwa útpaas.

It was a beautiful blanket, yes, the old man was all warmed up. You will see it today, he has a beautiful robe.

Íkw’ak íkush, anakúsh, wáḵ’ish aníya tmáynan, ku inátɨma. Ku íchi íkuuk awkú tmay iwá, anakúsh, ayáyat.

Now, in this way, he brought out the woman and made her alive, and still today she is a beautiful maiden.

Áyatma pat áwisx̱ta táatpaspa, awkú íkush awkú itx̱ánana íchi kw’ɨnk tmay, Áx̱shax̱sh.

Women sew her on their clothing; that is what that maiden, Dentalium (and her sisters), became.

Íkw'ak nam ák̲'inuta táatpaspa, awkú, iwá wísx̲i, ayáyat k̲'ínupa.

So you will see them now, sewn onto dresses, very beautiful.

Tɬ'áax̲wnam shínɨm i'ayáyanita imanák táatpas.

Everyone will admire your dress.

Íkw'ak iwá watít, kwnak iwá sápsikw'at: Chaw nam ásap'awita táaminwa shíx̲tx̲aw k̲'ínupa ɨwínsh, shíx̲tx̲aw k̲'ínupa ásham. Paysh pawá chaw shix̲ k̲'ínupa kútya áwa shix̲ tɨmná, yuk'áat tɨmná, shix̲ nam inaknúwita kwɨnkínk, chaw nam kw'áx̲i pawyáalakwta.

In this legend there is a lesson: Do not only go after the best-looking man, the best-looking wife. A person may not be good looking but yet they have a good heart, a soft heart, and they will look after you, they will not abandon you.

Anam k̲áwata imksá kw'áx̲i, ku nam iwyáalakwta palaláay myánash, míshkin nam awkú naknúwita kw'ɨnk íkush? Iwá sápsikw'at íkwnak watítpa.

A person you value only for their looks will soon run off on you and leave you single with a lot of children; how then will you care for them? This is the teaching of the legend.

Wáaax̲włała!

(An old word, a traditional ending for a legend. It has no translation.)

Anakú Itx̱ánana Aan

(Related to "Legend about the Sun and Moon")

Míimi, cháwx̱i íx̱wi iwachá ḵayx̱ íchna tiichámpa, ku cháwx̱i iwachá sts'at.

A long time ago, there was not yet daylight on this land, and there was not yet night.

Ku íkwna winátshapa ákwiitama tíinma ku kwnak pawíihaash-haashna sts'átpa.

And there, at Winátsha, the people were coming, and they rested there in the dark.

Ku kwnak tł'aax̱w mish pawímishana anakúsh pawisalílx̱ana, pax̱níx̱ana, tł'áax̱wtun, anakúsh, ḵḵanáywit.

Everyone did the things needed to provide their livelihood, like hunting and digging, everything.

Ku palalíwashana ḵáyx̱yaw.

And they were longing for the daylight.

Íchi íkuuk pawachá nápu x̱áyin kuuk piníich'ax̱i pakwíitama paháykshama íchɨn, wanapáynk pakwíitama.

That day there were two brothers, and those two also were meandering along, coming down this way, coming down at the river.

Ku kwnáx̱i awkú pawyách'aaka, "Íchi pawá winátshapa tíinma, ku tawnáapak'a kwnak pápawilaalakwshana, mun aw iwáta táaminwa łkw'i uu mun iwáta táaminwa sts'aat."

They came to a place and said, "Look, here are the people of Winátsha (the Pouring Out place). It looks like they are having a contest about when it will always be light and when it will always be dark."

Ku íchi x̱áyin pawaníkshana Aan, ku nax̱sh iwaníkshana Álx̱ayx̱.

And these two brothers, one was named Sun and the other was named Moon.

Ku áwku pawyánawya íkwɨn, ku ii, íkwnak íchi mɨx̱ísh kákya pina'ináwisha, "Ink nash wáta łkw'i."

And when they arrived there, yes, there was a bright yellow bird challenging, "I will be the daylight."

Iwiilúuka x̱wíiiimi ku wáawk'a ilák̲ayx̱ya k̲ayx̱. Itapch'íitiya tíinmaman. "Aaah, aw nam wíihaykɨmta. Wáawk'a nam wa k̲ayx̱. Tapch'íitishaam."

He flew up high and he burst into blazing light. He blinded the people with his light. And they told him, "Oh, come down now. You're too bright. You're blinding us."

Ku Spilyáyk'a awkú iwiilúuka. "Ink nash wáta k̲ayx̱." Ku awkú iwiilúuka.

Coyote also flew up to try. "I will be the daylight." And he flew up.

Ku kwnak awkú tł'áax̱wmish iwímiya. Ku chaw pat átk̲'ix̱na anakú, anakúsh k̲niip iwachá.

But he did all kinds of foolish things up there. They did not want him because he was too foolish.

Pat áwɨna, "Chaw matash tk̲'íx̱sha imk nam wáta k̲ayx̱. Wíihaykɨm kw'áx̱i." Ku pat ánakhaykma.

They told him, "We don't want you to be the daylight. Come down again." And they brought him down.

Ku kwnak awkú x̱áyin, Aan ku Álx̱ayx̱, patk'íshana Nch'iwánapa, awkú kwnak ts'aa íkwna tnánpa, anakwnák iwá anakúsh waníki Ribbon Cliff, kwnak pak̠'ínuna, "Kwnak nax̱sh íchi iwá kákya. Ilá'ayksha."

And the brothers, Sun and Moon, looked around there by the Columbia River at the cliff that is named Ribbon Cliff and saw, "Here is a bird. She is perching there."

Kwnak íchi ánch'ax̱i pak̠'ínuna, "Íchi iwá, aa, k̠'ínupa pu'úuɬ k'usík'usi." Ilá'ishana ɨmíti kwnak k̠'míɬpa.

There also they saw, "Here is a dog, it looks like he is blind." He was lying there below the cliff.

Ku pa'ɨ́na kákyanan, "Mish nam íchi lá'ayksha?" ku pá'ɨna "Ink nash wa tiix̱waɬá."

And they said to the bird, "What are you doing perching here?" and she said, "I am the informer."

"Uhn, mish nam awkú túuman átiix̱wax̱a?"

"Oh, whom do you inform?"

"Aah, anakwmák pakwíitamta íchɨn wánapa, wanapáynk íkwna." Ku pa'isíkw'ana íkwɨn, "Ikw'ak iwá k'usík'usi nch'ii, ku kwnak pat áwyawawnx̱a kwnak. Kush ink átiix̱wax̱a awkú tiin-mamíki, áx̱mikan, túnishiknik."

"Well, when some people come along the river here," she pointed, "over there is a big dog and they pass him there. I warn him about the people and the directions they are coming from, up from the river, or upstream."

"Uhn, íkw'ak mash wa kútkut."

"Oh, so that is your work."

"Ii."

"Yes."

Kúx̱ashtx̱ panashɬá inúk̠w'k-ɨnx̱ana anashín ikwíitamsh, iháykshamsh wánapa.

And the monster swallows who-ever comes along or down to the river.

Ku áwku x̱áyin pawínayka áwku, kwnak pa'iyáx̱na Yiityíitnan, kw'ɨnk iwá patíix̱wał́á.

Pa'ɨ́na, "Aw matash wapíitata." Awkú shápɨnchaashki pashapámłka ku tł'áax̱w awkú pashapámɨnka pɨnmínk wáptas ku áchaashpa. Tł'áax̱w pat shix̱ anakúsh áshapamx̱shka.

Ku pinák̲'inuna "Uuu, shix̱ nash wa k̲'ínupa!" Awkú iwáynana, pɨlksá pináwyak̲'inusha. Iláakna awkú, "Wash nash waachiłá."

Ku awkú x̱áyin pawínanuuna kwnak k'usík'usinan. Łuuwáaayki pawínanuuna. Chaw patk̲'íx̱na pa'ítax̱shita.

Anakú awkú cháwk'a áwacha tiix̱wałá, ku awkú kwaat ipnúshana kw'ɨnk k'usík'usi.

Kúx̱ashtx̱ ishúkwaana mish tunx̱ iwá, tun, ku itáx̱shya ku pináshukwaana, "Aw nash winanínsha" ku iwinanína awkú.

Ku Álx̱ayx̱in páwat'ana, páwat'ana ílkwaaski. Mɨláam páwat'ana ku awkú áwanana palaláay tilíwal.

And the brothers arrived, and there they found Sandpiper, the aforementioned informer.

They said, "We will help you." Then they used Indian paint to dip and smear her wings and eyes. They spread it, grooming her.

And she looked at herself, "Ohh, I look good!" And then she flew off; she went away looking at herself. She forgot she was a watcher.

And then the brothers came up to the dog. Slowly, slowly they crept up because they didn't want to wake him.

And he was sleeping soundly, that dog, because he no longer had an informer.

And the dog must have known something was different, and when he woke and realized something was different, he said, "I'm leaving!" And then he ran off.

And Moon hit him and hit him with a stick. He hit him many times and a lot of his blood flowed out.

Ku awkú pináwapyana, kwaat ápikshana napwák, ku awkú pat áwawyana, áwawyana, ánach'ax̱i, awkú pu'úuł. Ku íkuuni, íchiini awku tł'áax̱wkan miin huuy iwinanína, pat kwaat ápikshana.

He struggled to get away but the two both held tightly, and they hit him over and over again, but he was blind. And this way and that way, every way, he tried in vain to escape, but they held on tightly.

Awkú áwanana palaláay tilíwal, kwɨnmínk nam awkú ák̲'inuta, áwa pɨnmínk tilíwal Ribbon Cliffpa. Táaminwa íkw'ak nam ák̲'ínuta anámku kwnak wínata, Entiatpa.

Then a lot of his blood flowed. You will see it there; his blood is at Ribbon Cliff. You will always see that when you go there to Entiat.

Awku itłúpwiliina, itłúpwiliina chíishyaw, Nch'iwánayaw, ku awkú iwinanína ku pat huuy átwapatya ku aw pat áwapawx̱ina awkú.

Then he jumped into the water, jumped into the water, into the Columbia River, and then he escaped. They couldn't catch him, so they let him go.

Awkú pawináyka awkú Winátshakan x̱áyin, ku kwnak pawyánawika. "Palaláay tíinma íchi. Pawáwtuksha."

Then the two brothers arrived at Winátsha, they reached their destination. "There are a lot of people camping here."

Kwnak aw tł'áax̱wkan miin pawítk'ina, ku pat napwiinanák áshix̱na, pax̱ɨtwáyna ku pax̱ɨtwáyaka tł'áax̱wnan shiin.

They looked all around at everything there. The people there admired those two, and they in turn acknowledged them and visited around.

Kux̱ashtx̱ páyu páshix̱na náx̱shin áyatin anakúsh páwantwinshana Áannan. Iwaníkshana Aluk̲'át.

So one woman must have really liked Sun, and she was paying attention to everything he was doing. She was named Frog.

Páyu pátk̲'íx̲na Aluk̲'átin, páyu pá'atawya, anakú iwachá shix̲ k̲'ínupa. Ku kúshx̲i pɨ́nch'a Álx̲ayx̲ iwachá k̲ayx̲ ku shix̲ k̲'ínupa, kútya awkú páyutx̲aw pá'atawishana Áannan.

Awkú kwnak pawyánawika awkú ana'íkwɨn pakwíitana. Pátwananax̲it Aluk̲'átin, anakú páyu pá'atawishana awkú.

Awkú x̲áyin pa'aníya smaas ku kwnak awkú tun pawínicha, ku piiních'a awkú Aluk̲'átin páwyanawiyuuna. Shápi smaas, kwnak tł'áax̲wtun áwiwacha anakúsh chák'uki, ku pat ishápnya, "Mɨnán nash ínch'a anítax̲nay smaas?"

Ku Álx̲ayx̲ itíyana, anakúsh mish isápilɨmna, ku i'ɨ́na "Íchna!"

Ku icháx̲ɨlpa áchaash ɨmíti, íchi ɨmíti icháx̲wɨtka, ku i'ɨ́na "Íchna!" Anakúsh mish isápilɨmna áyatnan.

Ku átłupwinaynaka Alx̲ayx̲-míyaw áchaashyaw.

Huuy awkú icháx̲włka. Tł'áax̲w-ma pat awkú áwapiitana, huuy pat áchawinatanya. Kwaat pináwɨnpa Aluk̲'át áchaashpa.

Frog really loved Sun. She was in love because he was really very good looking. The other brother was also shining bright, also nice to look at, but she loved Sun the most.

Then they arrived at the place they were traveling to. Because she really loved him, Frog must have followed him.

Then the brothers made a bed there and put their things away, and she, lowly Frog, must have come along to them. She was carrying a pack with her bedding, and in it she had all kinds of things bundled up, and she asked them, "Where can I put my bed?"

And Moon laughed, like he was making fun of her, and he told her, "Here!"

He pulled his lower eyelid open, pulled it down in the middle, and he told her, "Here!" In this way he made fun of the woman.

And she jumped into Moon's eye.

He couldn't pull her apart from his eye! Everyone helped him, but they couldn't pull her out. Frog held on determinedly to his eye.

"Aw nash íchna táaminwa wáta, aw nash áwatawisha íchinak ɨwínshnan."

"I will always be here, now I love this man."

Awkú tł'áax̱wma awkú pahúuyna, awkuníik awkú ilá'ayksha Aluk̠'át.

And they could not do it, could not get her out. Frog has been sitting there ever since.

Ku pat awkú ásapilɨmna, "Tun mash íkw'ak wa áchaashpa?" Awkú pinátł'uyana awkú Álx̱ayx̱, awkú íkuuni wíyatyaw awkú mɨnán piná'ila'aykx̱ana. Chaw awkú itk̠'íx̱na ák̠'inuta pat tíinma.

And everyone made fun of Moon, "What is that in your eye?" Because he was ashamed, he would seat himself far away from everyone. He didn't want the people to see him.

Ku pat awkú átusx̱n awkú nax̱sh x̱ay, pat átusx̱nani awkú, "Imk nam aw wáta k̠ayx̱. Wátaam waníki k̠ayx̱."

And they appointed the other brother, "You will be the daylight. You will be named daylight."

Anakú awkú Álx̱ayx̱ inátx̱anana "Chaw nash ink wáta, aw nash wáawk'a wa ta'áash."

Then Moon declared, "I will not be, now I am too dim."

Ku mun nam awkú átk'ita Álx̱ayx̱nan, ku nam ák̠'inuta sts'áatpa, áwa kutł'k tpɨsh. Íkw'ak awkú iwá Aluk̠'át. Íxwi pinápiksha Alx̱ayx̱mípa. Awkú áyat átx̱anana Aluk̠'át Alx̱ayx̱mí.

And when you now look at Moon, you will see in the night that he has a part of his face that is dark. That is Frog. She is still holding herself onto Moon. Frog became Moon's wife.

Íkushx̱i iwá anakúsh tálax̱ikt tíinmaman. Chaw pam pápatalwaskta. Piná'ishix̱ita táaminwa, ku chaw nam ásapilɨmta túuman. Ikwɨ anakúsh iwá íchna tálax̱ikt.

This then is the admonishment to the people: Do not gossip. Always work to better yourself, do not make fun of anyone. That is the warning here.

Sɨ́kni

(Related to "The Wild Spring Flowers")

In her introduction to telling this legend, Virginia related how she learned it as she traveled for the original version of Anakú Iwachá. *She went to Nespelem, where a lot of Yakama Nation Elders from the Wenatchee and Lake Chelan areas lived. The storyteller whom she heard this legend from was a descendent of the Wenatchee band. Virginia says, "Children just love this story. It interests them in wild flowers. It is a story of our roots that we have, that we harvest in the spring."*

Pawachá ttmayíma. Panisháatuna x̱álukt tiichámpa, ku papnúshana, paháashhaashshana.

There were maidens. They were living underground, and they were sleeping, they were resting.

Chaw íx̱wi pa'átshama, anakú íx̱wi iwachá k'pɨs, k'pɨs iwachá íchi tiichám. Chaw íx̱wi itsts'úupshana puuy. Ku pt'ilíma íx̱wi papnúshana.

They still weren't coming out, because it was still cold, this earth was cold. The snow had still not melted. And the girls were still sleeping.

Íkuuk awkú iwíihaykma, iwináchika wináawa hulí. Winaawayáy, anakw'ɨ́nk pawaníkx̱a Winaawayáy, iwináchika. Iwá ts'muuy hulí Winaawayáy.

That's when the warm wind came blowing down, arriving. Warm Wind, the one they call Warm Wind, arrived. Winaawayáy is a warm wind.

Awkú iwináchika ku ishapápuxna awkú ts’muuuy tł’áax̱w-
tuun, ku puuy awkú itsts’úupna.
Awkú iwánana chíish.

Then he came and blew warm air over everything and melted the snow. Then the water flowed.

Ku iwinachikúuna ttmayímaman ku i’ɨ́na, “Aah, lɨ́tsama, áw pam pimáwɨshuwata, ku pam aw átɨmta. Aw itx̱ánasha ts’muuy ku áw matash wa íchi íkuuk att, ku pam tiinmamíyaw pima’-isíkw’ata. Pimá’iniix̱ita pam shix̱.”

Then he came up to the girls, and he told them, “Ahh, little sisters, it’s time for you to prepare your-selves, and then you come out. Now it’s getting warm, and it’s time for you to come out and show yourselves to the people. Fix yourselves up real good.”

Ku íiix̱wi patáwḵ’umshana, ku awkú pawinátax̱shya.

And they were still lazing about, and then they started to wake up.

Pawípshanata awkú wapáwat, ku pimáwapawana awkú tł’aax̱w túkin wapáwatki.

They started bringing out their outfits and dressed themselves with all their decorations.

Ku nax̱sh awkú kwnak tmáy awkuuníik ipnúshana. Pat huuy áwitax̱shix̱ana. “Ámash táx̱shik! Aw iwá pináwɨshuwat, áwna iwánpisha yáyanɨm áwna yakút átta.”

And one girl still slept. They were having difficulty waking her. “Wake up now! Now it’s time to get yourself ready, now older brother is telling us to go out.”

“Aah, táaminwa pam imách’a kkáasa túkin. Íx̱wiish pnuwát’asha.”

“Oh, you’re always in a hurry about something. I’m still sleepy.”

Ku kw’áx̱i awkú pinátama-sklikɨnkika ku ipnúnkika. Tł’anx̱ awkú pátma ápimawɨshuwana.

And instead she turned herself over and went back to sleep. Meanwhile her older sisters were readying themselves.

Íkush awkú íkw'ak iwá Síkni íchi ikúuk. That's how Yellow Bell is today.

Ttmayíma papnúshana x̱álukt tiichámpa. The maidens were sleeping underground.

Winaawayáy iwináchika. Warm Wind arrived.

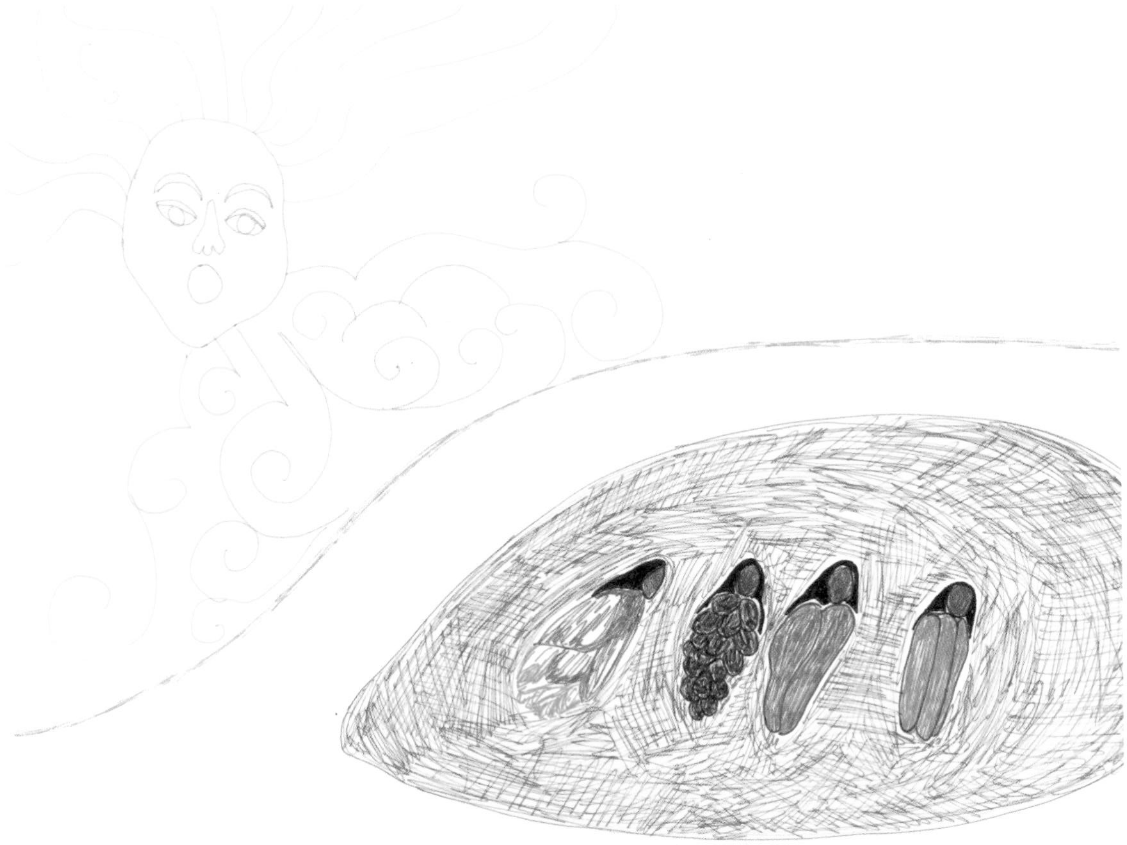

Ishapápuxna ts'muuuy tɬ'áax̱wtuun. He blew warm air over everything.

Ámash táx̱shik! Wake up!

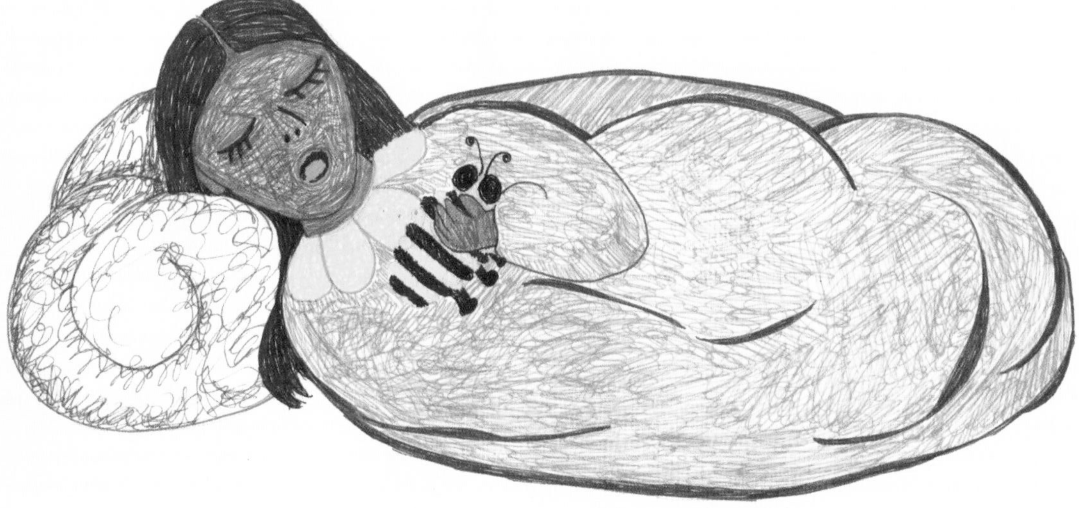

Ku na̱xsh tmáy awkuuníik ipnúshana. One maiden still slept.

Pimawɨshúwankika. The maidens readied themselves.

Iwyákw'miłkshana Sɨ́kni. Yellow Bell was late.

Pyax̱í ayáyat ilát'x̱sha. Bitterroot shines beautifully.

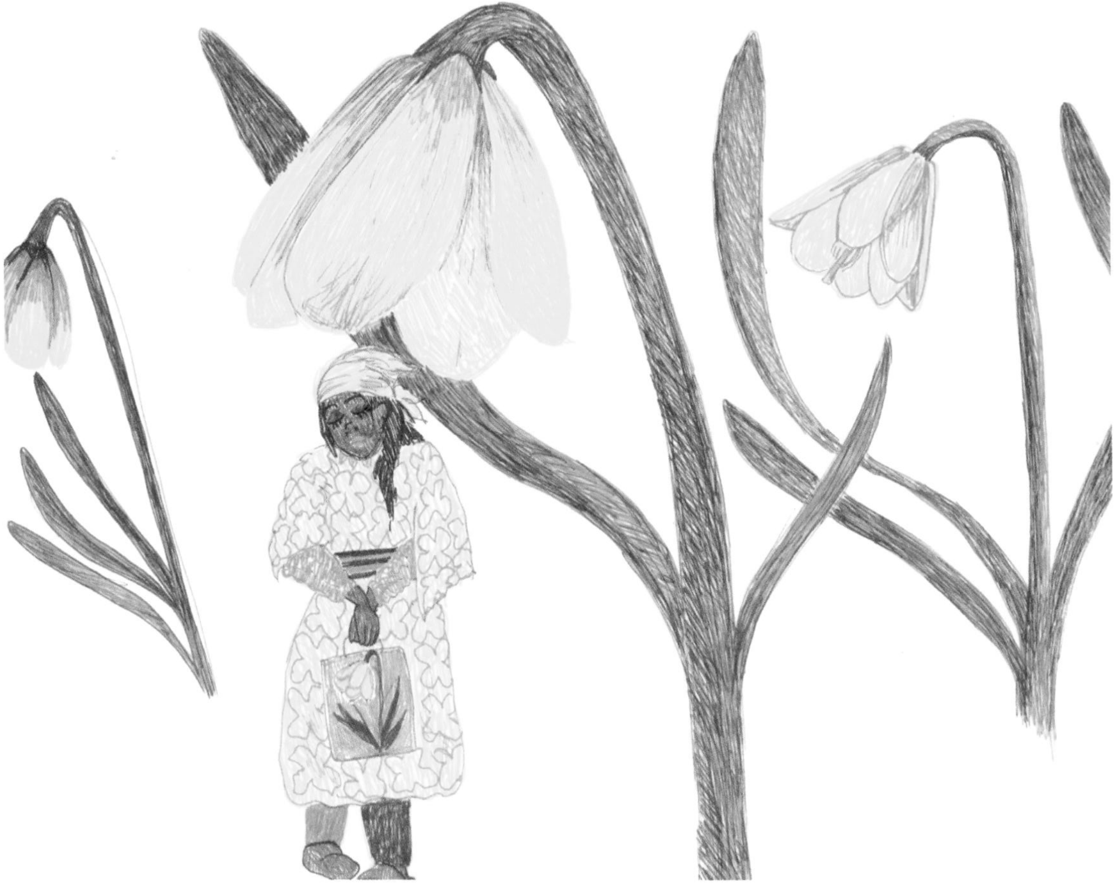

Sɨ́kni chawmún pináchax̱ɨlpanita tpɨsh Aanmíyaw. Yellow Bell never opens her face to the sun.

Spilyáy ku Ḵ’áx̱nu

(Related to “Legend of Prairie Chicken”)

Ichí iwá watít Winatshapammamí ḵ’ax̱numamíki.

This is a Winátshapam legend about the prairie chickens.

Áwacha nisháykt íkwnak k’pɨ́spa, ku kwnak áwacha ishích x̱wíimi íkush ɨlp p’ushtáypa, anakwnák iwánashamsh Nch’iwána.

They had a home over there up north, and they had a nest way up high on top of the hill, where the Columbia River flows this way.

Ku x̱wíimichnik kwnak áwacha nisháyaas.

They had a nest high up at their camping place.

Ku kwnak áwacha ishích káakɨm myánashma.

There they had a nest full of babies.

Ku awkú ɨ́na ḵ’áx̱nu áyatnan. “Aw na wíitł’x̱wsha tkwátat. Aw na waḵítatasha tkwátat kú na sáypta awkú myánashma. Aw pa’anáwisha.”

Then Prairie Chicken told his wife, “Our food is getting low. Let’s go look for food, and we will feed our children. They are hungry.”

Awkú pawínana, pawaḵítatana tkwátat.

And so they went. They went to look for food.

Pawyáalakwa myánashmaman,

They left the children.

ku áwacha wat’uymá myánash.

And they had an oldest child.

chaw áshukwaashana sɨ́nwit, chaw pasɨ́nwishana íx̱wi.

He was still unable to speak, they (all the children) didn't speak yet.

Kwmak myánashma íx̱wi pawachá wáawk'a ikks, ístamama pítpitma.

Those children were still too little, newborn chicks.

Ku pá'ɨna pshɨ́tin, "Shix̱ nam ánaktkwaninta. Chaw nam miin áshapawinata. Chaw nam shiin áshapa'ashta."

And the father told (the oldest), "Take care of them. Don't let them go anywhere. Don't let anyone inside."

Ḵa'áwtya awkú iwachá paykłá kw'ɨnk wat'uymá.

He was quick and obedient, that oldest one.

Awkú pawyáalakwa.

So they left the children.

Ku pɨ́nch'a Spilyáy ikwíitama, Nch'iwánapa.

In the meantime, that Spilyáy was coming along down the Columbia River.

Uuii ḵw'á'ash ḵw'á'ash iwyatkw'anátisha.

He was strutting along.

"Ínk nash wa shíx̱tx̱aw tł'aax̱wmaamíknik. Ínk nash wa wát'uy tł'aax̱wmaamíknik," iwyáwanpsha.

"I am the best of all. I am better than everyone," he comes along singing those words.

"Ink nash wa shíx̱tx̱aw ḵ'ínupa tł'aax̱wmaamíknik. Ink nash wa wapsúuux̱ tł'aax̱wmaamíknik," iwyáwanpsha.

"I am the best looking of all, I am the wisest of all," he comes along singing.

Ḵw'á'ash ḵw'á'ash ináwatiksha.

Strutting, strutting, he comes stepping along singing.

Awkú "Aah ínx̱ay ḵ'áx̱nu íchna mɨnán inisháatwa. Pa'ínx̱anash íchna mɨnán áwa nisháykt. Áw nash áwii'ashuuta kush paysh laak pasáypta, awsh anáwisha."

And so, "Ah, my friend Prairie Chicken lives here somewhere. They told me his home was here. I'll stop and visit a while; they might feed me, I am hungry."

Awkú iwyánawiyuuna. "Aah, íchix̱ash áwa nisháykt."

And he arrived there. "This must be his house."

Ku kwnak i'ashúuna, "Myánashmasim. Mɨnán iwá ɨtút?" ishápnya.

He went in. "Only the children are there. Where's your father?" he asked.

Chchúuuu, chaw pat áwiinpa.

Quiet, nobody answered him.

"Shápnisha mash, mɨnán iwá ɨtút?"

"I'm asking you, where's your father?"

Chchuu, pak'úsha, awkú mayk nch'íki, "Mɨnán iwá ɨtút? Páysh nam chaw páwiinpta, ku matash tíwita!"

They huddled together, then a little louder, "Where's your father? If you don't answer me, I will beat all of you up!"

Awkú wat'uymá iyíkshana. Ku chaw ishúkwaashana sɨ́nwit.

Then the oldest understood. He didn't know how to talk.

Ku itɬúpwiiɬtx̱a kwnak ishíchpa, ku iwápwiluuka Spilyáynan anakú iwachá iksíks íx̱wi, ku iwápwiluuka . . .

He jumped up to the edge of the nest, he looked up at Spilyáy, he was little yet, and he looked up at him . . .

"Ḵunḵúun shɨ́papap! Ḵunḵúun shɨ́papap!"

"Ḵunḵúun shɨ́papap! Ḵunḵúun shɨ́papap!"

Ku pátk'ina Spilyáyin, "Mísh nam nuu? Ḵunḵúun shɨ́papap! Tun awkú kw'ink íkw'ak iwá sɨ́nwit, Ḵunḵúun shɨ́papap?

Spilyáy stared at him, "What are you saying? Ḵunḵúun shɨ́papap! What kind of language is that? Ḵunḵúun shɨ́papap?

Ɨ́nx̱a mash, shápnisha mash, mɨnán iwa ɨtút?"

I'm saying to you, I'm asking you, where is your father?"

"Uu tł'aax̱w mish?" ánach'ax̱i nch'íki, iháashɨnkika wíyatyaw ku ishapá'atma "Ḵunḵúun shɨ́papap!"

"Oh, how to do this?" Again, louder, he took a deep breath, way down deep, and then let it out, "Ḵunḵúun shɨ́papap!"

"Aah pawawtk'íwishaam! Mísh nam awkú íkush páwiinpsha? Cháw nash áshukwaasha tun aw kw'ɨnk íkw'ak iwá, Ḵunḵúun shɨ́papap.

"You're trying to make a fool of me! Why are you answering me like that? I don't understand what that is, Ḵunḵúun shɨ́papap.

Áw mash tł'áax̱wsimk'a shápnisha, páysh nam chaw pá'ɨnta mɨnán iwá ɨtút, ku matash tł'aax̱w ítł'yawita, wáwtł'ikta matash."

I'm asking you for the last time, and if you don't tell me where your dad is, I'll kill you all; I will club all of you to death."

Uu awkú iskáwna pítpit. Awkú nch'íkitx̱aw wíyatyaw iháashtkw'ka awkú ishapá'atma "Ḵunḵúuuuuun shɨ́papap!"

The chick became frightened. And with the loudest voice, he took a deep breath, way down deep, and then let it out, "Ḵunḵúuuuuun shɨ́papap!"

"Áah matash tł'aax̱w wáwtł'ikta!"

"I'm going to beat you all to death!"

Tł'áax̱w awkú iwáwtł'ika myánashmaman. Iwɨ́npa ílkwaas ku iwáwtł'ika tł'áax̱wmaman, ku iwáanakwa kwnák papúxsha.

Then he beat all of the children to death. He grabbed a stick and beat them all to death, and he left them there, scattered everywhere.

Awkú itkw'á'anaakwa. "Ḵunḵúun shɨ́papap. Tun awkú kw'ɨnk Ḵunḵúun shɨ́papap? Pawawtk'íwishaash."

Then he walked away and left them. "Ḵunḵúun shɨpapap. What is that, Ḵunḵúun shɨpapap? They're making a fool out of me."

Awkú itkw'á'anaakwa.

And he walked away.

Patúx̱shana awkú ḵ'áx̱nu áyatin. Uuu! Aah, tł'áax̱wpa ápuxsha myánashma, tł'yáwiyi.

Prairie Chicken and his wife came home. Their children were dead and scattered all around.

"Áana, mish na tx̱ána myánashma, tł'áax̱w wáwtł'yawiyi." Uuu, ayatúks ináx̱tisha.

"What has happened to our children? They are all dead from a beating." The female is crying.

Paḵ'ínaniya wátiksh Spilyáynan. "Aah Spilyáyx̱ash íchi íkush ikúya. Aw na áwaḵitatasha."

They saw Spilyáy's tracks. "Ah, Spilyáy must have done this. Let's go look for him."

Pat awkú áshyaka.

Then they scouted for him.

"Iii, íchi ákwiita íkuuni." Pat áwiyax̱nanya.

"Oh, here the tracks are going that way." They found him.

Awkú pawiilúuka x̱wíimi ku pawíihaykma. Páwiipt'ana, náx̱shin chɨ́nik páwiihaykuuna ku páwiipt'ana.

They flew up and then came down. The first one hit him on one side and the other from the other side.

"Mísh pam mísha, x̱ay, aa, x̱ay, íchiish wa x̱ay! Mísh pam tx̱ánasha?"

"What are you doing friend, hey! I am your friend! What's happening to you?" (Coyote whimpers.)

Pat áwiipt'ax̱ana. Huuy piná'iłamaykanishana łamtɨ́x.

They collided again. He tried in vain to protect his head.

Pat áwiipt'ana, pat awkú ána-nayka, awkú ánanayka, ts'áa wánayaw. Ku kwnak iwachá k̲'mɨł.

They hit him and forced him along, forced him along, close to the river. And there was a cliff there.

Kuuk pat awkú nɨmnawít áwinanp'ana papúuchnik tł'áayawit. Ku tilíwal tł'áax̲wkan áwit'iishka.

Then they really hit him; they were attacking fiercely, coming together from both sides until he died. And his blood spilled everywhere.

Ku ix̲átamawiyawnana íkuuni wánakan. Awkú kwnak k̲'mɨ́łpa awkú áyawiihaykma.

He fell over that way towards the river. And there his blood poured down the cliff.

Tł'aax̲w awkú tł'áyawyi ik̲á'ɨsha Spilyáy. Kwnak awkú ilá'ɨshana.

All dead, Spilyáy lay crumpled there. There he lay.

Kwak maal. Mɨł kwak putáptit anwíkt tł'aax̲w x̲yáawk'a awkú iwachá íkush.

No one knows how long, probably hundreds of years. He dried up as he lay thus.

Ikwíitama Luts'ayáy, páwya'iyax̲na.

Red Fox came along; he was going along and found him.

"Aa, mishx̲ash íchi ínx̲ay imíya pɨ́nx̲i? Áwx̲ash iwyákwshtikshana."

"Oh, my friend, what must he have done? He must have been doing wrong."

Ku páwiiyawnana páx̲aam. Kw'áx̲i itáx̲shiya Spilyáy, mmm.

And then he stepped over him five times. Spilyáy woke up.

"Aah, áwx̲ash shaláwiya ku x̲átikw'ika pnúna."

"I must have gotten tired and fell over and slept," said Spilyáy.

Luts'ayáyin pá'ɨna, "Aah, x̱átikw'i-kaam. Wyákwshtikshx̱aam. Nah, túpan nam wyákwshtika? Túpan nam wyákwshtika? Mísh nam míya?"

Fox replied, "Ah, you 'fell over.' You must have done something wrong. Nah, what did you do now? You must have done something. What did you do?"

Awkú pinátamapayshka. "Íkush nash kúya."

And then Spilyáy confessed. "This is what I did."

"Aw mash íchi ítax̱shi, kú nam aw kw'áx̱i wa wák̲'ish. Ku chɨ́nik łkw'íknik chaw nam mun ánach'ax̱i áwitł'yawita k̲'áx̱numaman." Tamánwitki pá'iskawka.

"Now I have awakened you, and you have become alive again. And from this day on, you will never again kill prairie chickens." Red Fox issued Creator's words.

"Kuu mish, kuu mish," inánax̱tya Spilyáy.

"Okay, okay," whimpered Spilyáy.

"Páysh nam chaw páykta, ku mash shapátux̱ta íkwɨn anam kwnak wachá."

"If you don't listen, I'll put you back to where you were."

"Chaw, áw nash . . . áw nash shix̱ wáta! Cháw nash ánach'ax̱i mun áwitł'yawita k̲'áx̱numaman."

"No, I'll be, I'll be good! I'll never again kill prairie chickens."

Íkush awkú iwá íchi íkuuk. Cháwmun spílya ítł'yawita k̲'áx̱numaman. Íchi ikúuk, táaminwa.

That's the way it is now. A coyote never kills prairie chickens. That's the way it is today and forever.

Notes on Culture, Education, and Language

In this section, we present additional information to show the importance and depth of the legends and lessons and to help readers understand their ongoing relevance. We also include information about the Yakama Ichishkíin language.

ABOUT THE LEGENDS

The Elders and storytellers stress that the legends have a deeper purpose than entertainment (although they should be entertaining!). Here we explain some of the cultural traditions and contexts that are the foundation of Yakama legends.

Experiencing a Legend

In the following, we describe the importance of legends and the traditional and contemporary settings in which legends and stories are told. In doing so, we portray the storytelling/listening experience as it has always been experienced by Yakama people as well as how these traditions are carried on in contemporary times. Storytelling has always been a treasured form of education and community-building for our people and continues to serve these important functions today.

In the section "Traditional Child Raising," a storytelling setting is described, with children listening attentively to an Elder. The legends are presented here in written form, but it is important to keep in mind that they are intended to be experienced through listening. In recalling her experiences as a child, Virginia notes that Elder storytellers (then and now) move around as they relate the story. They illustrate the legends with their body movements and facial expressions as well as the tone of their voices. They pretend to be Coyote sneaking up or a threatening creature. And the children are engaged by the Elders' actions because they have to respond verbally (*nay!* or *ii!*). They have a role as well, something to wait for, wondering "when will it be our time to speak?" This tradition also affirms that each individual at the gathering in which a story is told is an important part of the collective.

Multiple versions exist of each legend. They vary by storyteller and family as well as setting, as an Elder may adapt the telling to a particular audience. Because of the tradition of visiting and sharing across Tribes, some Tribal peoples may have similar versions as well, depending on whether storytellers were traveling and sharing the legends. A version included in this book may not be exactly the same as you have seen or heard it elsewhere. This variation adds to the richness of the stories and storytellers. This is apparent in the legends we have added in the Ichishkíin language; they are slightly different than the ones in the 1974 text.

Repetition is an important part of each legend. It is used for emphasis and to heighten the drama as well as to help the children remember things. Things may be repeated three times, sometimes five times, maybe more or less, depending on the legend and context. Virginia explains that when someone is brought back to life in the legends, they are stepped over three, four, or five times. This is just one example of how numbers are important in our culture. In the legends, repetition reconnects listeners/readers with these important numbers. Sometimes phrases or episodes are repeated word for word, and sometimes there's a rephrasing to help emphasize an important point or to fix it in the listener's mind.

The number five is meaningful in our religion and connects back to legendary time, when the animal people were here, and the First People established the days of the week, composing of five days. What we now refer to as Saturday and Sunday did not count, as these days have special meaning: *Tamáts'aakt* (Saturday; from the verb *tamáts'aak-*, approach) means it is getting closer to Holy Day, and *Sapálwit* (Sunday) is Holy Day. Virginia explains that in her childhood, she was taught not to do anything on Sunday but rest, as it is a Holy Day of rest. When she was a little girl, Virginia was told all beings were worshipping on that day, including grasshoppers and ants. “Don’t step on them or kill them,” she was instructed, and she remembers having to be very careful when outside to not step on the beings who were worshipping. In Virginia’s youth, most of the Holy Day was spent inside, with singing and praying taking place.

Legend Locations and the Natural World

Storytelling is a winter activity, but the events of the legends take place year-round and seasonally, according to the traditions we follow each year. The legends help listeners to be aware of the seasonal round, even though they are perhaps sitting indoors and far from where the legend takes place. You are walking through the forest, you are by a lake, you are going over the mountains—even as you sit indoors on a dark and cold winter day. Within these stories, humans are humble creatures who only exist in our region today because other beings permitted this to be so (Jacob 2020b). Familiar geographic places gain a deep significance.

In this book, legends are located particularly along the Columbia River, which separates present-day Oregon and Washington, but Yakama stories have as far a geographic reach as the Rocky Mountains and Great Plains, to the Pacific Ocean and all the way to Hawai’i, to what is now Southern Oregon and Northern California, to what we now think of as the U.S.-Canadian border. Learning about the Yakama cultural, historical, and philosophical meanings of place allows us to “see” the natural world differently and increases our sense of relationship and responsibility to place and the environment (Jacob 2013). Such lessons are important for all humans to learn but especially for children who today often spend most of their time indoors. Stories can be a powerful way to reconnect people with place. When one drives along the Columbia River with the legends in mind, Lyle, Washington, is not just a small town but the place that Eel slid into the river, winning his race with Rattlesnake. The map highlights some legend locations, and place-names are identified in the glossaries.

Gender Roles and Power

Sometimes students begin reading *Anakú Iwachá* and notice how there is a gendered social order in some of the stories. Questions can arise: Are women really expected to walk behind men? Do men hit women? These examples are in the stories. Gender is important in Yakama culture. It is a way of connecting, and when a gender identity is nurtured in a supportive way, it is a proud part of a person's identity—to be a strong Yakama woman or a strong Yakama man is a high honor. Other scholars have written about gender roles in Plateau culture (e.g., Ackerman 1996; Jacob 2013, 2016). Here we will encourage readers to thoughtfully engage with the legends and find the multiple messages contained within them. For example, male figures are more prominent in visible public leadership roles; we see that Coyote is highly visible as a main character in many stories. Yet when he is in a jam, Coyote consistently turns to his sisters for counsel. He recognizes the superior wisdom of his sisters but is often too conceited to fully acknowledge this. We encourage readers to witness the power of the beautiful stories in this book and to understand the central cultural teaching of the unique and necessary gifts of all genders.

Body Parts and Sex

Oh no! Did we write *sex* in this book? Ii! (Yes!) We know that some students and readers will associate sex and body parts related to reproduction with being "naughty." Yet in Yakama cultural teachings, all children and adults are encouraged to be knowledgeable about their bodies and to take care of themselves. If children do not know the names of their "private parts" and what their functions are, how can they be expected to be responsible? How can they be expected to know their bodies are sacred and should be respected by everyone? Their bodies should never be violated. No human should ever violate another. In some of the stories within this book, sex organs are named and discussed. This was the way that Elders and storytellers traditionally educated children.

When asked, Virginia tells students about storytellers who used to provide all of this instruction. The storytellers would educate the girls: When a man touches you there (and points to her body) without your permission then you fight! The storytellers would educate the children through talking about nature and reproduction, using birds, horses, and other animals as examples, and explain that sex is part of marriage and producing children. That was one way that children were taught about life. Virginia said she grew up with this instruction and that all children were taught their responsibilities; boys were taught how to responsibly treat girls. When Christianity became more prominent in our communities, children became more ignorant about their bodies, and without basic teachings, there is easily a sense a shame around one's body.

There are clear lessons about the consequences of disrespectful behavior in the stories. For example, T'at'ałíya is sexually aggressive, and this leads to her getting killed. The lesson is to not get involved with bad people, to not be overly sexual, and to not overwhelm people. It is an example meant to educate children to make good decisions with their bodies and to understand their bodies are precious; they need to respect themselves and others. Today, Virginia instructs students and teachers to check with their schools and communities about what they want taught. We hope that the stories in this book will encourage all readers to be educated about their bodies and how precious they are, to carry themselves respectfully, and to respect all other beings.

Violence and Trouble

Virginia has explained that lessons about violence and trouble are also contained within the stories. Terrible things sometimes happen in legends, teaching us that life will not be 100 percent positive. Bad things happen, along with good things. There are many ways to get into trouble or for trouble to find you. Coyote often dies from getting into trouble. Readers can learn from his mistakes and also reflect on how different characters handle the trouble in their lives.

Another lesson found in legends is that death is a part of life. Death in legends does not necessarily last forever—and we see this when the same characters show up in multiple legends or when Red Fox wakes Coyote, who has been lying dead. Virginia contrasted this to the prophets who died and came back with a message for the people—but after that they died for good. Virginia has reminded us that we see related examples in other stories as well, for example, with Jesus, Lazarus, and other Bible stories. The legends are a wonderful source of entertainment, yet they also have deep lessons that can provide us with good opportunities to reflect on our own lives and how we want to conduct ourselves.

ABOUT THE LANGUAGE

The Elders from whom the legends were collected spoke a number of dialects of Ichishkíin (also called Sahaptin). Ichishkíin is spoken and taught at Tribal areas and Nations along the Columbia River and its tributaries. People refer to the dialects by their individual names or by the collective terms *Sahaptin* or *Ichishkíin*. There are approximately thirteen dialects. The dialects are mutually intelligible, meaning that a speaker of one could readily understand a speaker of another. Typically Elders knew multiple languages and dialects.

Members of the fourteen bands and tribes of the Yakama Nation speak predominantly Ichishkíin and also Salish and Chinookan languages. Virginia's language is Yakama Ichishkíin. We have used the Yakama practical alphabet for all of the Ichishkíin in the book. Across the dialects of Ichishkíin are slight differences in some of the words and the spelling systems that are used. For that reason, you will not find all of the words included here in other Yakama materials, like the dictionary (Beavert and Hargus 2009).

The Yakama Ichishkíin Sound System and the Practical Alphabet

The Yakama practical alphabet was developed by Tribal Elders with linguist Dr. Bruce Rigsby in the 1970s. This spelling system is now used in other published works (Beavert and Hargus 2009; Beavert 2017) and teaching and learning materials. Each letter represents one sound in Ichishkíin. Many of the letters and sounds are similar to English language sounds. Other sounds are new to learners.

All of the letters of the Yakama practical alphabet are presented in the following chart:

’	a	aa	ch	ch’	h	i	ii	ɨ	k	k’	kw	kw’
k̲	k̲’	k̲w	k̲w’	l	ł	m	n	p	p’	s	sh	t
t’	tł	tł’	ts	ts’	u	uu	w	x	xw	x̱	x̱w	y

Below are example words from *Anakú Iwachá* for each letter:

LETTER NAME	LETTER	EXAMPLE WORD	TRANSLATION
glottal stop	’	a’a	crow
short *a*	a	ámash	owl
long *aa*	aa	aan	sun
soft *ch*	ch	chcháya	juneberry, service berry
hard *ch’*	ch’	ch’íya	woodpecker, flicker

LETTER NAME	LETTER	EXAMPLE WORD	TRANSLATION
h	h	hulí	wind
short *i*	i	íkuuk	now, today
long *ii*	ii	ii	yes
barred *ɨ*	ɨ	ɨwínsh	man
soft front *k*	k	kákya	bird, animal
hard front *k'*	k'	k'álas	raccoon
soft front *k w*	kw	kwikwɬá	whistling marmot
hard front *k w'*	kw'	kw'áykw'ay	wren
soft back *k̠*	k̠	k̠ayx̠	light, daylight, brightness
hard back *k̠'*	k̠'	k̠'áx̠nu	prairie chicken
soft back *k̠ w*	k̠w	K̠wilkúla	name of a rock at Wíshx̠am
hard back *k̠ w'*	k̠w'	k̠w'áshk̠w'ash	crane
l	l	lákas	mouse
barred *ɬ*	ɬ	ɬkw'i	day
m	m	mɨsís	ground squirrel, chipmunk
n	n	nank	cedar tree
soft *p*	p	Pátu	mountain, Mount Adams
hard *p'*	p'	p'ushtáy	hill
s	s	sɨ́kni	yellow bell, buttercup
s h	sh	shɨ́shaash	porcupine
soft *t*	t	tax̠ús	milkweed hemp
hard *t'*	t'	T'at'aɬíya	Witch Woman
t barred *ɬ*	tɬ	tɬupwináynak-	jump into
hard *t'* barred *ɬ*	tɬ'	tɬ'aax̠w	all
soft *t s*	ts	tsúɬim	buffalo
hard *t s'*	ts'	ts'muy	warm (of weather or comfort)
short *u*	u	útpaas	blanket, robe
long *uu*	uu	uu	or
w	w	wáx̠push	rattlesnake
front *x*	x	xyaaw	dry
front *x w*	xw	xwyach	sweathouse
back *x̠*	x̠	x̠awsh	breadroot
back *x̠w*	x̠w	x̠wɨ́ɬx̠wiɬ	meadowlark
y	y	yiityíit	sandpiper

VOWEL SOUNDS

There are four vowel sounds. They are represented by the letters *i*, *u*, *a*, *ɨ*.

- *i* is pronounced like the vowel in the English word *ski*.
- *u* is pronounced like the vowel in the English word *moo*.
- *a* is pronounced like the first vowel in the English word *father*.
- Depending on what sounds are around the vowel and how fast the speaker is talking, the sound may change slightly—the *i* may sound more the vowel in the English word *bit*, the *u* like the vowel sound in *foot*, and the *a* like the vowel sound in the English word *pup*.
- *ɨ* (barred *i*) is close to the sound of the first vowel in the English word *supply*. It is barely there.

Vowel length is important in Ichishkíin—for example, the word *wásha-* means *ride*, but *wáasha-* means *dance*. Long vowels in Ichishkíin are *ii*, *uu*, and *aa*. The sound is held out for a longer duration than the corresponding short vowel. The vowel *ɨ* never occurs as a long vowel.

CONSONANT SOUNDS

For many of the consonants, your skills as a speaker of English will help you. Consonant sounds represented by the letters *ł*, *k̲*, *x*, *x̱* may be new to you:

- *ł* (barred *l*) is a voiceless lateral fricative. It is made by placing the tip of the tongue behind your upper front teeth and moving air through the sides of the mouth. Try setting your mouth to make an English *l*, smile slightly, then blow gently.
- *k̲* (back *k̲*) is a stop made farther back in the mouth than front *k* and *t*. It is a uvular stop, made with the back of the tongue pulled up and back to touch the far back of the mouth/upper throat. This is the area of the uvula. The sound is spelled with a *q* in other regional alphabets.
- *x̱* (back *x̱*) is a uvular fricative, made with the back of the tongue pulled up and back towards the far back area of the mouth, in the same area of the mouth used to pronounce *k̲*. The tongue does not touch the mouth to block off air.

- *x* (front *x*) is not a very common sound in Ichishkíin. It is a velar fricative, made by placing the tongue and mouth in the same position as you do to pronounce *k* but without blocking off the air.
- The apostrophe is a letter that represents a glottal stop. It occurs on its own and also with other consonants to indicate glottalized consonants. The glottal stop is made by closing the vocal folds to stop the air and the sound from coming out, as in between the syllables of the Ichishkíin word *a’a* (crow) or the English expression *uh-oh.* This same vocal fold action is used to create a glottal stop.

Some of the consonant sounds are written with two letters. These are called digraphs. For example, the letters *ch* and *sh* are digraphs. (The digraphs *ch* and *sh* are pronounced the same in Ichishkíin as they are in English.) Some digraphs include new sounds: *ḵw, xw, x̱ w,* and *tł*. When *ḵ*, *x̱* , or *x* are followed by *w*, it means the sounds are pronounced with the lips rounded, as with the beginning of the Ichishkíin word *kwyaam* (true) or the English word *quick*.

ACCENT MARKS AND STRESS

The writing system indicates with an accent mark which syllable of a word is stressed. Single syllable words are not always written with an accent mark. The stressed syllable has a raised pitch and intensity, so it is a little higher and louder than the surrounding syllables. Stress is important, as word meanings depend on it. The word *paḵ’ínusha*, with the second syllable stressed, means “they are seeing someone or something,” but *páḵ’inusha*, with the stress on the first syllable, means “s/he is seeing somebody.”

Legend Names

Names of legendary animals have the suffixes *-yáy*, *-yáaya*, or *-ya* added to a common animal name. *Spilyáy* (Coyote) from s*pílya* (coyote) is the best-known example. During the time of legends, animals had human characteristics; they could speak and reason as humans. They are treated as human in the grammatical markings of the language. There is variation between legend-tellers, dialects, and even within legends as to what version of the legendary name is used. For example, *Tiskáaya*, *Tiskayáaya*, and *Tiskayáy* from *tiskáy* (skunk) are all used by *X̠wáłwaypam* Klikitat speaker Joe Hunt in Melville Jacobs's 1929 texts. For Virginia, *Spilyáaya* is used to refer to Coyote as a holy man and *Spilyáy* to the Coyote with crazy antics who exemplifies ways not to behave.

The legendary animal names in *Anakú Iwachá* are listed below:

ámush – Amushyáy	monetaria shell
asúm – Asumyáy	eel/lamprey
átya – Atyayáaya	north wind
áx̠shax̠sh – Ax̠shax̠shyáy	dentalium
aykws – Aykwíisya	cottontail rabbit
k'álas – K'aláasya	raccoon
k'astilá – K'astilayáaya, K'astilayáy	crawfish
kw'áykw'ay – Kw'aykw'ayyáy	wren
k̠w'áshk̠w'ash – K̠w'ashk̠w'ashyáy	crane
lákas – Lakáaya	mouse
skɨlwisá – Skɨlwisayáy	ant
spílya – Spilyáy, Spilyáaya	coyote
t'wíita – Twit'áaya	grizzly bear
tsúłɨm – Tsułɨmyáy, Tsułɨmyáaya	buffalo
wawá – Wawayáy	mosquito
wáx̠push – Wax̠púshyay, Wax̠púuya	rattlesnake
wilalík – Wilaalikyáy	jackrabbit
wináawa – Winaawayáy	Chinook wind, south wind
wíx̠insh – Wɨx̠inshyáy	abalone
x̠átxat – X̠átx̠áatya	duck
yiityíit – Yiityíitya	sandpiper

Not all of the legendary animals have a legend suffix in the version of the legend in this book. For example, *Misís* (Ground Squirrel, Chipmunk) is sometimes called *Misisyáy*. Other legend characters have names that don't seem to be related to a common noun, like *Típikat* (Duck). And Red Fox's name, *Luts'ayáy*, is related to the word *luts'á* (red), not the common word for fox.

Humans in the Grammar

Throughout Ichishkíin grammar, a distinction is made among three categories of animacy: humans, other animate beings, and inanimate things. Humans—and legendary characters that are treated as human—have the most distinctive treatment in the grammar. One way this shows up is in a special set of numbers used only for humans.

	NON-HUMAN	HUMAN
1	*nax̱sh*	*laxs*
2	*niipt*	*nápu*
3	*mɨ́taat*	*mɨ́taaw*
4	*píniipt*	*pínapu*
5	*páx̱aat*	*páx̱naw*
10	*pútɨmpt*	*pútmu*

You can find the human number for two in the Ichishkíin legend "Anakú Itx̱ánana Aan" and the number for three in "Ḵw'ashḵw'ashmí Watít, ku Túyaw Alashikmí Psa Átx̱anana (Watít Atachiishpamá Ttmayimamíki)."

Family Terms

The Ichishkíin language has a large set of words for family members. This indicates the profound cultural importance of family ties and relationships. A child has specific and unique relationships with his or her *káɫa* (mother's mother), *tíla* (mother's father), *ála* (father's mother), and *púsha* (father's father). In "Ḵw'ashḵw'ashmí Watít, ku Túyaw Alashikmí Psa Átx̱anana (Watít Atachiishpamá Ttmayimamíki)," the older two girls were taught how to behave by their maternal grandparents.

Words for grandparent and grandchild relationships are the same. So, a man's daughter's child is *tíla*, as is a girl's mother's father. In "Legend about Winaawayáy," the grandmother calls to her grandson, "*Áana, chxw ála*" (Oh, my beloved grandson).

Virginia teaches the importance of maintaining all four titles and noted that the English language does not keep the distinction. This can lead to translation problems. For example, in "Legend about Winaawayáy," both maternal and paternal grandparents have roles. This information is included in the legend when the grandparents of the young Winaawayáy are introduced but not at each time they are mentioned. So, the reader has to keep track, which are the sea creatures? (His maternal grandparents, *káła* and *tíla*.) Which grandparents are Tick and Louse? (His paternal grandparents *ála* and *púsha*.)

There are specific prefixed terms for "my (relation)" and "your (relation)" and a special form of addressing the relative, used in speaking to or calling out to them. For example, *pat* (older sister of a man or woman) has the associated terms *nanánas* (my older sister), *anísh* (your older sister), and *nána* ("Sister!"). Siblings and cousins are often referred to with the same terms: *pat* could be an older sister or older female cousin.

Átway is used before the proper name or relationship term of someone who is deceased. And the terms for sister- and brother-in-law change to *awít* after the spouse's death. This word is used for both men and women. In "Legend of the Crane," Crane tries to steal Crow's *awít* (here it is his dead brother's widow, but in a different context the word could also refer to a male relative). The term *awít* reflects the traditional practice of maintaining family ties by marrying a spouse's sibling after the death of the spouse. The importance of traditional arranged marriage for strengthening families is described by Virginia Beavert-Martin as "a custom which reinforced the traditions, culture, and linguistic stability within their clans, and was usually done for sound economic advantages as well" (Beavert 1999, 65). Marrying a husband's or wife's sibling kept those ties in place.

NOTES ON LEGENDS IN ICHISHKÍIN AND ENGLISH

The cultural teachings of the four legends in Ichishkíin and English included in this new edition are described below. We also discuss language, location, and the significance of the characters and what happens in the legends.

K̲w'ashk̲w'ashmí Watít, ku Túyaw Alashikmí Psa Átx̲anana (Watít Atachiishpamá Ttmayimamíki)

In retelling this legend, Virginia noted that the three episodes in the version she told are sometimes related as stand-alone legends. "Amushyáy and Wɨxinshyáy" is the related legend in the 1974 edition.

CULTURAL TEACHINGS

This legend carries important teachings about humility and looking beyond physical appearance. Dentalium is self-absorbed and pays little attention to the world around her. She was not taught how to behave as were her older sisters. She was in a rush to get to Coyote's son. Crane calls her conceited and therefore flips her into the water. She has a lesson to learn. Coyote's son, too, is arrogant and conceited. He is violent towards the maidens, and even when he reconsiders his actions and tries to find them, it is because he heard they were good looking, not because he is repentant. Crane takes action against him as well, making him ill. When Coyote's son comes to face the Creator, there are further consequences. He is turned into a stone as an example of the importance of valuing people not for physical qualities but for their good hearts. Creator says, "Respect everybody. Take some time to see their heart. Don't think only of yourself."

Turtle shows that those who may not fit our mold of a strong, effective, or beautiful person may have qualities that make them best suited for doing what needs to be done. Turtle was the only one of all the creatures who could rescue Dentalium, even though he was old and had not volunteered for the task. The animals who dove into the water to show their strength all failed. Humble people can do things you may never expect of them.

THE SONG

The maidens sing a song after Coyote rejects them. A dance, the Cry Dance, accompanies the song and is performed by a group of young girls. The song begins as the girls leave Coyote's son: he has beaten and embarrassed them instead of marrying them. The beat is slow, and they cry as they sing. They move slowly, with sorrow in their postures, and they cry, wiping their tears, which flow constantly. However, as they sing, they realize that they are better off: "He must be a bad man, with a bad heart, we are happy to not be married to him!" The drumbeat picks up, and the dancers raise their faces and point their toes. They stand tall and are joyful in their movements, lightly bouncing and spreading joy first to the right and then to the left. The song helped them get beyond their hurt and realize their good fortune.

Anakú Itx̱ánana Aan

When you look up at the full moon after reading this legend, you will forever see Frog in Moon's eye. "Legend about the Sun and Moon" also tells the story of these two traveling brothers.

CULTURAL TEACHINGS

The lesson of this legend is to never make fun of somebody. Moon had a choice, and he chose to make fun of Frog. He did not work to better himself. As a result, he can only come out at night. Sun, who did not insult anyone, gets to be out in the daytime and did not sacrifice his beauty. To share this lesson, adults would take the children out at the full moon and show them Frog on Moon's eye, telling them, "Don't pull your eyelids down to people (make faces at people); it is insulting and it is not kind."

Another lesson, akin to those in other legends, is to not think too highly of oneself. The bird when painted became proud of herself, and she neglected her duty. The dog was then in danger and was attacked and hurt.

LOCATION

This legend takes place along the Upper Columbia River, and Ribbon Cliff, where the dog's blood was spilled, is around three miles north of Entiat, Washington. There is a highway pullout and information sign there. This is not the only story to explain how Ribbon Cliff came to be painted with blood; "Legend of Prairie Chicken" also tells of blood spilled to create Ribbon Cliff.

LANGUAGE NOTES

Verbs are complex and descriptive in the Ichishkíin language. Their intricate structure can include many parts, each contributing a particular meaning. A single word can express an entire sentence or thought, as with *pawisalílx̱ana* (they used to hunt) and *pax̱níshana* (they were digging roots). Many concepts that are built into the verb in Ichishkíin need to be expressed by additional words in English. In this legend, there are two examples with the verb *tłup-* (jump). This verb can be used on its own: *itłúpsha* (s/he is jumping). The prefix *i-* indicates that she or he is the actor, the main verb is *tłup-* (jump), and the suffix *-sha* is like English *-ing*, indicating that the action is ongoing. In the legend, we see two sentences that include the verb *tłup-* (jump):

Awku itłúpwiliina, itłúpwiliina chíishyaw, Nch'iwánayaw . . .
Then he jumped into the water, jumped into the water, into the Columbia River . . .

Ku átłupwinaynaka Alx̱ayx̱míyaw áchaashyaw.
And she jumped into Moon's eye.

In these sentences the core verbs are *tłúpwilii-* (jump into water) and *tłupwináynak-* (jump into). The difference in the suffixes on *tłup-* account for the difference in meaning. Both include a suffix *-wi*, which stresses movement and speed. The suffix *-lii* means "into water." The suffix *-náynak* also means into but into something other than water. It could be used for putting your foot into your shoe, for example. In this case, what is jumped into is Moon's eye!

USEFUL PHRASES

This legend contains a number of verbs and sentences to use regularly in everyday speaking:

Pawisalílsha.	They are hunting.
Paxnísha.	They are digging roots.
Lalíwashamash!	I miss you!
Aw mash wapíitata.	Now I will help you.
Chaw pam pápatalwaskta.	Do not gossip.
Piná'ishix̱ita táaminwa.	Always work to better yourself.
Chaw nam ásapiłimta túuman.	Do not make fun of anyone.

Síkni

Virginia notes that children everywhere love the story of Síkni (Yellow Bell). It is part of first-year university language curriculum, and students have developed artwork (like the artwork included here) and reenacted the legend to illustrate the story of Yellow Bell and her sisters. "The Wild Spring Flowers" is a related legend.

CULTURAL TEACHINGS

This legend provides important cultural teachings. At first glance, readers might assume the story is teaching about being "on time" as Yellow Bell is scolded by her relatives for being late and unprepared. However, a deeper cultural lesson exists about the importance of being "in time" with the seasons and being a responsible member of the community. In the story, Yellow Bell is accountable to her family and community, and her responsibility is to pay attention to the seasons and to fulfill her duties each season.

Note that Yellow Bell isn't expected to look at a clock and be at a specific place at a specific time. Rather, she needs to take her cues from her environment: Grizzly Bear rustling in the den; the warm Chinook Wind announcing that spring is coming; and even Yellow Bell's favorite time, sleeping on a comfortable bed of moss during winter. If she is paying attention to her environment, she will be prepared, and she won't have to be nagged by her relatives. The cultural lessons in the legend teach children (and all readers/listeners of the story) to read their environments to understand the seasons and the cycle of traditional foods gathering. Again, these important times cannot be marked on a calendar. We do not know the exact date that Chinook Wind will ask Yellow Bell to awake each year; her relationship with the environment and place will tell her.

Yellow Bell's relatives hold her accountable, insisting that she join them, as they know their collective will be stronger with her presence. They do not let her stay behind, as if she is expendable or doesn't matter. Although she is portrayed as "lazy" in the story, she is still important to her family, and they want her, even "sloppy," to be with them; they value her presence.

The legend also teaches us how to greet the world. Wake up and get out of bed. Bathe and groom yourself, get dressed, be ready for the day.

LOCATION

This legend takes place along the cliffs of the Columbia River between present-day Wenatchee and Lake Chelan, Washington. The high cliffs to the west of the river are visible from Highway 97 and Alternate 97. (Ribbon Cliff—we are told how it was formed in "Legend about the Sun and Moon" and in "Legend of Prairie Chicken"—is in this same area.) Roots are dug from very early spring to early summer.

PLANTS AND FOODS

Plants and foods mentioned in this version of the legend are shown in the table.

NAME IN LEGEND	OTHER COMMON NAMES	ICHISHKÍIN	SCIENTIFIC NAME	NOTES
Bitter Root	bitterroot	pyax̱í	*Lewisia rediviva*	An important food source and usually the first root to be named at traditional feasts. Harvested from mid-spring depending on elevation.
Camas	camas	wák̲'amu	*Camassia quamash*	Wák̲'amu grows in wetter areas. It is baked in the ground.
Lily	mariposa lily (probably)	nunás	*Calochortus macrocarpus*	Also called "starvation root," as it provides food in times of scarcity. Other lily foods are pananát (tiger lily) and sego lily.
Yellow Bell	yellow bell	sɨ́kni	*Frittilaria pudica*	As in the legend, sɨ́kni's flower is bell shaped and points to the ground.

LANGUAGE NOTES

In legends, storytellers figuratively put themselves into the setting of a story by using directional markers in the verb, based on the storyteller's perspective or the perspective of one of the characters. In "Sɨ́kni," the narrator positions herself at the place the roots will come up. Winaawayáy (Chinook Wind) comes to that place, indicated by the directional *-m* on the first verb below. This directional indicates movement towards the speaker: Chinook Wind is approaching the narrator.

Íkuuk awkú **iwíihaykma**, iwináchika winúawa hulí.
That's when the warm wind came blowing down, arriving.

The flowers are encouraged to come out to Winaawayáy's location above the ground, again, using the directional *-m* on the verb *at-* (exit):

> Aw pam **átɨmta**, aw iwá ts'muuy.
> *You come out now, now it is warm.*

But when the roots themselves, still underground, announce they are going out, they do not use *-m* on the verb *at-* (exit) because from their perspective, they are simply exiting their beds.

> Aw natash **átsha** . . . !
> *We're going out now . . . !*

After the flowers have emerged from the ground, the narrator remains figuratively in the initial location. In their most brilliant stage of bloom, the flowers shine out away from that place and from the narrator to the rest of the countryside, here indicated with *-kik*, movement away from the speaker.

> Latít tɬ'áax̱wpa mɨnán awkú **pattáwax̱nkika**, ayáyat k̲'ínupa.
> *Flowers were growing all over the place, looking beautiful.*

In this way, the presence of the narrator and her use of the directional markers allows the listener as well to have a place on the hillside of the spring flowers.

Spilyáy ku K̲'áx̱nu

The legend "Spilyáy ku K̲'áx̱nu" (Coyote and Prairie Chicken) is filled with emotion: the fear of a chick about to be eaten by a predator, the heart-wrenching sorrow of a bereaved parent, the silliness of an oblivious prankster. The intonation and actions of the storyteller bring this legend to life. It is related to "Legend of Prairie Chicken."

CULTURAL TEACHINGS

This legend illustrates the care and concern that the Prairie Chicken parents hold for their nest of babies. They instruct them to be careful and leave the eldest in charge, saying "Shix̱nam ánaktkwaninta. Chaw nam miin áshapawinata. Chaw nam shiin áshapa'ashta." (Take care of them. Don't let them go anywhere. Don't let anyone inside.) This enforces the idea that the home should be a safe place for children. Virginia recalls other teachings about keeping children safe at home. Children were instructed not to be outdoors alone after dark. When it becomes dark, they should come inside and stay in through the night, as there are evildoers who want to exchange their spirits with those of good people. In addition, children should stay away from places where dead bodies are. Today as well, it can be dangerous for our children, and they need to be both looked after and taught to look out for themselves.

In the legend, we also see Coyote's laziness, and he gives an example of how not to behave. His main reason for stopping by his friend's home seems to be that he is hungry, and perhaps he will be offered something to eat. Coyote often wants fish or food and help from others, rather than taking care of himself. In this way, the legends teach important culturally sustaining lessons: do your own fishing, take care of your own self. At the same time, help one another and help our Elders. For example, Elders are given salmon by those who fish. This giving happens within families but also with any Elder who comes along or who is in need. Virginia recalls her mother talking about this, "Whenever you go down to the river, they give the Elders salmon, that is our culture."

PRAIRIE CHICKENS

The word *k̲'áx̲nu* is translated as prairie chicken in this legend. The term can also refer to sharp-tailed grouse (Beavert and Hargus 2009, 83; Rude and CTUIR 2014, 520) and also prairie grouse or prairie fowl in general. This legend tells why coyotes do not eat prairie chickens. Red Fox delivered the Creator's message, and Coyote agreed so that Red Fox did not turn him back into a dried-out husk. We learn, "Íkush awkú iwá íchi íkuuk. Cháwmun spílya ítł'yawita k̲'ax̲numaman. Íchi ikúuk, táaminwa." (That's the way it is now. A coyote never kills prairie chickens. That's the way it is today and forever.)

Virginia recalls creeping up on prairie chickens as a child to see their elaborate mating rituals. The males dance and display their feathers. They inflate colorful air sacs on their necks to amplify their cooing noises. However, with loss of habitat, the number of these birds has declined.

Currently recovery plans are in place. People take care not to disturb these creatures as they watch their displays, as Virginia took care as a girl.

LANGUAGE NOTES

Special forms of expression and sound symbolism are an important and expressive part of speaking Ichishkíin. For example, consonant sound changes can express that something is small, is making a louder or softer sound, or is moving with more or less force, as in *myánash* (child) to *myálas* (baby). A dog who is a treasured pet might be called *k'uɬík'uɬi* rather than *k'usík'usi* (dog). Vowels may be lengthened for emphasis or to describe a drawn-out action. Actions are also expressed through sounds, so that blowing on ashes or to cool something can be *pupupu* and the sound of rain *t't't't'*. Animals make particular sounds, like Sandpiper's call "*Yiit, yiit.*"

In legends, storytellers are very expressive in using sounds to represent characters and actions. Spilyáy sometimes has a particular way of speaking, often using diminutive alternations of everyday words. Storytellers are skilled at making use of the sounds of the language as they tell the story. In "Spilyáy ku K̲'áx̲nu," the nonsense words *K̲unk̲úun shɨ́papap!* are the only thing that the eldest chick can say in response to Spilyáy's repeated questioning. The legend-teller uses her facial expressions as well as the description in the legend to indicate just how difficult it is for the chick to say anything at all, and the chick's confusion and dismay when this is the only answer he can come up with. Spilyáy feels mocked by the innocent chick and ends up killing the whole nest.

The description of Spilyáy's walk is also a creative use of sound. Coyote struts along, singing his own praises, as he comes to Prairie Chicken's home. The storyteller uses the words *k̲w'á'ash k̲w'á'ash* to describe his strutting steps. Virginia ties this to the word *k̲w'áshk̲w'ásh* (crane or heron), as in "K̲w'ashk̲w'ashmí Watít, ku Túyaw Alashikmí Psa Átx̲anana [Watít Atachiishpamá Ttmayimamíki]" and "Amushyáy and Wɨx̲inshyáy") and the way cranes move as they step. Adding a syllable and repeating the word brings to mind a crane's jerky, stalking motion and describes how Coyote proudly struts along.

Repeating words and syllables plays a number of roles in the Ichishkíin language. Sometimes a full word or sentence is repeated to express repeated action. When the Prairie Chickens are attacking Coyote again and again, words are repeated: *pat awkú ánanayka, awkú ánanayka* (they forced him along, forced him along). Sometimes it is not the entire word that is repeated but just the verb, or even part of the verb. For example, *lik'p-* means "blink once" and *lik'plík'p-* "blink repeatedly"; *tłup-* means "jump" and *tłuptłúp-* "jump up and down."

Words or parts of words may also be repeated to indicate number or size, such as *tnán* (cliff) and *tnántnan* (cliffs). *Wix̱á* means "foot or leg" and *wix̱áwx̱a* "feet or legs." More than one willow or a bunch of willow branches is *ttax̱sh*, whereas the singular is *tax̱sh*. For some words, the repetition refers to size, sometimes in conjunction with a consonant change. A small house or hut is *ɨlíitliit*, from *iníit* (house, home).

Finally, many animal names have repeated syllables as their basic, singular form. Bird names especially are tied to the sound the bird makes. In this legend, *pítpit* is chick. In other legends, we meet *x̱wíłx̱wił* (meadowlark), *ḵw'áshḵw'ash* (crane), and *kw'áykw'ay* (wren). Consider as well the sounds made by *á'a* (crow) and *ákak* (Canada goose).

As you can see, there are many valuable learning opportunities when one engages our traditional legends and stories. Readers and listeners learn about the natural world, cultural values, and the relationships and worldviews that are important in our language and culture. We hope you enjoy these stories and the many lessons contained within them.

Glossaries

The glossary to the 1974 edition has been expanded to include all the Ichishkíin words in the legends from the original edition. Following this now-comprehensive glossary are short glossaries to the four legends provided in Ichishkíin in the new edition, with key vocabulary from the legends to assist readers and language learners.

EXPANDED GLOSSARY TO THE ORIGINAL EDITION

áchaash eye

ála paternal grandmother or woman's son's child. This is the term you use to address the relative "Grandmother!" or "Grandchild!" and also means "her/his father's mother" and "her son's child."

aluk̲'át frog

Álx̲ayx̲ Moon

Alíx̲shtaní the name of a witch woman

ámash owl

Ámash táx̲shik! Now wake up!

ámush monetaria shell. This deep-sea shell is used by Yakama people to decorate regalia.

Amushyáy Legendary Monetaria Shell Maiden

anipásh Indian potato, spring beauty (*Claytonia lanceolata*)

ánutaash winter living quarters framed with lodge poles covered with tule mats

Anwáx̲tasit (place-name) ancient name of a place on the south side of the Snake River

asúm eel/lamprey. Dried for food or cooked in oven or on cedar sticks over open fire.

Asumyáy Legendary Eel

atáchiish ocean

átya, 'átyasha, i'átyasha north wind; a cold wind is blowing.

Atyayáaya Legendary North Wind

Aw now, enough now, exclamation, "Oh!"

Áwacha nay! "It was like this, in legendary days of the animal world." Also an expression the storyteller uses to make sure the listeners are paying attention. They respond "Ii!" or "Nay!"

Awátam (place-name) Parker. Parker/Sunnyside Dam on the Yakima River. A fishing site, "kind of lake, resembling a lake."

awít a widow or widower who would traditionally marry an unmarried close relative of the deceased spouse. If a woman's husband dies, she might marry her deceased husband's brother. If a man's wife dies, he might marry his deceased wife's sister.

Áwna! Let's go now!

áx̱mi up from water

áx̱shax̱sh, áx̱sh'ax̱sh dentalium

Ax̱shax̱shyáy Legendary Dentalium

áyat woman

ayatúks female animal

ayáyat beautiful

Aykwíisya Legendary Cottontail Rabbit

aykws cottontail rabbit

aan sun

áana cry of pain or astonishment

áana naa naa expression of pain

Chakyáy a clown, a devilish character that influences somebody to do bad things. Name of a boy in a legend.

Cháwisha (place-name) a place near a canyon stream, meaning killing place or place where he breathed his last breath

chawmún never

Chawnápam (place-name) a place on the Columbia River, near Tri-Cities, Washington (Kennewick, Pasco, and Richland). Also refers to the people who live there.

cháwp'ɨx̱ disheveled

chcháya juneberry, service berry

chíish water

chux, chxw affectionate expression to a loved one

hwíik'kw poisonous plant used carefully for medicinal purposes

ilíi! an expression of surprise

inawawíksh male hope chest or dowry, gift endowment to bring in marriage (families save for years): blankets, parfleches (rawhide suitcases), man's buckskin suits, horses, cattle, bone beads, war bonnets, beaver skins, etc.

ishích nest

isht son, woman's daughter

íx̱wi yet, still, later

ii yes. Pronounced "ee!" Children respond to "Áwacha nay!" with "Ii!" Then the storyteller begins.

ɨmawí island

Ɨpushayáy Legendary Snake, Rattlesnake, also called Grandfather. Related to *púsha* (paternal grandfather) as snakes are old and to be respected.

ɨtút your father

ɨwínsh man

kákya bird, animal

káɫa maternal grandmother or woman's daughter's child. This is the term you use to address the relative "Grandmother!" or "Grandchild!" and also means "her/his mother's mother" and "her daughter's child."

kápɨn root digger

kátɫ'yaas spit, saliva

kawxkáwx palomino horse

ku mish, kúumish okay

k'álas raccoon

K'aláasya Legendary Raccoon

k'asáwi cold (animate)

k'astilá crawfish

K'astilayáaya Legendary Crawfish, also K'astilayáy

K'tɨ́taas (place-name) Kittitas, Kittitas County, where Ellensburg is located

k'usík'usi dog

kwíkw a whistling sound

kwikwɫá whistling marmot

kw'áykw'ay wren

Kw'aykw'ayyáy Legendary Mountain Wren. A plump stub-tailed warbler.

ḵayx̱ light, daylight, brightness

ḵaamúukii Indian hemp, milkweed hemp, hemp dogbane, in Palús language

K̲unk̲úun shípapap the sound the baby prairie chicken makes in the legend, has no particular meaning

k̲'áx̲nu prairie chicken

k̲'ɨx̲lí tule mat; a grass mat made with tules sewn together with hardwood needle and hemp. Used as tablecloth, mat, cushion, etc. K̲'ɨx̲li is a single-layer mat; łíim is woven and thicker.

k̲'mɨł cliff

K̲wilkúla name of a rock at Wíshx̲am

k̲w'áshk̲w'ash crane

K̲w'ayk̲w'áylɨm (place-name) place in K'úsi Creek area

lákas mouse

Lakáaya Legendary Mouse/Mice Sisters

Lalawísh Devil Wolf, oldest of the Wolf Brothers

latít flower

láymut youngest child

Lilíik (place-name) Little Lake

ltáyltay shoulder bag made of hemp, used for carrying things

lumt grey

luts'á red

Luts'ayáy Legendary Red Fox

łamtíx̲ head

Łátax̲at (place-name) Klikitat (Klickitat), also refers to the people who live there

łkw'i day

łk̲'am moccasins

łuuwáayki slowly

míimi long ago

mɨsɨ́s ground squirrel, chipmunk

myánash child

Myáwax̲ Chief, Chief Mountain

myáak̲in a child born out of wedlock

nank cedar tree (*Thuja plicata*)

napwák both people

Nax̲chíish (place-name) "Good water," Naches

Nch'iwána (place-name) Columbia River (Nch'i Wána)

nisháykt home

nunás an onion-like edible root, sometimes pounded into flour; mariposa lily, starvation root

núsux̱ salmon

páhaashtknik- take someone else's spirit by exchanging spirits with them, usually without their knowledge

palyuułá gambler, bone game player

palyúut bone game, stick game, also betting or wagering

panashłá monster

Pánatk̲'pt (place-name) Indian Springs on Goldendale/Bickleton Ridge. Refers to something, such as water, shooting out.

pank'ú button-like root vegetable, very tasty, dug only in early spring

Pátimas (place-name) in Hog Canyon near Medicine Valley. Means "drawn picture" or "written."

Pátu (place-name) mountain, Mount Adams

Páwankyuut (place-name) village where Satus and Logy Creeks join

páx̱aam five times

Páx̱utakyuut (place-name) Union Gap

Payút Paiute, neighboring Tribe and people

páax̱amuni five more times, a phrase used in ritual to break a cold spell

pinápx̱wini conceited, vain

pináwakwyakuunaash I was carried away, I lost control of myself

pítpit chick

Pityachíishya Ocean Woman

píwnash in-law, relative by marriage

pít'x̱anuk mountains, high country

Pshwánapam "shale rock people," a clan from the Northern Cascades, Ellensburg area

pt'ilíma girls (more than two)

pt'ilíyin two girls

pt'íniks girl

púkła the fluffy white feathers that grow next to the body of an eagle

púła turnip or parsnip-like root

púsha paternal grandfather or man's son's child. This is the term you use to address the relative "Grandfather!" or "Grandchild!" and also means "her/his father's father" and "his son's child."

puuy snow

pyax̱í bitterroot, a low trailing herb with bright pink flowers, a root food. Preserved by drying in the sun and stored for winter use.

sapk'tít breadroot, ground up and formed into small biscuits, dried in the sun

sikáwya, sikáywa breadroot (*Lomatium sp.*)

Siwáala (place-name) East Satus, towards Mabton, on Yakima River. A fishing site. A clan lived there.

síkni yellow bell, buttercup (*Fritillaria pudica*)

sɨnmí red squirrel, squirrel

skɨlwisá ant

Skɨlwisayáy Legendary Ant

sk'in cradle board, baby board

smaas bed

spílya coyote

Spilyáy Legendary Coyote, who talks and acts like a human

spilyáywi- pull Coyote tricks, act like Coyote

stínstins water chestnut

sts'at night, darkness

sts'aat dark

súnx̱ silver salmon

Shapáḵanaykaash (place-name) historical site off Highway 97 south of Toppenish, meaning "made to lie down on your back"

shápɨnchaash traditional clay makeup, "Indian paint"

shaptákay parfleche, rawhide suitcase

shapyashápya thistledown, the mature, silky pappus of a thistle

shayy, shay, shaay sound frequently used by storytellers to represent chime-like sounds or the sounds made by a rattlesnake

Sháapshish the name of a boy in a legend

shíwanish stranger

shix̱ ḵ'ínupa good looking

shíshaash porcupine

Shḵ'íyachash (place-name) ancient name of a place near the Columbia River with a view of Union Gap

shux sound of wind, "whoosh"

Tamanwɨłá Creator

Tamapáani (place-name) a place near the mouth of Rock Creek

Támchatani (place-name) Soda Spring, Soda Creek. Resembling an open receptacle something is poured into.

tamkw'íkw'i hail, showery precipitation in form of icy pellets

tamsháashu shk'apáshway, roseberry bush, thorny tree in "Raccoon's Grandmother"

Táptat (place-name) Prosser Falls on Yakima River. A fishing site of the Yakama Tribe.

táta daddy (baby talk)

Ta̠xtx̠t (place-name) meadow above Wenas Creek, probably Saw Mill Flats

tax̠ús Indian hemp, milkweed hemp, hemp dogbane

Tayatkíisya Legendary Icicle Maker, sister to North Wind

Táytnapam Band of people, Upper Cowlitz Sahaptin

táaminwa forever

táatpas clothing, dress, shirt

tíla maternal grandfather or man's daughter's child. This is the term you use to address the relative "Grandfather!" or "Grandchild!" and also means "her/his mother's father" and "his daughter's child."

tilíwal blood

Típikat Legendary Mallard Duck

tíshpun black widow spider

tiichám land, earth

tiin person, Native American person

tíinma people, Native American people

tiix̠wałá, patiix̠wałá sentry

tɨmná heart

Tɨmsk'aplúya Legendary Blue Jay

tkwínat Chinook salmon

tmay virgin maiden

tmayíksh female hope chest or dowry; articles representing female gender; beaded bags, dresses, shawls, basketry, dried roots, grass bags, dried fruit, dry goods, etc.

tnán cliff, bluff

tpɨsh face

ttmayíma virgin maidens (more than one)

Túlulkɨn Legendary name of Spilyáy's dog, an ancient word

túnishi up river

túx̠ɨn sky

twanít'aas fire stoking stick, a handy instrument with many uses. Besides stoking fires, it is used as a walking stick or paddle to spank children.

twáti a medicine man or woman with supernatural powers as a doctor. This power can be used to influence bad as well as good results.

Twit'áaya Legendary Grizzly Bear

Tx̱ápnish (place-name) Toppenish, meaning "jutting out"

T'at'ałíya Witch Woman

T'at'ałiyayáy Legendary Witch Woman

Tƚ'úmni (place-name) a place between Páwankyuut and Xátay in "The Stone Woman"

Tsiláan (place-name) deep water, Chelan, from Winátshapam language

tsúłim buffalo

Tsułimyáy Legendary Buffalo

ts'íx̱aas name of rock that controlled the rain and wind. Meaning "anus" because it was a hole in the butt end of mountain on the Oregon side. Sacred stone to the Wishx̱am people.

ts'muy warm

útpaas robe, blanket

wák'alask- strapping or hitting from one end to the other, the way raccoon was spanked by his grandmother, leaving those marks on his body

wak̲'íshwit life, spirit

Walawitís (place-name) Willow Creek, near Umatilla, Oregon

walptáykt song

wána river

wanuukshiłá person from the coast

wapáwani wearing regalia or finery

wapáwat regalia, finery, costume

wáptas wing

Wasco a clan residing across the Columbia River from the Wíshx̱am people, who speak the same language as the Wíshx̱ams

watít legend, story

wat'uymá eldest child

wawá mosquito

wawachí acorns, pickled acorns, a delicacy which is usually stored in volcanic ashes buried in the ground

Wawayáy Legendary Mosquito

wáwnakwshaash body

Wawyúuk (place-name) upper part of creek near Sheep Camp, location of spring in "The Stone Woman"

wáx̱push rattlesnake

Wax̱púshyay, Wax̱púya Legendary Rattlesnake

wax̱tx̱t a prickly plant (thistle) having showy purple flowers

Wayámpam name of a band of Columbia River Indians residing at Celilo, Oregon

waykáanash religious name for salmon, used at ceremonies

wilalík jackrabbit

Wilaalikyáy Legendary Jackrabbit

Winátsha (place-name) Wenatchee, "Water pouring out, gushing out" from a mountain

Winátshapam people from Winátsha

winááwa Chinook wind, warm wind, south wind

Winaawayáy Legendary name for Warm Wind

wíshpush giant beaver

Wíshx̱am (place-name) village on the Columbia River, fourteen miles above the Dalles Dam (Washington side), and the name of the people from there

wítx̱uupt gentle cold wind that blows in the early spring

wíwnu huckleberry

wíix̱ish dowry, gifts brought to bride or groom in marriage

wɨx̱á foot, leg

wɨx̱ínsh abalone

Wɨx̱inshyáy Legendary Abalone

x̱aslú, x̱aaslú star

X̱aslúwaykt (place-name) Star Crossing Place, a place near Wíshx̱am

X̱átash (place-name) a nest-like place. Also the name of a star, sister to Yáslams.

x̱átx̱at duck

X̱át X̱at Sparrow Hawk, in Winátshapam language

X̱atx̱áatya Legendary Duck, Legendary Mallard Duck

x̱awsh breadroot (*Lomatium cous*)

x̱ay man's close male friend, "brother"

x̱áyin two close male friends, brothers

X̱líipx̱liip Open and Shut, the name of a young girl in a legend. X̱liip means "opened."

x̱tú strong

X̱ux̱ux̱yáaya Legendary Crow or Raven, Old Man Crow or Raven

x̱wayamá golden eagle

x̱wíɬx̱wiɬ meadowlark. In stories, Meadowlark gossips and reports on people.

x̱wísaat old man

X̱yámush tiichám (place-name) Toppenish Ridge
x̱yaaw nɨkwɨ́t dried meat
x̱yaaw núsux̱ dried salmon
Yáslams the morning and evening star
yaay bear grass (*Xerophyllum tenax*)
yiityíit sandpiper
Yiityíitya Legendary Sandpiper

GLOSSARY TO THE LEGENDS IN ICHISHKÍIN

K̲w'ashk̲w'ashmí Watít, ku Túyaw Alashikmí Psa Átx̱anana (Watít Atachiishpamá Ttmayimamíki)

Alashík turtle
ámush monetaria shell
Amushyáy Legendary Monetaria Shell
atáchiish ocean
ax̱sháx̱sh dentalium
Ax̱shax̱shyáy Legendary Dentalium
haasht breath
isíkw'at lesson
ɨmawí island
kátł'yaas spit, saliva
k̲w'áshk̲w'ash crane
K̲w'ashk̲w'ashyáy Legendary Crane
k̲w'laapsh bare
lalíwa- miss, yearn for
láymut youngest child
łp'uł tears
pshwa stone
sápalɨm- tease, make fun of
shix̱ k̲'ínupa good looking
talwásk- gossip
táaminwa always
tɨmná heart
útpaas blanket, robe
walptáykt song

wapíita- help
watít legend
wat'uymá eldest child
wisalíl- hunt for, hunt around
wɨx̱á leg, foot
Wɨx̱inshyáy Legendary Abalone
x̱ni- dig roots
x̱nit root
x̱wayamá Golden Eagle

Anakú Itx̱ánana Aan

áchaash eye
Aluḵ'át Frog
Álx̱ayx̱ Moon
áx̱mi up from water
Aan Sun
k'usík'usi dog
ḵayx̱ light, daylight, brightness
ḵ'mɨł cliff
łkw'i day
łuuwáayki slowly
napwák both people
Nch'i Wána Columbia River
panashłá monster
smaas bed
Spilyáy Coyote
sts'at night, darkness
sts'aat dark, after dark (time of day)
shápɨnchaash traditional clay, make up, "Indian paint"
tilíwal blood
tiichám earth, land
tíinma people, Indian people
tiix̱wałá, patiix̱wałá sentry
tnán cliff, bluff
túnishi up river
wána river
wáptas wing

x̱ay man's male friend

x̱áyin two male friends

yiityíit sandpiper

Sɨ́kni

Ámash táx̱shik! Now wake up!

anakú when, because

anakw'ɨ́nk the aforementioned

át- go out

áwi- search for

awkú then

awkuuníik still

ayáyat beautiful

chawmún never

cháwp'ix̱ disheveled

cháx̱ɨlp- open

haashháash- rest

íkush thus

Íkush awkú íchi ikúuk iwá pɨ́nch'a And this is the way this one is

ímałak- clean

íniix̱i- fix up, make presentable

isíkw'a- show

íx̱wi yet, still

Íx̱wiish pnuwát'asha I'm still sleepy (I still am wanting to sleep)

ɨmítichan downward

kkáasa- be in a hurry

kpáylk later

kúshx̱i also

kw'áx̱i again

ḵḵanáywi- be busy

ḵ'ínu- see

láḵayx̱i- shine

latí- bloom

Láymut youngest

lɨ́tsama little sisters (when addressing them)

łḵ'am moccasins

náktkwanin- take care of

pat older sister or they

patún this and that, things

pinátamasklikɨnkik- turn oneself over/away

pinatwakushiyáɫ uncombed

pinátɫ'uya- be ashamed

pɨ́nch'a that one—humbling

pnu- sleep

pt'ilíma girls (more than two)

pt'íniks girl

pyax̱í bitterroot

sikáwya breadroot

sɨ́kni yellow bell, buttercup

shapápux- blow

shapap'ikáɫ having unwashed clothes

shix̱ ḵ'ínupa good looking

táwḵ'um- oversleep, sleep late

táx̱shi- wake up

táaminwa always

táatpas clothes

tk'i- look at

tmáy maiden

tpɨsh face

ttáwax̱- grow

ttmayíma maidens

tɫ'anx̱ meantime, rather

tɫ'áax̱wtun everything

tsts'úup- melt

wáḵwnayk- bend head

wána- flow (as a noun: river)

wánpi- call or summon

wapáwani costumed, wearing regalia

wapáwat costume, finery

winách ik- arrive

winachikúu- arrive to someone

winaniináɫ unbathed

winátax̱shi- awaken, begin to wake up

Winaawayáy Legendary Chinook Wind

wíihayk- go down
wɨshúwa- ready
wyáalakw- leave
x̱álukt underneath
yáka older brother
yakút reported speech marker (she, he, they say, it is said)

Spilyáy ku K̲'áx̱nu

anáwi- be hungry
ayatúks female animal
ílkwaas stick, wood
íɫamayk- hide
ishích nest
íyax̱- find
ɨlp at the peak, top
ɨn- tell
k'pɨs cold
kwíita- walk by, be on the way to
K̲unk̲úun shípapap! nonsense words spoken by oldest prairie chicken baby
k̲'áx̱nu prairie chicken. Also refers to sharp-tailed grouse, prairie grouse, prairie fowl in general.
k̲'ínu- see
k̲'mɨɫ cliff
lá'ɨsha- lie around, relax
Luts'ayáy Legendary Red Fox
ɫamtɨ́x head
Mɨnán iwá ɨtút? Where's your father?
myánash child
náx̱ti- cry
Nch'iwána Columbia River
nisháykt/nisháyaas home, home site
nɨmnawít really, a lot
páx̱aam five times
pítpit chick
putáptit anwíkt one hundred years
p'ushtáy hill
sáyp- feed

skaw- be afraid
shaláwi- be tired
shyak- scout
táx̱shi- wake up
tilíwal blood
tkwátat food
tkw'anáti- walk along
túx̱- return home
tł'yáwiyi dead
wána river
wanp- sing a power song or medicine song
wátiksh footprints
watít legend
wat'uymá eldest
wáwtł'ik- beat with a stick, club
wáawk'a too much
wíit'iishk- splatter
wɨ́np- take
wyákwshtiksh- do wrong
wyáalakw- abandon, leave
x̱ay man's male friend
yik- hear, understand

Additional Readings and Resources

Ackerman, Lillian A., ed. 1996. *A Song to the Creator: Traditional Arts of Native American Women of the Plateau.* Norman: University of Oklahoma Press.

Beavert, Virginia. 1999. "Native Songs Taught by Ellen W. Saluskin (Hoptonix Sawyalilx̱), 1890–1993." In *Spirit of the First People: Native American Music Traditions of Washington State*, edited by Willie Smyth and Esmé Ryan, 62–71. Seattle: University of Washington Press.

Beavert, Virginia. 2011. *Tiinmamí Tɨmnanáx̱t: Legends of the Sahaptin Speaking People.* Lake Forest Park, WA: Northwest Heritage Resources. CD.

Beavert, Virginia. 2012. *Wántwint Inmí Tiináwit: A Reflection of What I Have Learned.* DPhil diss., University of Oregon.

Beavert, Virginia. 2017. *The Gift of Knowledge / Ttnúwit Átawish Nch'inch'imamí: Reflections on Sahaptin Ways.* Edited by Janne Underriner. Seattle: University of Washington Press.

Beavert, Virginia, and Sharon Hargus. 2009. *Ichishkíin Sɨ́nwit: Yakama/Yakima Sahaptin Dictionary.* Toppenish, WA, and Seattle: Heritage University and University of Washington Press.

Beavert, Virginia, and Bruce Rigsby. 1975. *Yakima Language Practical Dictionary.* Toppenish, WA: The Consortium of Johnson O'Malley Committees of Region IV, State of Washington.

Beavert, Virginia, and Deward E. Walker Jr. 1974. *The Way It Was (Anakú Iwachá): Yakima Legends.* Yakima, WA: Franklin Press, The Consortium of Johnson O'Malley Committees of Region IV, State of Washington.

Hargus, Sharon, and Virginia Beavert. 2014. "Northwest Sahaptin." *Journal of the International Phonetic Association* 44, no. 3: 319–42.

Hugo, Russell. 2017. *Endangered Languages, Technology and Learning: A Yakama/Yakima Sahaptin Case Study.* DPhil diss., University of Washington.

Hunn, Eugene S., and James Selam. 1990. *Nch'i-wána, "The Big River": Mid-Columbia Indians and Their Land.* Seattle: University of Washington Press.

Hunn, Eugene S., E. Thomas Morning Owl, Philip Cash Cash, and Jennifer Karson Engum. 2015. *Čáw Pawá Láakn–They Are Not Forgotten: Sahaptian Place Names Atlas of the Cayuse, Umatilla, and Walla Walla.* Pendleton and Portland, OR: Tamástslikt Cultural Institute in association with Ecotrust.

Jacob, Michelle M. 2013. *Yakama Rising: Indigenous Cultural Revitalization, Activism, and Healing.* Tucson: University of Arizona Press.
Jacob, Michelle M. 2016. *Indian Pilgrims: Indigenous Journeys of Activism and Healing with Saint Kateri Tekakwitha.* Tucson: University of Arizona Press.
Jacob, Michelle M. 2020a. *The Auntie Way: Stories Celebrating Kindness, Fierceness, and Creativity.* Whitefish, MT: Anahuy Mentoring.
Jacob, Michelle M. 2020b. *Huckleberries and Coyotes: Lessons from Our More Than Human Relations.* Whitefish, MT: Anahuy Mentoring.
Jacob, Michelle M., and Stephany RunningHawk Johnson, eds. 2020. *On Indian Ground: A Return to Indigenous Knowledge-Generating Hope, Leadership and Sovereignty through Education in the Northwest.* Charlotte, NC: Information Age.
Jacobs, Melville. 1929. "Northwest Sahaptin Texts." *University of Washington Publications in Anthropology* 2, no. 6: 175–244.
Jacobs, Melville. 1931. "A Sketch of Northern Sahaptin Grammar." *University of Washington Publications in Anthropology* 4, no. 6: 85–291.
Jacobs, Melville. 1934. "Northwest Sahaptin Texts (English Translations)." In *Columbia University Contributions to Anthropology,* vol. 19, part 1. New York: Columbia University Press.
Jacobs, Melville. 1937. "Northwest Sahaptin Texts (Indian Text)." In *Columbia University Contributions to Anthropology,* vol. 19, part 2. New York: Columbia University Press.
Jansen, Joana. 2010. *A Grammar of Yakima Ichishkíin/Sahaptin.* DPhil diss., University of Oregon.
Rigsby, Bruce. 1965. *Linguistic Relations in the Southern Plateau.* DPhil diss., University of Oregon.
Rigsby, Bruce, and Noel Rude. 1996. "Sketch of Sahaptin, a Sahaptian Language." In *Languages,* edited by Ives Goddard and William C. Sturtevant, 666–92. Vol. 17 of *Handbook of North American Indians.* Washington, DC: Smithsonian Institution.
Rude, Noel, and Confederated Tribes of the Umatilla Indian Reservation. 2014. *Umatilla Dictionary.* Seattle: Confederated Tribes of the Umatilla Indian Reservation in association with University of Washington Press.
Uebelacker, Morris L., and Jeffery S. Wilson. 1984. *Time Ball: A Story of the Yakima People and the Land: A Cultural Resource Overview.* Yakima, WA: Yakima Nation.

Contributors to the New Edition

Deward E. Walker Jr. received his PhD in Anthropology from the University of Oregon in 1964 and is Professor Emeritus at the Department of Anthropology, University of Colorado, Boulder. He has conducted research among Tribal populations of the Columbia Basin, Western Plains, Northern Great Basin, and Southwest. He is frequently retained by Tribal governments and agencies to conduct research related to planning, program development, treaty rights, and Tribal environmental initiatives. He was the technical consultant to the original edition printed in 1974 and contributed to the new edition.

Robert K. Elliott (MA, San Francisco State University) has been involved with language teaching for over twenty years. At the University of Oregon, Robert works at the Northwest Indian Language Institute (NILI), where he partners with numerous tribes in the Pacific Northwest and beyond on Indigenous language revitalization. His technology and computer-assisted language learning (CALL) background keep him involved in a wide variety of digital projects, such as film, e-books, mapmaking, and the development of a digital resource center for Indigenous language teachers.

Editors of the New Edition

Virginia R. Beavert, Tux̱ámshish, is the foremost scholar and an enrolled member of the Yakama Nation and a highly respected Tribal Elder. She is a teacher and fluent speaker of her language, Yakama Ichishkíin. She has been an integral part of documentation, description, and revitalization efforts for her language since 1934, first working with the anthropologist Melville Jacobs and working with nearly every researcher of the language since. She has witnessed the dramatic changes in education for our people, experiencing the traditional teachings by Tribal Elders as well as working her way through the Western education system, culminating in a PhD in linguistics. Beavert has a bachelor's degree from Central Washington University and a master's degree in Bilingual/Bicultural Education through the University of Arizona's American Indian Language Development Institute (AILDI). She holds a Doctorate of Humane Letters (Honorary PhD) from the University of Washington and a PhD in Linguistics from the University of Oregon. From 1974 to 1985, she held an elected position on the General Council of the Yakama Indian Nation. She was the Project Director of the 1974 edition of *Anakú Iwachá* and in this capacity collected, transcribed, and translated all of the included legends; authored the introduction and conclusion and the introductions to sections and legends; and edited the legends as requested, as some committee members felt that there was inappropriate violence and sexuality for schools. Beavert authored *The Gift of Knowledge / Ttnúwit Átawish Nch'inch'imamí* (2017) and coauthored *Ichishkíin Sínwit: Yakama/Yakima Sahaptin Dictionary* (2009) with Sharon Hargus. In 2015, the Yakama Nation dedicated the Tux̱ámshish Higher Education Center, named in her honor.

Michelle M. Jacob, PhD Sociology, is an enrolled member of the Yakama Nation and is Professor of Indigenous Studies at the University of Oregon's

College of Education in the Department of Education Studies, where she also serves as the Director of the Sapsik’ʷałá (Teacher) Education Program, which trains American Indians and Alaska Natives to become teachers who serve Indigenous communities. The Sapsik’ʷałá Program is a successful collaboration between the University of Oregon and the Nine Federally Recognized Tribes of Oregon. Jacob is also affiliated faculty with the Department of Indigenous, Race, and Ethnic Studies and the Environmental Studies Program at the University of Oregon. She has extensive experience with grant-funded research, as well as in leading projects into academic publication, including her five books: *Yakama Rising*, *Indian Pilgrims*, *On Indian Ground: A Return to Indigenous Knowledge-Generating Hope, Leadership and Sovereignty through Education in the Northwest* (coedited with Stephany RunningHawk Johnson), *The Auntie Way*, and *Huckleberries and Coyotes*. Jacob thinks Auntie-ing is awesome and she is very proud of her niece and nephews. One of her greatest joys is to camp in the many beautiful places around the Columbia River Basin. To learn more about Jacob’s work please visit https://anahuymentoring.com.

Joana W. Jansen, PhD Linguistics, is the Associate Director of the University of Oregon’s Northwest Indian Language Institute (NILI) and served as Senior Research Associate of the Sapsik’ʷałá (Teacher) Education Program. NILI is internationally known in the fields of Indigenous language revitalization and teacher development. Jansen’s contributions to these programs and partnering Tribal communities are teacher education, descriptive linguistics, curriculum development, and project planning and management. Her research includes linguistic description, analysis, and revitalization of the Ichishkíin language. She also investigates the development and impact of local, culturally informed place-based curriculum. She was instrumental in bringing the Ichishkíin language class and its instructors, including Virginia Beavert, to the University of Oregon. Jansen and Beavert have worked together for more than sixteen years on Ichishkíin language projects. Together they transcribe, translate, and edit the Ichishkíin language, and work on language documentation, description, and curriculum. Jansen has served as principal investigator or co-principal investigator on numerous grant projects. She loves hiking and being on and around the waters of the Pacific Northwest.